Andrew Billingsley,
Scholar and Institution Builder:
Essays and Tributes

Books by Andrew Billingsley

The Role of the Social Worker in a Child Protective Agency:
A Comparative Analysis
(1964: Society for the Prevention of Cruelty to Children, Boston)

The Social Worker in a Child Protective Agency New York
(1965: National Association of Social Workers, New York)

Black Families in White America
(1968: Prentice-Hall, Upper Saddle River, New Jersey)

Illegitimacy: Changing Services for Changing Times
(1970: National Council on Illegitimacy, New York)

Children of the Storm: Black Children and American Child Welfare
(1972: Harcourt, New York)

Black Families and the Struggle for Survival
(1974: Friendship Press, New York)

The Evolution of the Black Family
(1976: National Urban League, New York)

Climbing Jacob's Ladder: The Enduring Legacy of African-American
Families
(1992: Simon and Schuster, New York)

Mighty like a River: The Black Church and Social Reform
(1999: Oxford University Press, New York)

Yearning to Breathe Free: Robert Smalls of South Carolina and His
Families
(2007: University of South Carolina Press, Columbia, SC)

Andrew Billingsley,
Scholar and Institution Builder:
Essays and Tributes

Editor

Charles Jarmon, Ph.D.

Assistant Editors

Samantha Obuobi, M.P.H.

Jo Von M. McCalester, Ph.D.

Bathsheba Bryant-Tarpeh, Ph.D.

Black Classic Press
Baltimore

Andrew Billingsley, Scholar and Institution Builder: Essays and Tributes

Library of Congress Control Number: 2020950294

Print book ISBN: 978-1-57478-201-1

Ebook ISBN: 978-1-57478-202-8

Printed by BCP Digital Printing (*www.bcpdigital.com*), an affiliate company of Black Classic Press, Inc.

To review or purchase Black Classic Press books, please visit *www.blackclassicbooks.com.*

You may also obtain a list of titles by writing to:

Black Classic Press
c/o List
P.O. Box 13414
Baltimore, MD 21203

CONTENTS

Contributors

Janell Walden Agyeman
D. Kamili Anderson
Lois Benjamin, Ph.D.
Andrew Billingsley, Ph.D.
Bathsheba Bryant-Tarpeh, Ph.D.
Greg Carr, Ph.D.
Congressman James E. Clyburn (D-SC)
Douglas Davidson, Ph.D.
Ambassador Amy Ruth Davis
Howard Dodson, M.A.
Lawrence E. Gary, Ph.D.
Ralph Gomes, Ph.D.
Sheila Heatley, M.B.A.
Evelyn Brooks Higginbotham, Ph.D.
Robert B. Hill, Ph.D.
Reverend Kenneth F. Hodges

Ralph Hurtado, M.S.W.
Charles Jarmon, Ph.D.
Joyce A. Ladner, Ph.D.
Ana Lopez-DeFede, Ph.D.
Haki Madhubuti, Ph.D.
Jo Von M. McCalester, Ph.D.
Edna Greene Medford, Ph.D.
E. Ethelbert Miller
Patricia Motes, Ph.D.
Joshua Myers, Ph.D.
Samantha Obuobi. M.P.H.
Percy A. Pierre, Ph.D.
Wornie Reed, Ph.D.
Roger H. Rubin, Ph.D.
Kesho Scott, Ph.D.
Eleanor W. Traylor, Ph.D.
Ronald Walters, Ph.D.

Acknowledgments

*A*ndrew Billingsey, Scholar and Institution Builder: Essays and Tributes would not have been written without the contributions of close associates of Dr. Andrew Billingsley. At two major events in which he was honored—the occasion of his April 2010 retirement from the University of South Carolina and the symposium at Howard University honoring his 90th birthday in April 2016— former students and colleagues recognized him for his scholarly, professional, and personal contributions. Their papers have been presented in this *festschrift*. We also recognize the commitment of the organizers of these events for their herculean efforts to bring together many of his former students and colleagues from his years at Hampton University, Grinnell University, University of California at Berkeley, Howard University, Morgan State University, University of Maryland, and the University of South Carolina. As their presentations were about Andy's contributions to their personal or professional lives, we are provided a view of the many roles that he played. They also remind us of our debt to him for his contributions to the doctoral program at Howard University and Morgan State University. It is because of the participation in the two symposia attended by his former associates and students that this work was possible. Finally, I express my gratitude to Dr. Gregory Carr for providing accommodations in the Department of African American Studies, where we spent months and weeks planning for the completion of this project.

The organizers of the symposium at the University of South Carolina in 2010 included:

Dean Mary Ann Fitzpatrick
Dr. Patricia Motes
Ms. Sheila Heatley
Prof. Bobby Donaldson
Prof. Valinda Littlefield
Prof. Todd Shaw
Prof. Kimberly Simmons

At Howard University, the Billingsley 90th Birthday Symposium Committee included:

Dr. Andrew Billingsley, Honoree
Dr. Greg Carr, Associate Professor and Chair of the Afro-American Studies Department
Mrs. Amy Billingsley, Chair, Billingsley Symposium
Dr. Bathsheba F. Bryant-Tarpeh, Co-Chair, Billingsley Symposium
Ms. Donald'a Gaddy, Administrative Assistant to the John and Eula Mae Cleveland Distinguished Chair

Ms. D. Kamili Anderson, Media Coordinator and Program Editor
Mrs. Patricia Walters, Program Advisor
Mrs. Carolyn Smith, University and Community Outreach
Dr. Karen Miller, University and Community Outreach
Mrs. Shirley M. Hausley, Volunteer Coordinator
Mrs. Altheria Myers, Volunteer Coordinator

Foreword

Greg Carr, Ph.D., J.D.
Chairman, Afro-American Studies Department
Howard University

The question of the scholarly evolution of African American thought pertaining to higher education in Black colleges and universities has been a subject of debate for many decades. As early as 1933, W. E. B. Du Bois commented on what should be the primary focus of the Negro college. In 1933, he stated:

> "When the southern Negro college changed from a missionary school to a secular college, there was a tendency continually to say: This college is not a Negro college; it is a college; we are not teaching Negro science nor Negro art; we are teaching art and science. To this I wanted to oppose a word of warning. I wanted to say in all kindness and cooperation: You are and should and must remain a Negro college; but that involves no low ideals." ("The Field and Function of the Negro College," in Herbert Aptheker, Ed., *The Education of Black People: Ten Critiques, 1906-1960*, 2001, pp. 11-12)

In the same vein, Lerone Bennett Jr., in 1969, expressed his view of the complexity of the concept of Blackness as it had evolved in the 1960s. He made the following comment about the meaning of blackness:

> "What is the true meaning of blackness? It is too soon to say. Let us say, provisionally, that blackness is that universe of values and attitudes and orientations which rises, like dew, from the depth of our undergraduate experience and pulls us toward the distant shores of our destiny. Let us say provisionally, that it is a totalizing and enveloping force, and ambiance, and a milieu. But let us also say that there are depths beneath the depths in blackness and that the first challenge of blackness is the challenge of defining blackness. We believe that this challenge will require the long and careful collaboration of many

minds, and that we can no longer afford the luxury of doing our own thing in our own private pastures. By this we mean to say that we believe that that community has a prior claim on our time, our talents, and our resources, and that we must respond when it calls." (The Challenge of Blackness. Chicago: Johnson Publishing Company, 1972, p. 34)

Andrew Billingsley, as much as any other Black scholar and educational administrator in the second half of the twentieth century, explored and expanded the possibilities of institutionalizing collaborative Black intellectual work in the American academy. A product of master teachers who taught in the American apartheid-era schools of his native Alabama, he used his academic and administrative talents to help midwife the birth of Black Studies in elite white institutions of higher education. Poised to enjoy a lifetime of academic distinction as a pioneering African American in those spaces, he answered the call to lead the significant problem of building the Black University concept at Historically Black Colleges and Universities (HBCUs). Dr. Billingsley continues to instruct and inspire in his mid-nineties; his ideational and literal fingerprints are firmly affixed to the institutions he served and in the minds of the generation of scholars he has helped to shape.

In the spring of 2013, I met with the family and representatives of the estate of John and Eula Cleveland, two giants of African American organized labor, whose 1.2 million-dollar bequest to Howard's Department of Afro-American Studies established our first endowed chair. In thinking of watershed figures in our intellectual genealogy that have been underresourced and that Cleveland Chair resources should support, my first phone call was to Dr. Billingsley. On behalf of our Department, I asked him to consider an offer of resources and support for helping him complete the task of writing his memoirs. As an academic who was of the first generation of academics to receive the Ph.D. in the field and discipline of Africana Studies, I am an intellectual son and beneficiary of Dr. Billingsley and his comrades. As an apprentice who had studied and sat with many of his comrades, such as John Henrik Clarke, Ron Walters, Joyce Ladner, Vincent Harding, Lerone Bennett Jr., W. Paul Coates, and Howard Dodson, I knew the indispensable importance of creating institutional spaces at HBCUs for Black Studies scholarship and activism.

We had also begun the task of building Howard's Department of Afro-American Studies into one of the country's only units to have a faculty comprised primarily of doctoral degrees in the discipline. With the enthusiastic support of Howard's 16th President, Sidney Alan Ribeau, himself a former Black Studies faculty member and department chair, we seized this moment to provide Dr. Billingsley with help to complete his project as well as to integrate him once more into the regular life of the university he had so deeply impacted.

In 2013, the legendary Reverend Dr. Jeremiah Wright became the first John and Eula Cleveland Chair Scholar-in-Residence. Shortly thereafter, Dr. Billingsley accepted our invitation to follow Reverend Wright as a Scholar-in-Residence in the Cleveland Chair office on the third floor of the Founder's Library. Over the next several years, enabled by his ever dependable partner, Amy Billingsley; his collaborator, Dr. Charles Jarmon; and a coterie of assistants that included Donald'a Gaddy, Samantha Obuobi, Dr. Bathsheba Byrant-Tarpeh, and Dr. Jo Von McCalester, Dr. Billingsley began mapping and producing the remarkable project you now hold.

In April 2016, the Andrew Billingsley 90th Birthday Symposium and Celebration forged the missing link in Dr. Billingsley's recorded intellectual journey as well as documented his role in operationalizing the Black University concept. Visions of the Black University that emerged during the Black Power/Black Studies movement of the late 1960s-early 1970s were born out of a global intellectual thrust that imagined a world after colonization and apartheid. This vision has largely receded in the institutional memory of the campuses on which it was born. A handful of academic books and articles on the subject, cobbled together out of archival traces of the era by scholars with no living link to this movement or its institutional afterlives, fail to capture the movement or its living legacy at HBCUs. At our Black institutions, the faculty recruited into that movement has almost all transitioned into retirement or the eternity beyond. Most of them made their exits with little or no fanfare, a testament to a structural failure of institutional memory across our HBCUs. They have left in their wake those of us who served and apprenticed directly with them to face the challenge W. E. B. Du Bois revisited time and again in his public speeches from the nineteen-teens to the nineteen-sixties: What are the possibilities of purpose and meaning for a Black university in an increasingly non-white country or world?

Partial answers to this question are to be found in these pages. I remain in awe of the giants who participated in the symposium, some of them now ancestors and each of them overjoyed at the time to convene, assess, debate, and remember what they had achieved. The Billingsley years at Howard saw him recruit and/or support watershed figures in the intellectual history of African America. Many of their ideas were influenced by the pragmatic Black nationalism of the Institute of the Black World, such as ideas informing the establishment of the Institute for Arts and Humanities, the Urban Institute, the Moorland-Spingarn Research Center, and the Institute for Black Music. The most compelling of his creativity was the building of Howard into a world-class university. Those who gathered at the Symposium provided much of the dialogue provided herein.

The record of accomplishment during the Billingsley's years at Howard stand as witness to, and case study for, how this effort flowered across HBCUs from the early 1970s. It is also both an indictment and challenge to Black institutions that have yet to match, much less exceed, the convergence of will, ability, and collaborative vision of that apogee. As you read this volume, understand that the challenge to match and exceed what Billingsley and his comrades achieved still remains. The work of realizing the promise of the Black University, as Du Bois declared many times during his 95 years, is the central *raison d'etre* for their existence. To not understand this fundamental conceptual reality is what E. Franklin Frazier referred to as "the Failure of the Negro Intellectual."

Faculty members are, by definition and, more importantly, by nature, thinkers, teachers, and researchers. These are frequently solitary exercises, even when comingled with team pursuits. When done to its greatest impact, intellectual work requires the highest level of skill development. Such development is not a requirement for professional success as much as it is a necessary element of personal conviction and aspiration. In a moment when commodification of labor and branding of the appearance of excellence can take the place of the thing itself, we must not lose sight of the fact that these appearances, like any mirage, do not endure. The greatest institutions do not survive, thrive, or otherwise subsist on fakery and devoting primary energy to the appearance of excellence.

The greatest academic institutions create space and support for a mutually reinforcing community of thinkers. Andrew Billingsley's life example demonstrates an expenditure of spiritual and cultural capital whose model is more valuable than even the material form of compensation and material benefits, which have never been the principal institutional attraction for any but vulgar careerists. As you read these pages, understand that his expenditure of this ethereal capital was the principal catalyzer of "The Black University" and draw from his life the lesson that we can resume this work, with immediate attention and great declarative effort.

The future for higher education in America in this technological age is not predictable and even more so for the Black University. The future of HBCUs should lie with a revival of the Black University concept. When discussed at all, this concept only serves as archival fodder for scholars working at and/or with white universities, archives, and publishers. The irony of this development is not lost. What was gained by the disruption and renegotiation initiated against hierarchical power structures by Black liberation leaders through struggle is now being met with resistance by the leaders of the of these institutions. It is not lost that these are the very same institutions they struggled against decades ago. This was predictable.

If we do not locate the restorative sources of our collective social and intellectual inheritance as Black institutions, our best schools will not endure nor even thrive in the immediate future. They will do so, however, as something other than sources for transformative global change fed by larger visions born of the best and deepest of the long arcs of African intellectual work. This will occur even as our "sister HBCUs" in Africa and the Caribbean turn toward the truly transformative work of grounding their futures in a renewed engagement with the oldest, longest continuous and most important and impactful traditions and caches of human knowledge. It is what Jacob Carruthers called the "deep well" of African thought. So read this book, written by a contingent of Black scholars, about institutionalizing an expansive vision of Blackness in the academy and published by a legendary Black publishing house. Read it, not as a collection of reminiscences but as a roadmap, a battle cry, an inspiration to support and renew our collective commitment to this work. Long live Baba Dr. Andrew Billingsley! Long live the Black University!

Andrew Billingsley

Introduction

Charles Jarmon, Ph.D.

I welcomed the opportunity to participate in the celebration of the distinguished life of Professor Andrew Billingsley, an esteemed colleague and friend. This book of essays is in recognition of his stellar career and life of service as experienced by his former students, colleagues, and friends. It is a *festschrift* on his life and times. Most people in the general population have not heard of the uncommon German word, *festschrift*. In the sense of its German origin, it refers to a book written in celebration of someone of great accomplishment. This book honors Professor Billingsley for his accomplishments over his long professional career. The authors of the essays and articles contributed for this volume have had deep and significant relationships with Professor Billingsley. They have previously given presentations at symposia in his honor, either at the University of South Carolina or Howard University. In addition, I solicited a few others. The first symposium, organized and held at the University of South Carolina, celebrated his retirement in April 2010; the second, at Howard University, was held on the occasion of the celebration of his 90th birthday in April 2016.

The essays included in this *festschrift* capture parts of his life from his childhood experiences growing up in Alabama to the salient accomplishments of his later professional life. In the Prologue, Professor Billingsley discusses his life and times from early childhood to high school. We get a glimpse of the hardships of farm life on his family during the Great Depression, the impact on the family of the unfortunate injury to his father while working in the coal mines at Acmar, and his successful navigation of Lincoln High School in the urban slums of Birmingham. It reveals a very determined youth, who was drafted to serve in the U.S. Army after the tenth grade, and who returned two years later to complete his final two years. However, after he successfully passed the GED examination while in the eleventh grade in high school, he was allowed to bypass his final year of high school. He enrolled in Hampton Institute, where he spent the first two years of college before transferring to Grinnell College for his remaining two years. Andy completed his doctoral degree in the Department of Social Policy and Social Research at Brandeis University in the Florence Heller School for Advanced Studies in Social Welfare in 1963. His quest for further intellectual growth and professional development is evident in his post-graduate studies at Harvard University, where he spent the summer of 1981 at the Institute of Educational Management; his summer as a Rockefeller Foundation Fellow at the Aspen Institute for Humanistic Studies in 1979; and his time at the Leadership Workshops sponsored by the American Council of Education from 1977 to 1982.

Like so many other scholars and professionals in the academic world, my first awareness of Andrew Billingsley was related to his first major publication, *Black Families in White America,* which was published in 1968. I had begun my first full-time teaching position at Southern University in Baton Rouge, Louisiana, and had not been pleased about the availability of books on the Black family. While searching through new book announcements made available by publishing houses, I learned of Billingsley's nationally acclaimed book. He had taken one of the mainstream sociological functionalist approaches to society and adapted it to the African American family. However, in his use of this systemic approach, the Black family became the center of a social system in a way that had not been considered in mainstream sociology. He reversed the notion of the dysfunctional Black family, creating a fresh dialogue on its nature and role in the American society. I adopted it for class reading assignments, and continue to read the book today.

In 1978 ten years after having adopted his book, I joined Howard University's, graduate faculty with an appointment to the graduate faculty in the Department of Sociology and Anthropology. In this context, through conversations with members of the faculty of the department, I learned that Professor Billingsley had been the Vice President for Academic Affairs at the University and, in this role, how he had played a significant role in the development of Howard's graduate program. He had been particularly supportive of the development of the graduate program in sociology, playing a significant role in the establishment of the doctoral program.

Further, I learned of the role Andy had played in his leadership role in the development of doctoral programs in the other social science departments as well; this was particularly evident in the number of new distinguished faculty he had recruited to the departments of Political Science, African Studies, and History. He had also been committed to the development of the departments in the natural sciences, which was evident in the expansion of the faculty in the Department of Physics and in the School of Engineering.

In 1975, three years before my arrival at Howard, Professor Billingsley had left to become the president of Morgan State College in Baltimore. As President of Morgan State, he was active in its successful effort to obtain university status, which was essential for the development of a doctoral program at the University. Many years later, at one of the professional sociology meetings, I asked Billingsley why he had not been honored at Howard University for the role he, in partnership with James Cheek, played in creating a new intellectual climate at that university—in particular, for the establishment of doctoral programs in the social sciences and for the development of other academic and research centers as well as the Howard University Press. In a witty reply, he said, "I don't know, but you can make it happen."

What manner of man is Andrew Billingsley? There is no easy answer to this question; however, one approach to the question is to judge him by his deeds. In moving through the chronology of events over the span of his life, as described in the different essays and articles encompassed in this book on his life, we are made aware of an unassuming intellectual, a brilliant administrator, a pioneering sociologist of the Black experience, a caring civil servant, and a visionary. Each of the authors provides the reader with a piece of the answer to this question—providing insight into different dimensions of the question, but still leaving the reader with the obligation to arrive at his own conclusions. Beyond this, through the recognition of the many honors that he has received over his lifetime, the reader gains a greater appreciation of the breadth and depth of his achievements. These include two honorary Doctor of Humane Letters degrees and none more important than the one awarded to him by his undergraduate college, Grinnell College in 1991. His second honorary degree was awarded to him by Mercy College in 1982.

He has been recognized by numerous other professional organizations in sociology and social work. These include recognition for his public service by the South Carolina State Legislature; recognition by the Boy Scouts of America, Birmingham Chapter; recognition for his community leadership by the National Council of Negro Women; and recognition by Howard University for professional service to the School of Architecture. This selected listing of the range of his accomplishments more than justifies why the contributors to this book came together to recognize him and were generous in their accolades.

As an illustration of his influence in the area of sociology and the broader area of social sciences between 1970 and 2006, Professor Billingsley's scholarly works were cited at least 856 times in the Social Science Citation Index and the Arts and Humanities Citation Index. The citations primarily reflected the importance of his research on the family, church, and education, the primary subjects of his eight books and other journal publications.

He is an established public intellectual on matters pertaining to the Black family, the Black church, and the education of Black youth. His first major book, as previously cited, was *Black Families in White America,* published in 1968. In later years, his books, *Climbing Jacob's Ladder,* published in 1992, and *Yearning to Breathe Free: Robert Smalls of South Carolina and His Families,* published in 2007, attracted national attention.

The authors of the chapters in this book, which follow the chronology of his life events, provide views from different points in the life and times of Dr. Billingsley, and we owe them a great debt of gratitude for participating in the symposia and for agreeing to share their experiences with Professor Billingsley. From their collective contribution, we gain a deeper understanding of the pathways he took to gain insight into ways of conceptualizing and strengthening the Black family; understanding the role of the church and its relationship to the Black community; and understanding the prologue of history for continuing to push further for more comprehensive studies for advancing the future of the Black community. The authors have done this in different ways.

Prologue

The prologue consists of an autobiographical essay of Professor Billingsley's early youth in Alabama through the years of the Great Depression and his later years in World War II. Dr. Billingsley and Dr. Bathsheba Bryant-Tarpeh tell of a family that struggled mightily after the Depression years. Andy recalls that he was born, according to the family Bible (written in the handwriting of his father), on March 22, 1926. However, his family's oral history gives alternative birth dates: March 20 and March 21. No official record was made of his birth. He, along with his father, mother, and brother, grew up poor on a farm in Marion, Alabama. During this period, they relied on growing food crops to help sustain the family. However, the Great Depression in 1929 changed their lives. Billingsley was still young when the Depression created an economic crisis across the country. As President Theodore Roosevelt's New Deal Policy did not rescue farmers, things fell apart, and families were forced to leave the farm.

In 1934, his father moved to Acmar, Alabama, a coal-mining town 25 miles from Birmingham. There is where Andy entered school for the first time. His father, after several years with the company, broke his leg in the mine and consequently could not work at his job at the coal-mining company. His father moved the family to Birmingham, where they discovered that they were too poor to live in public housing. His father had no substantial employment and therefore, did not have a job that provided the minimum income level to qualify for public housing. Thanks to the temporary assistance of his father's brother, a steel worker, they were able to acquire an apartment. During this period of hardship, his mother worked as a domestic worker for white families. This was a time, as Andy recalls, that taxed his father's sense of pride and independence.

As there were no schools for Blacks in Marion, Alabama, during the years of his youth, Andy and his brother depended on Andy's father to teach them the rudimentary skills expected of one with a primary-level education. His father had completed six years of education and felt that it was necessary to be able to read and write. It was not before Andy was eight years old and his brother was ten years old that they first entered school. With the education provided by his father at home, they mastered the basics of reading, writing, arithmetic, and grammar, and were permitted to skip grades appropriately. They acclimated well to Lincoln High School in Birmingham, and Andy joined the marching band. During a session with the band on Sunday morning, December 7, 1941, someone shouted: "The Japanese have bombed Pearl Harbor! The President has declared war."

A few years later, his brother William was drafted in the military. Six months later, Andy received his draft letter to enter the Army. After his discharge from the Army, he returned to his former high school, Parker High, where he returned as an eleventh-grade student. In March of that year, he requested to take the General Education Development (GED) test. He passed the exam. He was subsequently exempted from his senior year of high school. Having received his high school diploma at the end of junior year, he applied for admission to Hampton Institute and was accepted.

Part I: Undergraduate Studies

Professors Lois Benjamin and Kesho Scott, in Chapters 3 and 4, respectively, discuss Andy's experiences as an undergraduate student in college. Benjamin writes of his experiences at Hampton Institute during the years 1947-1949. After two years, Andy transferred to Grinnell College for the final two years of his undergraduate education, graduating in 1951. Scott writes of his experiences during these two years. In both chapters, we get a feel for the ideas and ambitions that consumed him as an undergraduate student.

Part II: On Becoming A Teacher Scholar: University of California, Berkeley, 1964-1970

After earning Master's degrees in social work (1955) and sociology (1960), and completing his Ph.D. in child welfare and public policy studies in the Heller School at Brandeis University in 1963, Professor Billingsley began his academic career in 1964 at the University of California at Berkeley, in the Graduate School of Social Welfare. In 1968, the assassinations of Dr. Martin Luther King Jr. and Senator Robert Kennedy were followed by a period of national turbulence and Civil Rights activism. At the University of California at Berkeley, Dr. Billingsley was appointed by Chancellor Roger Haynes to become Assistant Chancellor for Academic Affairs, with the responsibility of assisting the University in responding to the demands of ethnic minority students whose aim was to establish Ethnic Studies programs. Established in 1970, it included programs in African American Studies, Hispanic American Studies, Asian American Studies, and Native American Studies. It would be the second such department established in the nation (after San Francisco State). It would become a model for other universities.

Chapters 3 and 4 provide different perspectives from which to understand Dr. Billingsley's leadership role at Berkeley. Douglas Davidson and Howard Dodson provide insights into different aspects of Professor Billingsley's determination to include the African American experience in the curricula. As a result of his leadership and activism, Billingsley was elevated to the position of Vice Chancellor and charged with the responsibility of developing a Black Studies Program. Davidson aptly describes the struggle for the inclusion of the study of the African American experience as a movement "from Black Power to Black Studies." Dodson provides a view of the many sides of mentorship, which he illustrates in his discussion of the long and symbiotic relationship that existed between him and his professor, Dr. Billingsley.

Part III: Institution Building at Howard University, 1970-1975

The next ten chapters focus on Andy's years as the Vice President for Academic Affairs at Howard University following the turbulent years of the 1960s. Andy arrived at Howard in 1970 and recruited most of those contributing to this discussion on Howard University. These include Dr. Ronald Walters, former Chairman of the Department of Political Science; Dr. Percy Pierre, former Dean of the School of Engineering; Dr. Joshua Myers, Assistant Professor of Afro-American Studies; Dr. Joyce Ladner, sociologist and former Acting President of Howard University; Dr. Ralph Gomes, sociologist; Dr. Eleanor Traylor, former Chairman and Professor Emeritus of the Department of English; Dr. Edna Medford, former Chairman of the Department of History and former Interim Dean of the College of Arts and Sciences; Lawrence Gary, former Director of the Institute of Urban Affairs and Research and Professor Emeritus of Social Work; and Janell Walden Agyeman, Literary Agent. This was the beginning of a period of "enlightenment" and change in the evolution and development of Howard University as a major university. Professor Walters provides a quote of a statement made by Andy to *Ebony* magazine. It summarizes the essence of his vision:

> We must be sure that we put Blackness into the curriculum, and that we do it in a manner that is a move toward excellence. We don't want to cripple Black students with a watered down curriculum that doesn't really speak to their needs. We have to be very hard-headed about scholarship. We can't be soft, call it Black, and just dismiss it like that, because we're going to be liberated by training our minds and then moving into the community.[1]

The remaining chapters provide examples of how his vision was transformed into his legacy.[2]

Part IV: Institution Building at Morgan State University, 1975-1984

In the two essays presented in Part IV, Dr. Clara Adams and Wornie Reed tell the story of Professor Billingsley's accomplishments as President of Morgan State University. Andy served in this position for nine years, 1975 to 1984. During this period, as Professor Reed sets forth in his article, "Morgan State University and the Urban Mission," Billingsley established Morgan State as a major urban research university, attracting nationally recognized scholars. Reed discusses the significant role of the Institute for Urban Research (IUR) in assessing the status of African Americans in urban areas. The Institute's Baltimore Area Study was an exemplary example of this mission.

Part V: A Return to Scholarship at the University of Maryland, College Park and, University of South Carolina

Part V presents commentary on Billingsley's return to scholarship, which he pursued at the University of Maryland, College Park, and the University of South Carolina. While at the University of Maryland, College Park, he was able to return to his research on the Black family and publish two books: *Climbing Jacob's Ladder: The Enduring Legacy of African American Families* and *Mighty Like a River: The Black Church and Social Reform*. With reference to the importance of Andy's research, Paula Giddings, in her Foreword to

Climbing Jacob's Ladder, comments: "Where a previous generation of scholars saw deviation and weakness, the new scholars saw resourcefulness and resilience…and looking at the African-American family through the lens of what it has done, against all odds, …brings one to a very different conclusion than looking at it as merely a deficit model." Evelyn Higginbotham and Roger Rubin, two of Andy's colleagues while he served as the Chairman of the Department of Family Studies, continue to provide accolades in honor of Andy's career. Dr. Higginbotham, whom he has known since his years at Howard University, comments on Andy's influence on the development of her professional career, particularly during her years at the University of Maryland. Roger Rubin, who became Andy's colleague in 1986, was first influenced by Andy's first major publication, *Black Families in White America.* He was "profoundly influenced by the theoretical framework and context of this work" and used it as a theoretical framework for his own research on the Black family. Their colleagueship bloomed into a lifetime friendship.

During Billingsley's years at the University of South Carolina, he would enjoy his longest tenure at any institution of higher learning, and he has taken particular pride in this fact. He was, for the first time, free of administrative constraints. He has taken particular pride in ending his long and distinguished career at the University of South Carolina. He served there from 1997 to 2010. During this tenure, he served simultaneously as Professor of Sociology, Professor of African American Studies, and Senior Scholar in Residence at the Institute for Families in Society. While at that university, he also managed to publish *Yearning to Breathe Free: Robert Smalls of South Carolina and His Families,* which includes an introduction by Assistant Democratic Leader James Clyburn of South Carolina and a cover designed by the distinguished artist, Jonathan Green.

In this section of the *festschrift,* Assistant Democratic Leader James Clyburn provides an official Congressional statement in which Professor Billingsley is praised highly for the significance of *Yearning to Breathe Free.* Congressman Clyburn's comments are followed by Professor Billingsley's telling of his serendipitous discovery of a story about Harriet Tubman in a Columbus, South Carolina, newspaper. He was captivated by the role she played in the Civil War. In addition to serving as a spy, scout, and nurse to the Federal Army Command in South Carolina, Tubman was instrumental to the Command for her invaluable role as a recruiter of Black male slaves. She influenced them to join its ranks at a crucial period when the Federal Army faced a shortage of Union soldiers. It was a necessity to get Black males to join the ranks. She is most remembered for her role in leading three army war ships on Beaufort, freeing the slaves and sacking the town.

She was an extraordinary woman who could not read or write but was foremost in her leadership for the freedom of Black slaves. A laudatory chapter is provided by Patricia Motes, Ana Lopez-DeFede, and Sheila Heatley, concerning Professor Billingsley's stay in South Carolina. For his colleagues at the University of South Carolina, his role as a mentor, teacher, and scholar endeared him not only to the Institute for Family Services but also to the wider community. It is remarkable that Andy ended his professional career in the same way that it began: as an activist scholar.

Following this discussion, Andy and Reverend Kenneth Hodges give us their perspectives on much of Dr. Billingsley's research in South Carolina. The final perspective in the book is provided by Robert Hill. He comments on Billingsley's successful contribution to our understanding of the Black family, both its strengths and weaknesses, and how it helped to redefine the Black family in the literature in both the disciplines of sociology and social work.

As primary editor of this *festschrift* honoring Andrew Billingsley, I appreciate the opportunity to participate in recognizing the works and deeds of one of our foremost scholars of the African American family. When we consider the impact that he has had on the research accomplishments of generations of scholars, think tanks, research centers, and even universities —as his colleagues noted in recognition of his years at Howard University, Morgan State, University of Maryland, College Park, and the University of South Carolina—we fully sense the depth of this man. They help us to understand the answer to the question, "What manner of man is Andrew Billingsley?" I attempted to provide my answer to this question at the celebration of his 90th birthday at Howard University, as I had been amazed at his ability to move into uncharted territories and have the capacity to build foundations for change and new beginnings. I concluded that he was one of our intellectual giants in the disciplines of Social Work, Sociology, African American Studies, and in the broader area of higher education. In reflecting on the comments of my colleagues, I have concluded that they do not fully measure the breadth of Andrew Billingsley's accomplishments.

Andrew Billingsley, Sixth grade graduation picture from Acmar Junior
High School, Acmar, Alabama, 1940.

An Autobiographical Essay: Growing Up in Alabama, 1926 -1947

Andrew Billingsley, Ph.D.*

I was born on a farm in the rural sector of Marion, Alabama, in March 1926. Through the years, relatives have differed as to the exact date—with some of the family saying March 20 and others saying March 21. I remember at a very young age seeing the date listed in my father's handwriting in the family Bible as March 22. I was told that I was delivered by an older woman of the family, not by a midwife. No record was ever made of my birth in official records.[3] There is a consensus that my brother Bill was born June 16, 1924, which made him a year and nine months older than me. And until he was drafted into the U.S. Army, we were virtually inseparable in all we did. He was drafted at the age of nineteen-and-a-half years. I was drafted six months later.

I did not always appreciate the significance of the place of my birth; however, when I met with Dr. Horace Mann Bond (Julian Bond's father) in his office at Atlanta University, he told me of some path-breaking research in which he was then engaged. Dr. Bond, a sociologist, historian, and educator, was then at Atlanta University. He was formerly President of Lincoln University in Pennsylvania (1945-1957).

In his mid-1960s, study titled "A Study of Factors Involved in the Identification of Unusual Academic Achievement Among Underprivileged Populations," Dr. Bond highlighted some historical facts about Black families in Marion, Alabama. He had found that a substantial proportion of his subjects, Black holders of Ph.D. degrees, medical doctorates, and other high-level professionals, were descended from parents or grandparents who were born and raised in Alabama in the early years after the Civil War. Among those with roots in Alabama, an unusually high proportion had been born and raised in Perry County, Alabama, where Marion is located. Of the major factors he found boosting an achievement orientation among Blacks in Perry County was the Lincoln Normal School, named for the U.S. President during the Civil War.

Dr. Bond was alerted to the significance of Lincoln Normal School in the achievement of contemporary Blacks in letters from the subjects in his study. He rose from his desk to show me the map he had constructed in the shape of the state of Alabama and its 67 counties, on which he had placed little dots representing high achieving Black persons with family roots in Alabama and Perry County, where Marion is located. Then he said to me with feeling: "All of those dots represent Black persons with doctorates from Alabama and Perry County, and they came directly or indirectly from the Lincoln Normal School in Marion, Alabama."

Now, I was not a subject of Dr. Bond's study, and it was only then that I dared to interrupt the Professor, shouting, "Dr. Bond, you have to add another dot to that map!" He looked puzzled. "You have standing before you another confirmation of your thesis." Then, with excitement, I said something like, "I, Andrew Billingsley, am a freshly minted Ph.D. from the Heller School at Brandeis University. I am now a University of California Professor, and I was born in Marion, Alabama, in 1926."

My father, Silas Billingsley, who only had a sixth-grade education from the Lincoln Normal School in Marion, raised his family there probably from 1926 to 1934. I have always considered him to be a very learned man. It was remarkable that he was able to spend his life as a farmer, coal miner, and laborer; yet, he was able to teach his children the basics he had learned at Lincoln School. In Marion, there were no schools for Blacks when we were younger. He taught us to stand on his shoulders and reach for the stars. My brother Bill and I were both high achievers.

Marion, Alabama, 1930-1934

I remember moving to and living on a farm in Marion when I was about four years old. Life was pretty good, considering the nature of that time in our nation's history. We lived in the country several miles from the town of Marion. My father was a sharecropper. The white owner of the farm provided the land and seeds for planting. When the crops were marketed, the owner would get half the proceeds and my father the other half. I do remember that for several years we were prosperous. My father planted cotton, corn, and sugar cane. At harvest time my father made little sacks for my brother and me to pick cotton along with — or way behind — him. I do not remember my mother working in the fields. Her specialty was the gardens and the home. She planted Irish potatoes, sweet potatoes, tomatoes, green peas, and okra. She also cultivated blueberries, blackberries, grapes, and strawberries. We also had several cows, which provided milk and butter. Horses and mules were there for riding and for work. In the nearby woods we went hunting for birds, rabbits, squirrels, and an occasional opossum.

My father, using his Lincoln education, taught us all the basics he had learned at Lincoln. He also taught us repeatedly the facts about life. My mother made all the children's clothes, except shoes, raincoats, and winter coats, which she ordered from the Sears Roebuck catalog. (We also used its back issues as toilet paper.) She was a moralist, and wanted us to be good. My father, however, wanted us to be smart. Both parents read the Bible and were church-going Baptists. Both taught us to "do unto others as you would have them do unto you." We learned that lesson well.

During the year 1933-1934, conditions got worse. We actually went hungry some days. All the animals, chickens, and gardens had been devoured or had died. My father, given that most of what we learned came from him, must have told us that the nation was undergoing a depression. For several years, after it began in 1929, we barely survived. Surely, after 1932, he told us about FDR and the New Deal. But whatever it was, the New Deal had not come to the farms of Marion, Alabama, and we were desperate.

The time came when we had to abandon the farm and head for more fertile ground. In early 1934, my father came home from somewhere and announced that we were moving. He said we should pack all our belongings and a few kitchen items and wait until around midnight. We packed hurriedly without asking any questions. My mother silently took charge of the packing. As we were going to her sister's house, her sister's husband Johnnie had come home with Daddy to help us move. At midnight, we were all packed and ready to move. In anticipation of our arrival, her sister had prepared a large and wholesome meal for all of us. Uncle Steve, her husband's father, had learned that the government, under President Roosevelt, was giving away food to poor families, and he had acquired a barrel of food for each of his families. We ate hearty and prepared for bed. My father hugged everybody goodbye. Then, while it was still dark, he went outside and sat on the front steps, facing the highway. Soon an open-bed truck came along. My father hurried down to the highway and boarded the bed of the truck, pulling down a tarpaulin over himself along with five or six other men. The truck did not tarry long. It had to be on the highway headed north out of town before sunrise.

For days and weeks we did not know where he was, but we had no doubt that he would come back and take us with him. Finally, he did come for us, and he took us to a place called Acmar, Alabama, a coal-mining town some 25 miles from Birmingham. He had found a steady job as a coal miner, a house for his family, and a school, which would be the first school for his two boys. Although we had begun to feel the effects of the Depression, we were now somewhat sheltered from its worst effects.

The Alabama Coal Mine and Railroad Company (ACMAR) owned everything; thus, the name of the town). For the next five years ,we lived relatively comfortably. We had electricity for the first time. My father had a steady yet low-paying job. My mother did not have to work outside the home. We purchased food and other necessities from the company-owned commissary. My father taught us how to shop and count change, saying that would prevent us from being cheated by the clerks. It also prepared us for school.

Acmar Junior High School was the most important thing about Acmar, Alabama. It was located in a church building, up a hill in a neighboring community. It was the first schoolhouse that we had ever seen. In the fall of 1934, my brother Bill, age 10, and I, age 8, entered school for the first time ever. There were no schools for Blacks in our part of Marion. It would be a most joyous next six years. All students beginning school for the first time were entered into the primary grade. It was a yearlong course of study to prepare for promotion to the first grade. However, long before the end of that first year, the teachers had discovered what my father tried to tell them at the beginning.

My father had taught us the basics of reading, writing, spelling, arithmetic, and grammar. We, of course, excelled at the grammar school and were at the head of our class. At the end of that year, the teachers skipped us both over the first grade and placed us into the second grade. As I remember, we floated through the second grade at the top of the class as well. My father was so proud of us. Thus, in May 1940, we graduated with certificates from the sixth grade at Acmar Junior High School.

That last year at Acmar Junior High was great for us in school, but things were very difficult at home. During that year my father broke his leg in the mines. The company doctors treated and set his leg and provided him with a set of crutches. His leg healed slowly. He received no worker's compensation and no salary while he was off work. He was a very proud man. After five years of a very good, steady livelihood and family life, we were now thrown back into the deepest poverty. Neighbors helped out as they could, but that was limited. Worse yet, since the company owned everything in town, including the housing units in which we lived, we had to move out of town.

My father's half-brother, Emerson Billingsley, lived 25 miles away in Birmingham. He worked in the steel mill, which was owned, not surprisingly, by the same company that owned the coal mines in Acmar. He rented a two-room apartment for us on the second floor of a building on 17th Street and 8th Avenue North, near the downtown area of the city. I had never heard the word "slum," but during that early period in Birmingham we were miserable. My father's brother gave us a little money for food, but my proud father, who was still on crutches, began to pound the pavement looking for work. His utter dependence and inability to provide for his family, which included being dependent on his half-brother, affected him deeply. He believed that it was *his* responsibility to provide for *his* family.

The last straw came when my mother began working in domestic service again. It only intensified my father's concerns about providing for our family, consisting of him, Mother, Bill and me. During this time, my father's mother, Leah Billingsley, became ill, and she came to live with us, which made our lives very hard. Our family was once again in deep crisis. Although my father had great faith in President Roosevelt, who was completing his second term and getting ready for his third, he was apparently no help to us.

By September, my father could walk with his cane. Immediately, he went down the street to join the Macedonia Baptist Church (St. James Baptist Church would come later). I do not remember where he found work. However, soon after, he found us a better apartment, but still with only two rooms, on the ground floor and more spacious. We could now play in the yard. We could also walk to school.

In the fall of 1940, my brother and I entered seventh grade at Acmar Junior High School for Colored. It was located on 8th Avenue adjoining a public housing project in the Smithfield Section of the city. The school was located just off a busy highway that separated the town's two Black communities. Our section was in the flatlands; the Smithfield section was on higher ground, which we later learned was occupied by older established and prosperous neighbors. I remember coming home from school one day to tell my father about the public housing project I had learned about from one of my teachers. President Roosevelt had built these houses for poor people. I said, "Aren't we poor? Can't you get us a house there?" My father told me sadly, "Yes, son, we're poor, but you have to have some steady income to get in there. I have already checked it out." We were not able to live up to the income requirement standards of the new public housing projects. This was a conundrum that I would not completely unravel until years later when I entered college at Hampton Institute in 1947.

Bill and I attended Lincoln High School, which offered a tracking system and in addition to academic classes, trade and workshop classes from which students could choose. My brother chose to take classes in tailoring.

I chose to take music classes, which consisted of school band training and performance. Mr. Handy, my instructor, was the nephew of the Father of the Blues, William C. Handy of St. Louis, Missouri. He was also a native of Alabama. Because I had had piano lessons in my earlier years, I knew a lot of the fundamentals of music and learned rapidly. By the end of my first year, I had mastered the trombone enough to fill a vacancy in the school marching band.

In the eighth grade, school officials made the decision to separate my brother and me into different classes, skipping my brother a grade ahead of me. For the next few years, even in high school, my brother and I would invariably be elected (or appointed by teachers) as presidents of our class. I suspect our leadership skills were partly a result of being older than most of our classmates and the sound educational training that had been given to Bill and me back in Marion. Acmar had been a school noted for its exceptional educational programs. Our math teacher at that time was Mr. Davis. My brother remembered later that Davis would become the father of Angela Davis, the noted Civil Rights activist. Further, my music teacher, Mr. Handy, in addition to his Lincoln school band, was also instructor of a band of men who worked in the steel mills. On Sundays, he would meet and instruct those men, and he included me in the band to fill a trombone position.

One Sunday afternoon, while the band was practicing, a man burst into the room and shouted, "The Japanese have bombed Pearl Harbor! President Roosevelt says that this means war!" It was Sunday, December 7, 1941. I was 15 years old. My brother was 17.

After graduating eighth grade from Lincoln, we entered the ninth grade at Parker High School Annex. It was a cluster of frame buildings near Lincoln School, while in the main building of Parker High School the tenth to twelfth grades were in the large, new, white stone-and-brick building a little way up Eighth Avenue. I played trombone in the Parker High School Band and did well in school. My family was active in the St. James Baptist Church, three blocks from our house. In 1944, when my brother turned 20 years old, he was drafted into the U.S. Army. I was proud; I wanted to go and do whatever my brother did. Before the end of the school year, at eighteen years old and in the tenth grade, I too was drafted. Our family, neighbors, and the church people were proud of us. They said we were a credit to our nation and our race!!

It was not long before I had to report for induction. I went up the street to see Dr. Ballard, a Black physician, and the first physician I had ever seen, for my physical exam, and, before school began, I too was in the U.S.

Army. At the induction center, I was frightened yet determined to serve my country. I inquired if I could join my brother's outfit, which still had not shipped out oversees. "No," I was told. The Army had a policy against assigning brothers to the same unit. At the induction center they gave me many tests and admitted me to the hospital to remove a cyst that had grown on the back of my head. After a few days, I was off to basic training at Fort Devens in Ayer, Massachusetts.

Training was very difficult, but I was determined to do well; not nearly as well, however, as Ralph David Abernathy, who would rise to become top sergeant of my company. One time a soldier from another unit came over to visit someone in our unit. When he met me, he said there was another soldier named Billingsley in his unit. My brother and I not only got to visit frequently, we got passes to go into Boston on weekends. We heard Marion Anderson sing and saw Paul Robeson play the role in Shakespeare's *Othello*. Also, on weekends my outfit was frequently assigned guard duty on Saturday nights at the Roxbury Hotel. What a treat!! Best of all was that in 1944 at Christmas time, we both got to go home on three-day passes. We enjoyed being home again and being addressed as heroes, but we were soon back at our separate training units.

A few weeks later, my brother's outfit was shipped overseas. Word had it that they were bound for Germany. Ralph David Abernathy was appointed platoon sergeant over my platoon. The *Stars and Stripes* Army newspaper blared the headlines. Captain Pletz called the company into formation. Lieutenant Swanson read the official communiqué outlining that on April 12, 1945, President Franklin D. Roosevelt had died at his summer cottage in Georgia. The war was winding down. We would be sent overseas, nevertheless.

Our platoon shipped from the U.S. and landed at Le Havre, France. We were met by U.S. Army trucks, which carried us into Germany. We were instructed to carry our weapons loaded and at the ready during the entire trip. We were assigned occupation duty, urged to watch out for German snipers and urged to stay away from German civilians, especially females. We served for short terms variously in Bonn, Dusseldorf, and Durin. At one post, one of the other units assigned to the city included my brother Bill. He had already become acquainted with the city and showed me around. They were amazingly civil to us. The German armies surrendered to the U.S. and Russian forces on May 8, 1945. Abernathy became ill and was returned stateside for treatment and discharged.

The second surprise came on August 6, 1945. We were in the midst of the Pacific Ocean headed toward Japan when the news came over the ship's radio. The U.S. had detonated the atomic bomb over the Japanese mainland city of Hiroshima. In this city of half-a-million population, over 100,000 Japanese were killed. Before we could digest the impact, three days later, on August 9, a second atomic bomb was detonated over the city of Nagasaki, a city with a population of 400,000 in which another 100,000 Japanese were killed. The cities were destroyed. With the enormously high casualty rate, the war was over. The Japanese surrendered unconditionally on August 15, 1945, and ended World War II. The formal peace treaty was signed September 2 aboard a U.S. warship by President Truman. President Truman appointed General Douglas MacArthur as Commander-in-Chief over Japan and ushered in to that nation a democratic government whose military was forbidden to engage in warfare.

Our ship was diverted to the Philippines, and my unit was stationed in Manila, where I would serve for six months, mostly doing office work for the unit. My brother's outfit was sent to another island in the Philippines. After six months in Manila, I was transferred to Inchon, Korea, where I spent the last six months of my military career. I was promoted to the rank of sergeant and placed in charge of personnel records; however, when the six months were over, I was eager to be discharged. My brother remained in the army for twenty years before retiring.

I had heard about the GI Bill, which I learned would support military veterans who chose to return to high school or attend college. I took that opportunity to return to high school with the expectation of also attending college. It was a great feeling to return for my last two years of high school, which would provide me with an opportunity to go to college. In that regard, in my last deployment to Korea, in 1946, I served under two Black officers. One was a certified public accountant who had graduated from University of Michigan. He urged me to pursue higher education under the GI Bill.

When I returned home to Birmingham after the Army, I threw myself back into civilian life with enthusiasm. I was discharged in August 1946, just in time to reenter Parker High School in September, where all my classmates had graduated. When I entered the eleventh grade to complete the last two years I needed to graduate, I did so without shame for being older but with enthusiasm and a sort of ease. I strived to do what I knew I could do, simply because everyone believed in me.

I missed my brother terribly. I had to make my way without his example and without the Army's explicit explanations about how to act in different situations. Birmingham was still a rigidly segregated city in 1946. The church and the school — still my primary connections to the world beyond my family — embraced me warmly. Though I was still remarkably shy, even after having traveled around the world, my veteran's status helped stand me in good stead in the community.

At the church, I was welcomed back and taken in as a member. I rejoined the youth choir, taught Sunday School, gave talks about my experiences overseas, and began to pay my dues. Moreover, the girls were respectfully receptive to my advances at Parker High.

At Parker High School, I picked up where I left off. I rejoined the school marching band and concert band. In March, when I turned 21, I was encouraged by my teachers to take the exam to become an eligible voter. The exam required the applicant to read and interpret any section of the Alabama State Constitution to the satisfaction of the examining officer. Some said this new law was aimed at keeping Blacks from passing. I passed and paid my $1.50 poll tax to become a registered voter in Alabama and for national elections in 1948. I also took and passed the GED which meant that I would be able to skip the twelfth grade altogether and go straight to college. Guess what? I passed that one too, and I do not know who was the proudest — my father, my teachers, or my pastor. My brand new girlfriend, sixteen-year-old Gwendolyn Strick, said that she knew all along that I would pass both exams.

With those accomplishments, while still in eleventh grade and enjoying it, I started applying for admission to college. I applied to only two. I thought I might like to be a CPA and applied to Michigan State University. I was rejected with the explanation that Michigan's universities were obliged to give preference to Michigan residents. The other college I applied to was Hampton Institute, now Hampton University, and I was accepted. The only other person in my Army unit who had been to college was my officemate, Bernard Jones. He had attended Hampton University and had sung its praises.

In the eleventh grade at Arthur Harold Parker High Sschool in Birmingham, I was admitted to college, which was truly a cause for celebration. As my homeroom teacher proposed, since I was going to college without finishing twelfth grade and because I had obtained the my GED, the school should award me the high school diploma at the very next commencement. The principal, Mr. Johnson, agreed, and so it was done!!! In the fall, I would be off to Hampton Institute.

Andrew Billingsley and brother William Billingsley, 1945, training at Fort Devens, Massachusettes, while serving in World War II.

PART I

UNDERGRADUATE STUDIES

"Hampton would become the foundational springboard for Billingsley's life path as a scholar/activist — the nurturer of his service orientation and his candle of consciousness and the whetstone of his political diplomacy and his leadership development."

Chapter 1

"A Life of the Mind": Andrew Billingsley's Hampton Years, 1947-1949

Lois Benjamin, Ph.D.

At the close of World War II, millions of returning veterans flocked to colleges and universities across the country due to the GI Bill. When Andrew Billingsley, at age twenty-one and a two-year veteran of the Army, headed to Hampton Institute (now Hampton University) in 1947, he was among that cohort. For the first time in the history of America, this watershed legislation helped to democratize higher education. Certainly, it was Billingsley's passport to college. "I would not have gone to college without the GI Bill. I never had any experience of college. The only people I knew who went to college were my teachers,"[4] said Billingsley, the son of working-class parents. Although his father had only a sixth grade education and his mother even less, his travels around the world while serving in the Army had broadened his sphere beyond the borders of Alabama. In the service, he had met Bernard Jones, a former student at Hampton Institute prior to being drafted for the war. Since Jones was the only person in Billingsley's unit who had attended college, Billingsley was eager to spend time with him. Often, Jones' conversations with Billingsley centered on the kaleidoscope of campus life — its challenges, its cultural activities, and its biracial experiences. Billingsley, who was drafted at age eighteen after completing the tenth grade, could not, however, begin to dream of college life until he completed high school. After his stint in the Army, he returned to Alabama to do just that. Two factors allowed Billingsley to graduate early: he passed the GED test and the voting rights test, becoming the only boy in his eleventh grade class who could vote. His teachers, so impressed with his accomplishments, allowed him to graduate early with his GED.

In 1947, Billingsley arrived on the Hampton campus, and there he found a "fantastically new experience, which was intellectually and socially challenging." It offered such enriched "cultural activities and such a mixture of people from everywhere, both faculty and students." In some ways,

1

he was not prepared for college life, particularly, its cultural changes and its academic challenges. Billingsley, who had never written anything more than one page, struggled to find his footing writing term papers during his first semester in college. In learning how to write, he spent several nights burning the midnight oil. But soon, he said, "I got the hang of it." Later, J. Saunders Redding, poet and professor of literature at Hampton, would also help him to get the hang of writing as well as literature.

Hampton would become the foundational springboard for Billingsley's life path as a scholar/activist: the nurturer of his service orientation and his candle of consciousness and the whetstone of his political diplomacy and his leadership development.

The Hampton Influence

Billingsley entered the Division of Business at Hampton Institute as a general business major, but when he came under the influence of Hylan Lewis, professor of social sciences at Hampton Institute from 1945 to 1948,[5] he caught the social science fever and developed an impressive sociological imagination. At the time, Billingsley was taking one of his courses in sociology, Lewis was conducting field research for his classic work, *Blackways of Kent*. He shared with Billingsley his field notes, which were based on an African American community in South Carolina. "I was particularly influenced by field studies and the importance of observing and recording what people say and what they do," Billingsley acknowledged. Under Lewis' tutelage, Billingsley also gained a deeper understanding of the social-class structure. "I knew that I was poor growing up in Alabama, but I did not fully comprehend structured inequality until I took that course with Hylan Lewis." In addition to introducing Billingsley to the conceptual framework for understanding social-class structure, Lewis also helped him to understand the concepts of slum and social mobility — the movement of individuals, families, and groups through a system — as well as helped him to understand community as a sociological construct. Armed with Lewis' transplanted sociological lens, Billingsley would employ the sociological insights harvested at Hampton Institute to effect social change.

Years later, the two men became reacquainted when, during the academic year of 1967-68, Lewis invited Billingsley to present a paper on trans-racial adoption. Billingsley was then at Berkeley and Hylan Lewis at Howard University. When Lewis moved to New York, he invited Billingsley to come there to work on a research project for a semester with the Urban League. Ultimately, Billingsley's work on transracial adoption was informed by this assignment.

Unmistakably, the influence of Hylan Lewis' conceptual and methodological framework is evidenced in Billingsley's own scholarship. As Billingsley concedes, "Hampton introduced me to Hylan Lewis, and the influence endured."

Life of Service: The Hampton Influence

After Billingsley's freshman year ended, he planned to return to Birmingham, Alabama, to work as an accountant in a Black bank. However, Edward Miller, Dean of Chapel (Professor of Social Sciences with a degree in sociology), persuaded him instead to do volunteer work. Specifically, he suggested that Billingsley should volunteer his service to the Black bank as an accountant, and then use his experiential learning to better understand the principles of accounting. Miller, also a chaplain and a Quaker, would become a pivotal influence during Billingsley's time at Hampton. "He introduced me to Quakerism and the importance of community service. Being service oriented was strongly embedded in me by Miller, particularly service to Blacks."

The GI Bill paved the way for Billingsley's volunteerism. During another summer, he volunteered his service to build a center for war orphans in Ortona, Italy, with the American Friends Service Committee. Three Americans from diverse social and political backgrounds, along with other internationals, worked at the camp, which was overseen by Catholic priests. They included Billingsley, who was a Black Democrat; Sanford Kravitz, a Jewish progressive; and a white American woman, who was Catholic and a Republican. This experience helped him to appreciate and respect diverse perspectives. Billingsley stayed eight weeks in Italy and was able to travel throughout the country and the Adriatic Sea.

In a newspaper article dated November 6, 1949,[6] highlighting his work camp experience, Billingsley explained "the work camp philosophy of voluntary, unpaid, short-term service as a means of expressing one's faith in cooperation and brotherhood."[7] Billingsley, like the other campers who volunteered in Italy, noted that the "Italians…were highly suspicious at first, but came to like the campers later…The Ortona group constructed a center for boys: cleared rubble from the town, which had been the scene of heavy fighting during the war, and cleaned a German cemetery."[8] One camper was "a German whose home had been in the town which was occupied during the war by American troops. Another was an Italian who hated all Germans, Americans, and British because of his war experiences. The experience of working together on a common project, however, healed these wounds." "During the war, we were enemies," the German volunteer told Billingsley simply. "Now we are friends."[9]

Thereafter, for the next three years while in college, Billingsley performed some community service. He spent one summer in St. Paul and Minneapolis as an intern in cooperatives. There, he said, "I got religion on cooperatives." Later, he became an advocate, leader, and organizer for cooperatives in Berkeley. While volunteering in Mexico, he built a drainage ditch to prevent malaria. Another summer he spent working in Peoria, Illinois, in a mental hospital. "It made a deep impression on me. I worked later in a mental hospital as a social worker." That summer, Billingsley was among ten young people from nine southern states who participated in service projects sponsored by the American Friends Service Committee.[10]

Unarguably, Edward Miller had a far-reaching impact on Billingsley's professional and personal development at Hampton. Billingsley participated in the school's Exchange Student Program, headed by Miller. This program attracted "national attention as a possible bridge...between segregation and integration" for one to three students, generally in their junior year, who were interested in "problems of race and racial adjustment."[11] The participating colleges — Antioch, Bucknell, Denison, Grinnell, Heidelberg, Hiram, Oberlin, Ohio Wesleyan, Willimantic, and Wittenberg — sent a similar number of white students to Hampton for a semester.[12] During the spring semester of 1949, Hampton hosted four students from Grinnell and Oberlin. Billingsley and Wyvetter Hoover of East St. Louis, Illinois, along with Haywood Robinson of Lynchburg, Virginia, and Mildred Thompson of Paeonian Springs, Virginia, spent a semester as exchange students at Grinnell and Oberlin, respectively.[13]

From 1946-47 to 1958, except 1957-1958, the Exchange Student Program had "fifty Hampton students to participate and forty-seven from the aforementioned colleges...."[14] For Hampton students, scholarships were provided to cover the differences in cost of the selected colleges.[15] As Miller said of the Exchange Program: "[T]his experiment is a little seed of democratic understanding and practice from which 'giant sequoias' may grow."[16]

Billingsley's Political Diplomacy and Leadership Development: The Hampton Influence

Soon after Billingsley arrived on campus, he joined the frontline battle to protest the racist actions and policies of the last white president to serve Hampton, Ralph P. Bridgman (1944-1948). Since Billingsley had fought for democracy overseas, he was compelled to join the fight for justice at his "Home by the Sea." "It was time to have a Black president," argued Billingsley. Seemingly, the president's duplicitous manners abrogated the mission of the institution. "The students demonstrated against President

Bridgman because he was racist to students, arrogant and not supportive of the mission of the college. He made different kinds of speeches on campus to students, staff, and faculty than he made outside the campus to whites," Billingsley noted.

During his first year of college, Billingsley did not assume the mantle of leadership; however, when he became a sophomore, he took the reins as Class President. He was also active in the Christian Student Association, the jazz band as a trombone player, the men's choir, and the debate team. While Billingsley was an exchange student at Grinnell College in Iowa during the spring semester of 1949, he was elected vice president of Hampton's Student Council for the academic year of 1949-1950 over his female opponent, Dolores McNair. Haywood Robinson, a junior in the Division of General Studies and an exchange student at Oberlin College, was elected president of the Student Council in his bid over Rufus Grant. According to *The Hampton Script* on May 14, 1949, "Of the 792 votes cast, Robinson received 296, while his runner-up, Rufus Grant, received 259 votes. Billingsley received 246 votes, while his runner up, Dolores McNair, received 232 votes.[17]

After Billingsley's semester at Grinnell, he assumed the position as vice-president of the Student Council during the fall of 1949. However, when the elected president, Hayward Robinson, did not return to campus because of family matters, Billingsley was selected to take over the reins as acting president in Robinson's unavoidable absence. Although his junior status did not permit him to become president, he exclaimed, "I thoroughly enjoyed it!"

As acting president, he served on the inauguration committee for Alonzo G. Moron, the first African American president of Hampton; he was also selected as speaker to represent the student body at the inaugural ceremonies.[18] In his report to the Student Council as acting president, Billingsley discussed plans to conduct the Red Feather campaign and outlined a far-reaching agenda that included "membership in the NSA (National Student Council); establishment of a student court, whose function would be to handle cases of student misconduct; initiation of a Faculty Rating System, whereby students would have the opportunity to evaluate their instructors; initiation of an extracurricular point system, whereby the number of official positions held by students in extracurricular activities would be limited; and an honor system to govern examinations."[19] Of course, in Billingsley's report to the Student Council, he mentioned the proverbial thorn of college life: the state of the dining hall. Undoubtedly, his Vesuvius of ideas harnessed from his semester at Grinnell was in full gear — one of the purposes of the exchange program.

Debate Team

As a member of the debate team, Billingsley further honed his political diplomacy and his leadership development by engaging in the art of role playing and by learning "to stand toe-to-toe according to rules without animosity" with visiting debate teams from other historically Black colleges. Debating also helped him to have a "greater understanding of world government." One such debate on the topic, "Resolve: That a Federal World Government Should Be Established," took place between Hampton debaters and visiting teams from Morris Brown College of Atlanta, Georgia, and Virginia State University of Petersburg, Virginia. According to the *New Journal and Guide*, Hampton Institute's affirmative debating team won a 2-1 decision over the Morris Brown College negative team on the resolution…"[20] Andrew Billingsley was second to the lead debater, George Edmonds, for the affirmative side; and Robert Cole was an alternate. Earlier, Hampton's debaters — George Edmonds of Tillery, North Carolina; Andrew Billingsley, of Birmingham, Alabama; and William Dutrieuille, of Clinton, Connecticut — argued the affirmative side of the question against David Crew, Ernest Carter, and Leedell Neyland of Virginia State. On the one hand, Hampton's Edmonds and Billingsley, who, along with their alternate, prepared rebuttals, argued that "world government not only would offer security against the war and opportunity for economic stabilization, but that it is necessary to prevent world destruction."[21] On the other hand, Virginia State's Crews', Carter's, and Neyland's rebuttals argued that "nations are too jealous of their national sovereignties to make world government practicable, and that there is no proof that a federal world government would prevent war."[22] The resolution ended in a non-decisional debate.[23]

The Hampton debating team not only hosted visiting teams, it also held debates on campus. In partnership with the Hampton branch of the State Students Sociological Association, it sponsored a mock debate modeled after the presidential campaign of 1948. Billingsley was instrumental in the mock presidential debate, which presented the views of four major parties and which was "designed to stimulate interest and develop an understanding of the national election among the student body."[24] The organization, as well as the platform of the four parties, was analogous to the national campaign. Billingsley played Thomas E. Dewey of the Republican Party; Haywood Robinson, who later went on to seminary and became active in the Civil Rights Movement, represented the Democratic Party; Robert Cole, who did advanced study at the University of Minnesota and became an architect, played Strom Thurmond of the Dixiecratic Party; and a female student debater represented Henry Wallace of the Progressive Party. "The campaign was fantastic," Billingsley glowed. "We had to memorize speeches, and I had to memorize Dewey's numerous speeches on the campaign. We got lots of attention across town, and we were written up in the newspaper. Robert Cole, whom I later attempted to recruit as vice-president of Howard University, got more attention in the local paper. What I learned from this experience was the passionate goal of politics, commitment to your text, and competitiveness." In the mock elections, *The Hampton Script* reported that "students representing the Democratic Party secured a comfortable voting edge over rival politicians in the...mock election sponsored by the Sociological Association and the Debating Club. The Democrats garnered 271 votes; Progressives, 189; Republicans won 137; the Dixiecrats, 48; and the Socialists, 14."[25]

Billingsley Leaves Hampton: Its Shadow Spirit Follows

From the Hampton experience, Billingsley garnered a bevy of life lessons, but the draw of his days at Grinnell as an exchange student was beckoning him back. Whether to return to Grinnell College or stay at Hampton weighed heavily on him. Edward Miller, Billingsley's professor, had always told him to use his "experiences, learn something, and come back to your school." He opposed, as did others, Billingsley's return to Grinnell, noting he thought that he should remain at Hampton to help "his people." Billingsley said of Miller, "He meant well, but he did not always understand things from the perspective of an insider." Still others, like Stephen Wright, Academic Vice President, encouraged him "to go and make the most of it." Billingsley admitted, "I am sure that I lost some friends because of my decision." Having fulfilled his obligation as an exchange student to return to Hampton for one semester, the season had come for Billingsley to depart after completing the first semester of his junior year. The shadow spirit of Hampton's treasure trove of knowledge and experiences would follow his path — "A Life of the Mind" — of scholarship, leadership, and service.

"I guess coming to Grinnell, in a way, prepared me for what the inside of a white-dominated world might be like. It also prepared me for life, which meant dealing with what white people controlled."

Chapter 2

The Grinnell College Years: The Pioneering Spirit That Came to Iowa

Kesho Scott, Ph.D.

Dr. Andrew Billingsley is one of Grinnell College's most esteemed alumni. When I was a graduate student in the 1970s, he impacted my life intellectually, emotionally, and spiritually. Andy, as those whom I have talked to called him, has a vibrant story on his way to becoming Dr. Billingsley. In my opinion, he is distinguished by a set of circumstances that made him special, not common in the descriptions of our Grinnell student body, then or now.

Andy came to Grinnell College in 1949 as an exchange student from Hampton Insitute (now University) in Virginia. He came with another Hampton student, Wyvetter Hoover, for one semester. After returning to Hampton for the required one semester, he transferred to Grinnell for the last year-and-a-half and graduated as a member of the Grinnell Class of 1951.

Upon his arrival, there were about 1,102 students and 107 faculty; the comprehensive fee was about $1,300 a year. Today, there are 1,630 students, 157 faculty members, and the comprehensive fee is about $45,000 a year. There were no other Black students, faculty, or staff at Grinnell when he and Wyvetter arrived. Thus, they were pioneers who brought integration to the College.

Andy was 22 years old when he arrived at Grinnell, and the College itself was 103 years old. He was a WWII Veteran of the Army, who had seen action in Germany, the Philippines, and Korea. He had finished only the tenth grade before the war broke out and he was drafted. He completed a GED after it ended. He paid his own way through school with the GI Bill and a part-time job on campus working before and after class as a waiter in the women's dining hall. There were 203 students who were veterans the year he arrived, all male.

The president of Grinnell College at the time was Dr. Samuel N.

Stevens, who presided over the College through World War II and the Korean War. He was responsible for bringing hundreds of young officers and servicemen to campus for training, and Andy came with a family mandate: "My parents, they wanted us to be somebody, not just exist and get through life, but to go places and do things."

Mind you, this Andy guy was deeply influenced by his father, Silas Billingsley, who had six grades of education at the historic Lincoln Normal School. Mr. Silas Billingsley even met Booker T. Washington when he came to visit the school.

Now, the historical settings, technical facts, and political capital that brought Andy to Grinnell College are simple — he volunteered. He applied to be part of a Hampton-Grinnell Exchange Program, which encouraged racial integration, as a social agenda, in a racially segregated America of the 1950s. Actually, Andy was pressed to consider it by his Social Studies professor, Edward Miller, who was also Hampton University's Chaplain, because he thought Andy would be a fine candidate.

Andy said later: "It was a social experiment to spend one semester at a white school aimed at improving interracial understanding. Dr. Miller thought I was an appropriate person because I was a veteran and was exposed to places and people outside of Alabama. I think this was a big red flag for me...the researcher," said Dr. Billingsley in an interview, when asked of his decision to come to Iowa. "I was mature, a veteran, pioneering, and a racial barrier breaker."

Andy recalls his trip to Grinnell from Virginia in January 1948: "I took a train from Hampton to Norfolk, Virginia, to Des Moines, Iowa. It was cold. I arrived in the cold and proceeded to get strep throat and was in the hospital for nearly the first five days."

He also laments about what he understood about Grinnell College at the time, continuing:

> Progressivism was "in the air" but not in the town. I felt it. We were called Negroes then. We were not yet Black or African Americans. There were only two of us around. We were a threat to no one. I immediately recognized privileges in the way people were supported by their parents...who came from professional backgrounds...and, after all, Grinnell was a congregational school. They had a very strong Christian Student Movement.

He continued, explaining that in the 1950s:

> Wyvetter and I spent time together but did not date, and did not separate ourselves from the other students. Some students thought I was exotic or special. I could read and write, and others thought I was special because I had been around the world and seen Army life...but

what I didn't have the words for then, which I now know as "white paternalism." It wasn't all bad...in fact, there was already a NAACP chapter on campus. They were all white, and I integrated it too!

In his senior year, Andy was elected president of the Grinnell chapter of the NAACP. After three months on the campus, he jumped right into the pecking order of social and extracurricular events. He had already adapted to the "gentlemanly behavior" and dress code of white shirts, ties, and dark slacks from Hampton University days, along with the habit of addressing his teachers as "professors."

He explained,

> I lived in Smith Hall and I guess I integrated that too. I worked as a waiter in the women's dining hall and I knew all the female students. I arranged a lot of the dates on campus. And because of that advantage, I was elected to the Council of Smith Hall as Social Chairman, responsible for organizing co-ed parties in our dorm several times a semester.

But also...Andy's rise to popularity and a campus "stature" was also "because he bonded with an inner circle of guys...who helped me build those social ties." During his years at Grinnell, the campus was also separated by gender. Racial divides were less significant because the numbers of non-white students were very few. Andy recalls "that race was not talked about a lot, but by being a 'firster'...I was in that era of being a firster...I went on to integrate the dorm and campus organizations and things like that." As well as all these firsts, Andy might not know it, but he would become the first Black to graduate from the Political Science Department of Grinnell College in May 1951.

The Department was headed by Joseph Dunner between 1949 and 1951. Dunner worked with the famous Brookings Institution in Washington, DC, and was a co-founder of the United Jewish Appeal. Later, he left Grinnell and worked as chief of intelligence in the War Office. Dunner's local influences on the department and College were only matched the following year when another Black American first (who also impacted Andy's life) appeared on the national front. In 1950, Ralph Bunche would become the first African American to win a Nobel Peace Prize for his work in negotiating "The Game of Peace" in the Israel/Arab conflict. Andy later met Dr. Bunche at the home of fellow classmate John Sly during Christmas break in 1950. He would speak of the many things that would influence his consciousness while at the College:

> I had already seen Marian Anderson, Paul Robeson and *Porgy and Bess*. I knew that Walter White was President of the NAACP...and I was living at a time when one occupational achievement as a Black man

could make an impact on the white world.

I had already grown up with a social consciousness about myself as a Black person in a predominantly Black world...but coming to Grinnell shaped my political awareness that someday I could be of public service in a larger context. I was an integrationist...and I wanted to be a skilled professional...and I guess that was a radical goal for me in the '50s.

Andy acted on his dream of multiple layers of public service in his campus life. He joined the Grinnell College Choir that went on tours through the Midwest. He was again a firster! His Smith Hall mate, Dick Braun, elected to be his roommate, as choir members stayed overnight with Grinnell parents and alumni during spring tours. Andy and Dick became good and long-time friends. When Dick and Trudy Camp got married in Missouri after graduation, they stayed in correspondence. In one letter to Andy, Dick wrote, "I could see the exasperated expression on my Uncle's face when he saw you (Andy) walking my mother down the aisle."

Andy's hopes of being "a well-trained professional" were confirmed when Donald Wilhelm, another political science professor, wrote a letter of recommendation for him for a federal government job after graduation. He was offered the job, but did not take it. Instead, his fascination with, and later commitment to, the principles and activism of the Quakers' faith led him to work with the American Friends Service Committee. Andy thus took his first "skilled professional job" in the Quaker's headquarters in Chicago right after graduation. Again, this was another first! He was the only Black professional on the staff.

While at Grinnell, Andy assumed copy editorship of the weekly paper, *Scarlet and Black*, edited by Kay Swartz, the first female editor of the paper. Swartz later married one of the most successful businessmen from Des Moines, where she grew up, and later donated a substantial contribution to the Bucksbaum Center — home to Grinnell's Fine Arts Program, which includes art, music, theatre, dance, and galleries. She also served on the Grinnell College board of trustees.

I asked Andy how he reconciled "the Grinnell experience" with his "real world experience" of a then-racially segregated Alabama. He commented: "Well, at Grinnell, nobody organized to keep me out and they (the whites) didn't lose anything to have me come. I was not any serious threat!"

Andy's pioneering spirit was tempered by his keen sense of pragmatism to succeed and to flourish where he could. He speaks about that: "I had a sense of belonging at Grinnell, even though where I was (in Iowa) was strange. I was an 'outsider' pushing the intellectual and physical boundaries of the 1950s conventions — to get a 'good' education...because I knew I could make it in the world."

I asked Andy what he thought this "good" education afforded him, and he answered pragmatically: "Acceptance! And that equals, in my mind, to jobs, money, security, predictability, and relative safety from white racism." Unfortunately, Andy's years at Grinnell did not always promise the social safety he would seek after leaving the college.

He also has a hair story! Not of a "bad hair day" but a "bad haircut day" when the white barber at the only barbershop in the town of Grinnell refused to cut Andy's hair, his white friends walked out of the barbershop with him and Andy immediately went to the dean of men to complain. The dean called the barber and said if he would not cut Andy's hair, then other white male students would be prevented from patronizing his shop. After all, this was the only barbershop in town. All the Grinnell male students and faculty members got their hair cut there, so the dean of men had a strong economic hand as he confronted the barber. Either the barber cut Andy's hair or the dean would forbid other Grinnell male students to get their hair cut in his shop. A few days later, the barbershop offered to cut Andy's hair. It was a political victory "but a cosmetic disaster," Andy recalled.

We both laughed in the interview when he told me: "It was a bad haircut! That's why I developed connections with the Blacks in Des Moines." Andy's account of how "the college ran interference on his behalf in the 1950s also demonstrated [to him] that he could wage polite, respectable political battles, win or lose!" Again, we both laughed out loud.

One of Andy's favorite teachers at Grinnell was Professor Charles Foster of the English Department, who often used to read Robert Frost's poem, "Home," out loud in the classroom and who also allowed students to visit his home. His favorite of Frost's lines was: "Home is where, when you go there, they have to take you in.

Andy's favorite place on campus was the library.

> It was a refuge for me. And of course, so was Herrick Chapel...because it was a chapel and a place to reflect on the Quaker spirit of mediate and reflection. I had come to this place in Iowa representing Hampton University, my family, my church, and my race; and I needed at times a place to reflect on that. I would come to the Chapel and hum my favorite hymn: "Take me to the water, none but the righteous shall see God..."

His least favorite memory was flunking swimming. He recalls:

> This was my only problem with the curriculum. All students were required to take a swimming class or pass the swimming test. The registrar informed me of this after the school was closed and a few days before graduation. I was a vet, and I could not get out of doing it, but

> I do remember how my friends, and even one of the teachers went out
> of their way to give me private lessons to help me get through the test.
> I surely needed it. That was just one way Grinnell folks responded
> when you were in a pinch.

As we closed the interview, Andy reflected on his honorary degree from
Grinnell College in 1971, his pioneering contributions to the fields of
Black sociology and American sociology, and his prolific scholarship on the
African American family. Andy articulated his take-a-ways from his "good"
education:

> I guess coming to Grinnell, in a way, prepared me for what the inside
> of a white-dominated world might be like. It also prepared me for
> life, which meant dealing with what white people controlled. I sure
> learned this at Grinnell. In the end, I guess I was a kind of "reverse
> diversity" for them. My experiences there exposed me to a very broad
> base of people and the concepts of critical thinking, lifelong learning,
> creating lifelong friendships and faith alongside my education. What
> was difficult at Grinnell made me more enduring because of the qual-
> ity of education, which wedded me to be a lifelong activist in one
> form or another.

Andy shared with me how his experiences at Grinnell introduced him
to integrated politics as well as the process of expanding political terrains
for leadership: "I think my liberal arts education experiences helped me
professionally and personally...and in relationships with people because I
remembered to remain faithful to my family and values...I have lived in the
spirit of giving back."

I have one final Andy story I want to tell, which explains why he is
a giant in my mind and memory. When I was a graduate student in the
1970s suffering from the pains of an American and Eurocentric education,
I had no theoretical framework to challenge my teachers and fellow white
students' weapons of analysis. They frequently used the pathological lens to
analyze my community, which I believed was inappropriate. For lack of an
appropriate tool, I was saddened and felt ill-equipped to address the underlying intellectual oppression of that "good education" I was supposed to be
getting. Fortunately for me, after we students took over some building on
campus (you know the rest of the story) things started to change, on campus and in the classrooms. Suddenly, I saw a Black woman's face on that of
my professor. I was listening now!

She was Dr. Shirley A. Lewis, who had been a student of, — guess
who? I can quote her words today:

"We will be reading a book called *Black Families in White America*, by
Dr. Andrew Billingsley, recently published in 1968. It will begin to help us

debunk the myths of the Black family, the Black community, and reexamine the politics of an agenda to destroy the spirit and resilience of the Black diverse family in America."

Lewis was a graduate student of Andy's at U.C. Berkeley in 1968 when that book was published. She had an outstanding career in higher education and was for a time president of Payne College in Georgia, where she invited me to spend time with her students.

I started to cry. When I looked around the room, the other four "colored folks" were also sobbing. I was not alone. I promised myself that, one day, I would go meet this Dr. Billingsley and I did — several times — and each time it was sweet.

When I asked Andy, since I finally got old enough to call him by his first name out loud and to his face, "Why did you decide to be part of my study of Black men who had graduated from Grinnell?" he stared back at me and, after quietly reflecting for half a minute or so, replied: "Well, because you asked me, and I've been thinking about Grinnell these days." As I have now spent my 24th year at Grinnell I, too know why.

Dr. Andrew Billingsley is a living hero. He is the pioneer who came to Grinnell College and left it a better place for all of us to claim.

Andrew Billingsley overlooking the campus of the University of California, Berkeley, while serving as its Assistant Chancellor for Academic Affairs, 1969.

PART II

On Becoming a Teacher-Scholar: University of California, Berkeley, 1964-1970

"...[Andy's] ability to navigate through the turmoil and competing demands confronting him provided a model of leadership, compassion, and Black professionalism I have attempted to emulate and pass on to my students."

Chapter 3

The Furious Passage of Black Studies at the University of California, Berkeley, During Dr. Billingsley's Administrative Tenure

Douglas Davidson, Ph.D.

Dr. Andrew Billingsley is one of the most gifted, committed, activist scholars of the Black Studies Movement and prominent Black university presidents. He has been, and continues to be, a major contributor to my personal and professional accomplishments. I had the pleasure of serving as his graduate assistant during his tenure as Assistant Chancellor for Academic Affairs at the University of California, Berkeley. As part of his duties and responsibilities, Dr. Billingsley was tasked with assisting students of color, faculty, and staff in organizing one of the most controversial academic programs in postsecondary education at that time.

The African-American Student Union had been in negotiations with the University administration about the creation of a Black Studies Department when I arrived on campus in the fall of 1968 to begin pursuit of doctoral studies in Sociology along with eight other similarly recruited African American students. Our arrival represented the culmination of the advocacy and activism of several members of the Sociology Department including Drs. Troy Duster, Robert Blauner, and others. Indeed, our collective presence on campus was part of the larger commitment made by predominantly white postsecondary institutions in the late 1960s as a result of the critique of U.S. society and culture emanating from the Civil Rights Movement and the struggle to end *de jure* or legal segregation practiced in the South and *de facto* segregation practices characteristic of the North. As Brother Malcolm X noted, there was not a great deal of difference between the racist practices "down South" and those less openly acknowledged "up South." This powerful political movement exposed the socially accepted racist practices of predominantly white postsecondary institutions of limiting or refusing admissions to African-American students, both undergraduate- and graduate-level. The decision to reverse these practices came in the aftermath of the 1954 school desegregation law and subsequent racist murders of Medgar Evers, Dr. Martin Luther King Jr. and countless others. Thus, African American students, many veterans of the Civil Rights Movement, and survivors of desegregation efforts arrived with heightened levels of political consciousness regarding these racist exclusionary practices. In the aftermath of Dr. King's murder, many of us were experiencing mixed emotions about our presence on these campuses. We recognized that our presence represented one of the many hard-earned victories of the Movement, but we were not sure that this was the right place for us.

Dr. Billingsley suggested that I should title this speech/essay after a presentation he asked me to do for a Black graduate student forum years ago. At that time, the University had admitted a record number of African American graduate students across various disciplines. Several of us were also active participants in the demonstrations and other political events associated with the strike called by the African American Student Union as result of the University administration's opposition to our demand to create a Black Studies Department. In his usual perceptive and caring style, Dr. Billingsley wanted to hear from the graduate students to determine their perceptions of and responses to their presence on campus and in departments where few, if any, African Americans had matriculated before. So I entitled this paper "The Furious Passage of the Black Graduate Student" to connect it to the domestic colonial model presented in the Carmichael and Hamilton classic, *Black Power*.

For many of us, that book became our political "Bible," as it armed us with a vocabulary, historical context, and political economic perspective to interpret and challenge much of the theoretical and methodological orthodoxy we were forced or compelled to engage in during the process of demonstrating our competency and proving to the powers-that-be that they had made a good decision by admitting us. As most are aware, that book and the concept of Black Power were extremely controversial at this time. It represented a major departure from the liberal, humanitarian, integration/assimilationist perspective associated with Dr. King's inspirational leadership of the Civil Rights Movement. It exhorted the Black community to assume control over its institutions — politically, economically, culturally, educationally. It was, for many of us, a new, exciting, and powerful idea, as it presented new ways of understanding and interpreting the world we inhabited.

Most of us had unquestionably accepted the vision of an integrated United States, in which Blacks and whites existed in egalitarian harmony. Yet, we were vividly aware of the horrors experienced by Civil Rights activists in their efforts to secure fundamental citizenship rights for Black

Americans. We witnessed the violence and racial hatred in whites' responses to court-ordered efforts to desegregate public schools, mostly in the South at this point in time. The book introduced us to the concept of covert or institutionalized racism and how it impacted our daily lives. This was especially illuminating to those of us entering predominantly white post-secondary institutions, as it made us conscious of the brainwashing and perpetuation of white racial superiority embedded in the standard academic process and content. It emphasized that we were victims of a colonial process that denied our humanity as it used our labor power and obedience to systemic demands to legitimize the economic dominance of the white majority while simultaneously convincing us to accept our inferiority and subordinate status.

Acquiring this previously unknown knowledge contributed to the righteous anger I experienced and shared in my earlier speech at the forum. Which was later published as an article in a very visionary and controversial text edited by my good friend, colleague, fellow panelist, and Tougalooian, Dr. Joyce Ladner. The text was aptly entitled, *The Death of White Sociology*.

The anger, frustration, ambivalence, and feelings of powerlessness I expressed in that speech/article were also alive in the leaders and supporters of the African-American Student Union. The document submitted to the University administration reflected the beginnings of what author and analyst Reiland Rabaka describes as "Africana Critical Theory." It benefitted from preceding efforts by African American students at Northwestern University, who had initiated a successful student movement to compel that university's administration to support the creation of an African American Studies Department. It also incorporated some of the intellectual justifications presented by the Black Student Union at San Francisco State University in its request for a Black Studies Department.

Yet, at the prestigious University of California at Berkeley, this proposal met considerable administrative and faculty opposition. The oppositional arguments provided by the University were perceived as racist in that they were couched in the language that supported the covert racism embedded in the system. In denying the students' demands and the rationale used to justify those demands, the University was essentially indicating that it did not accept the fundamental assertion that it, the University, was guilty of practicing, sustaining, and justifying racial oppression. Black student anger intensified, and ultimately the students called for a general strike at the University. Other students of color organizations made similar demands and were met with the same results. These groups united with the African-American Student Union and formed the Third World Liberation Front.

The demand shifted from a request for four independent departments to the demand for a College of Ethnic Studies.

As the Assistant Chancellor for Academic Affairs and the highest-ranking administrator of color at the University, Dr. Billingsley's office became centrally involved in these negotiations. This entailed numerous meetings with other administrators and community representatives from a variety of interested community groups as well as meetings with representatives of the various student groups. The larger political climate of the times included ongoing debates between groups and individuals supporting often-competing political ideologies and organizations. Thus, the Black Power advocates were suspicious of those who still identified with the goals and objectives of the Dr. King-led Civil Rights Movement and organizations. The cultural nationalists' organizations were at odds with Black Power advocates, as they considered Black Power advocates as not appreciating and respecting Black American culture and especially its connection to traditional African culture. Other nationalists identified with the teaching and philosophy of the Honorable Elijah Muhammad, which encouraged its members not to participate in Civil Rights political movements.

While these political perspectives represented great political vitality and were the source of enthusiastic political debates, they also led to tensions between individuals and groups. Often, this led to intense confrontations between individuals and the emergence of challenges for leadership among groups and increased tensions as individuals and students were subjected to judgments (or verbal "put downs") about the authenticity of their "Blackness." A friend and colleague, Dr. George Napper, who worked with Dr. Billingsley prior to my appointment, referred to this judgmental practice as one of the major sources of tension and turmoil among Black individuals and groups, dubbing it the "Blacker-than-thou" syndrome. Indeed, he did his dissertation research on this topic and later published it as a monograph under that title.

This negative label was discussed in the Carmichael and Hamilton text in their critique of Blacks who did not identify with nor accept the fundamental premises of the Black Power ideology. As domestically colonized people, they noted that Black Americans' responses were similar to the responses described by the philosopher and social analyst Albert Memmi in his text, *The Colonizer and The Colonized*. One of the seminal observations made in this text was that many of the colonized had internalized the values, beliefs, and perceptions of the colonizer to the point that they identified more with the colonizer than they identified with their own people — the victims of colonization. In more popular terms, it asserted that many Blacks had become "Oreos" and thus white "wannabees."

This term also had a political economic dimension, as it suggested that those who did not identify with the decolonization movements had not only internalized the colonizers' system of beliefs but also materialistic values. Thus, they wanted to become a part of their *bourgeoisie* or "bourgie." These verbal put-downs were also applied to Black faculty members and administrators. Needless to say, Dr. Billingsley and I were subjected to these disrespectful, disreputable identifiers as well, yet he maintained his calm. He continued to represent the interests and demands of the students with his usual intellectual depth, energy, and commitment to their goals and objectives.

Our work was also facilitated by the timely Black Studies Curriculum Development Conference convened by the Institute of the Black World. This conference brought together Black Studies directors and department chairs from around the country to convene in Atlanta. Early efforts at creating curriculum models consistent with an emerging Pan-African Nationalist political perspective were reviewed and critiqued, and recommendations for enhancing these initial efforts were developed. This conference also included several esteemed scholars: Dr. Joyce Ladner, Howard Dodson, and myself among them. We were all inspired by the intellectual, political, and spiritual leadership of the Institute's then-Director, the late Dr. Vincent Harding.

This movement, as labeled by Fabio Rojas in his monograph, *From Black Power to Black Studies*, was characterized by the intense energy, commitment, disagreements, and confrontations as well as the exhilarating sense of euphoria created when oppressed people struggle collectively to achieve highly desired goals against entrenched opposition. It was one of the truly high points in my personal, academic, and professional career. Dr. Billingsley's calm, steady presence and his deep commitment to the vision and promise embedded in Black Studies, along with his ability to navigate through the turmoil and competing demands confronting him, provided a model of leadership, compassion, and Black professionalism I have attempted to emulate and pass on to my students.

We were not successful in achieving the ideal goal we desired, as the students were not granted the sought-after College of Ethnic Studies. Instead, the University granted us a department, that would house four programs: Black Studies, Latino Studies, Native-American Studies, and Asian-American Studies. These programs (since our departure) have grown into nationally prominent academic specializations. The Black Studies Department ultimately became an independent entity from Ethnic Studies. Each of these departments have developed masters and doctoral degree programs; however, the fact that they exist in separate college divisions in the University indicates that the political struggles continued after we departed. Although the University refused to meet the demands of the Third World Liberation Front as originally proposed, students of color and faculty supporters as well as some cooperative administrators, continued to pressure the University. The current, highly respected academic units offering specialized studies in previously neglected areas of American life and culture — now have a permanent place in postsecondary education. This presence was not voluntarily granted by University authorities, but brought into being by the vision, courage, perseverance, and leadership of committed students of color and their faculty, administrative, and community supporters.

As noted above, Dr. Billingsley's teaching, mentoring, and administrative model is exemplary; and I am very pleased and honored to be a part of the career of this outstanding African American educator, administrator, researcher, and theoretician.

Chapter 4

Searching for Self, Searching for Heritage Following Andrew Billingsley

Howard Dodson, M.A.

Although I took my undergraduate and master's degrees in social studies and history and political science, respectively, I had no plans to become a historian of the African American experience or the custodian of the nation's premier research library on Black history and culture. Indeed, when I completed my master's in 1964, I put myself on a path that I thought/hoped would lead me to a diplomatic career or at least a career of public service overseas. Five years later, I met Dr. Andrew Billingsley on the campus of the University of California at Berkeley. Six years later, I discovered a potential vocation in the field of Black Studies or Africana Studies. Thanks to Dr. Billingsley, I was introduced to, and had the opportunity to study and work with, some of the leading Black scholars and intellectuals in the world, who had devoted their lives to rescuing and reconstructing the histories and cultures of people of African descent worldwide. Following Dr. Billingsley's own pioneering excursions in the field, I discovered my true vocation and purpose in life — the sense of vocation and mission that eventually led me to the Schomburg Center for Research in Black Culture. There, I have spent the last 25 years developing it into a resource that serves the research needs of the seekers after truth on the Black experience around the globe.

I have entitled this presentation "Searching for Self, Searching for Heritage Following Andrew Billingsley." It is at one and the same time a personal odyssey and an expression of my gratitude to Dr. Billingsley for the contributions he made to making me the person I have become. It is also a recognition/acknowledgment of the fact that Dr. Billingsley, perhaps without even knowing it himself, has played a similar role in guiding, directing, and shaping the lives and careers of literally thousands of students, colleagues, and peers over the years. It is, finally, my way of personally thanking him on behalf of all of his protégés — known and unknown — who have benefited from his generosity of spirit, his wise counsel, his probing, demanding intelligence and intellect, and his passionate commitment to the struggle for freedom, justice, and human dignity for all people, beginning with the oppressed and exploited people of African descent in the United States.

The year 1968 was traumatic for me — a decentering, disruptive, confusing year that literally brought me to the brink of insanity. First, came the assassination of Dr. Martin Luther King Jr. in April. Then I went to work on King's Poor People's Campaign to help myself recover from the trauma of his death. As many of you who were around at the time know, God opened up the heavens on the Poor People's Campaign that camped out on the Mall in the nation's capital and forgot to close them! The unrelenting rains during the Poor People's Campaign literally washed away Tent City and caused me to start questioning God's commitment to the poor and the oppressed. In the midst of the Poor People's Campaign, Bobby Kennedy was assassinated. I had signed up to go to work on his presidential bid as soon as the Poor People's Campaign ended. I was devastated. Then, in November, Americans elected Richard Nixon as President of the United States. I had confirmed offers from the State Department's U.S.I.A. and the Peace Corps to work in administrative capacities in those two agencies in Latin America. However, with Nixon as President, I could no longer work for the United States government in any capacity.

Depressed, confused, angry, and bitter, lacking in any clear sense of purpose in life and literally on the verge of going crazy, I decided to take a break and go in search of myself, my heritage, and my future. I had been collecting books on Black history since I had returned to the U.S. from the Peace Corps in 1966. I decided to pack up the books, ship them to Puerto Rico, and spend some time there reading Black history as a means of grounding myself in the Black experience. It was my firm belief that an immersion in Black history could help me rescue my sanity and sense of self. Prior to embarking on this Black history journey, I had only taken one course in my formal education having anything to do specifically with Black people. It was a political science course in African politics during the last semester of courses in my master's program. I shipped some 20 boxes of books on Black history to Puerto Rico and spent several months in San Juan in the mountains of Mayaguez reading Black history, hoping to read myself back into sanity.

When my money told me I couldn't complete this process in Puerto Rico, I decided that I would return to the mainland and head for the University of California at Berkeley, where a Peace Corps roommate of mine had encouraged me to go to pursue doctoral studies. I had learned that Berkeley had just established a new Ph.D. program (probably the first in the country) on the history of Black people and race relations. Some of the leading American scholars of the Black experience, including Kenneth Stampp, Leon Litwick, Nathan Huggins, Wintrop Jordan, and John Ralph Willis, were all in Berkeley's history department and part of this new Ph.D. program.

I arrived in Berkeley in time to enroll in the fall semester of 1969 and managed to get accepted into the program, even though I had missed the application deadline. I first met Dr. Billingsley when I was moving around the campus trying to figure out how to have this requirement waived. Andy was a tenured professor in the School of Social Work as well as Assistant Chancellor for Academic Affairs. He, and a dean on campus, Dr. Kenneth Goode, helped me deal with that late application as well as facilitated my introduction to the history department. Thanks to their intervention, I was admitted to the program with a full tuition scholarship and a living stipend.

My second meeting with Dr. Billingsley was indirect and extremely fortuitous. During registration for the fall semester, I met one of Andy's graduate student assistants, Ms. Jualynne White. She was a doctoral student in the sociology department who was assisting Andy with the registration process. I met and talked to her for about 20 minutes to a half hour, at the conclusion of which I declared my intentions to marry her. Three months later, she accepted, and four months later we were married in Andy's house. The marriage lasted 23 years.

My enrollment in the history Ph.D. program did not mean that I had committed myself to the field or to an academic career. My intentions, quite frankly, were to stay there for only a year and to spend that time continuing my self-administered psychotherapy. The doctoral program offered me a more structured way to delve into the Black past, and I found myself drawn deeper and deeper into the study of slavery and the slave trade and its African background. Significantly, when I applied to the department, I made it clear that I had no intentions of teaching in the field. I said, perhaps prophetically, that I wanted to use my administrative background to develop programs and activities that would teach the public about the Black past. I said further that I did not feel I could do this responsibly without substantive knowledge of Black history. In reality, at the time, I was just searching for my sanity.

Berkeley, California, was a good place to look for one's sanity in 1969. That's because Berkeley itself was so crazy. One quick story will make the point. I was walking down one of Berkeley's main thoroughfares, Telegraph Avenue, one afternoon when I saw this line of four people coming toward me taking up most of the sidewalk. There was a white female blonde, about

6'2", with hair down to her butt; a bearded white male, about three-and-a-half feet tall, who walked with a limp; a dark-skinned African American woman, about 5'8" tall with an Afro that made her look 6'2" or more; and a Black male, about 6'7" tall, counting his 'Fro. Each of them carried a tin cup and a sign. I came to understand, based on the signage, that they were demonstrating for their right to be nude and taking up a collection to support that cause. Not one of them had on a stitch of clothes!! But that wasn't what was strange. What was strange was that nobody else on the street noticed that there was something strange about their behavior. Most passersby didn't even seem to see them, even though they were making noise and shaking the few coins they had collected or with which they had seeded the cups. I determined there and then that Berkeley was insane and that I was on the road to recovery!

Throughout that first year at Berkeley, even though I did not take any courses with Dr. Billingsley, I found myself in regular conversations with him and some of my fellow graduate students about the emerging field of Black Studies. Berkeley had established a department in that field the previous year and Andy had been one of its faculty advisors, but he had thrown himself fully into the national debate about the viability of Black Studies as an academic discipline. He had been among those who attended the first National Conference of Black Studies at a place in Atlanta, Georgia, called the Institute of the Black World (IBW). The Institute, in addition to supporting the development of Black Studies programs nationally, had called for the conversion of the former "Negro Colleges" into "Black Universities." Andy met regularly with an organization of Black graduate students that we had formed. In mostly informal settings, we discussed and debated all of the questions that arose about the intellectual viability of Black Studies, the content of Black Studies curricula, the theory and methodology of Black Studies, and the relationship of this largely academic endeavor to the struggles of the Black community. Andy, more often than not, led those discussions; and in his quiet, deliberate and inquiring way, he challenged us to think deeply about these questions as we pursued our respective graduate school academic programs. Andy, as mentor and scholar, wouldn't let us get away with the overblown rhetoric and ideology that permeated the era. If, as he believed, Black Studies was worthy of serious academic pursuit, we were required, as future academics and intellectuals, to take it seriously ourselves — to question our assumptions, to support with evidence our assertions, and to wage serious intellectual warfare — if we believed Black Studies was worthy of defending and perpetuating.

Andy's commitment to the development of the field was not mere lip service. He saw in it a potential vocation for himself and acted upon it. He had a year-long sabbatical coming up in 1970-71, and he decided that he wanted to return to Atlanta and spend the year in residence at the Institute of the Black World, the newly established Black think tank whose mission included a firm commitment to the future of Black Studies. Wanting to support the development of the Institute as well as the field, Andy negotiated a sabbatical deal that included taking some graduate students with him to assist the Institute in helping define and develop the field. My wife Jualynne and I were two of the first graduate students he invited to join him.

Armed with this invitation, I walked boldly into the history department offices one day and proclaimed that one couldn't study the Black experience in California because there were no Black people in California. If one was serious about studying Black history (as I professed to be), then one had to go to the South. I either made a compelling case or Andy threw around some of his tenured faculty/Assistant Vice Chancellor muscle on my behalf. The bottom line is, the history department granted me permission to spend "a year abroad" in Atlanta studying at the Institute of the Black World with Dr. Andrew Billingsley as my faculty mentor. The sociology department granted Jualynne the same permission, and, by the spring of 1970, Jualynne and I (and a couple of other grad students) had signed up to travel to Atlanta in the fall to spend a year at the Black think tank searching for new perspectives on the study of the Black experience and searching for our heritage. Jualynne and I included in our study plans research on the historically Black colleges in the region and field trips to southern Black communities, where we used participant-observation methods to learn more about southern rural Black life and Black vernacular culture, the foundational setting/ context for the development of Black history and culture in the United States. Our respective departments were kind enough to fund this year-"abroad" experience.

Halfway through the summer, as we were making preparations for our southern sojourn, Andy received a call from Howard University. Its president was interested in exploring the feasibility of transforming century-year old Howard from a Negro University into a Black University, and he wanted Andy to help lead the effort. Andy was offered the position of Vice President for Academic Affairs with this transformation agenda as a part of his portfolio. He was gracious enough to discuss his dilemma with us — whether to go to IBW or take the offer from Howard, but there really wasn't much to discuss. The Howard offer was one he couldn't refuse. We decided that we would go on to IBW as planned, and he should see what the Howard opportunity had to offer.

So, Andy headed to Howard to see what he could do to make the vision of a Black University real, and we headed to IBW in Atlanta, in my case to see what this new Black Studies thing was really all about. I still had not committed to the field or to an academic career. I was still in search of my own sanity and some deeper understanding of the heritage of Black people.

We arrived in Atlanta in early October 1970 a few days before Amiri Baraka's Congress of African Peoples was slated to open. The Institute was providing administrative and logistical support for the Congress, and I was given the task of supporting the history workshop co-chaired by Dr. John Henrik Clarke and Dr. Josef Ben-Jochannan. Within days of arriving in Atlanta, I was plunged into the debate on the definition of Black history and the future of Black Studies. The Congress facilitated my personal entry into that debate.

My involvement with the Institute gave this intellectual discourse real substance and grounding. A month or so before we arrived in Atlanta, the Institute had declared itself an independent Black institution. Founded a year earlier as the research arm of the newly formed Martin Luther King Jr. Center, the Institute had spent the year in conflict with the King Center's board over the definition of its mission and role. The King family and the board believed that the Center's research arm should focus exclusively on preserving and interpreting Dr. King's legacy. IBW's staffers, led by Dr. Vincent Harding, firmly believed that Dr. King's legacy could not be understood outside of the context of the larger Black struggle for freedom, justice, and human dignity. They believed also that the times called for a fundamental rewriting of both African American history and American history. In addition to Harding, IBW's senior research fellows included historians Lerone Bennett and Sterling Stuckey; sociologists Joyce Ladner and Gerald McWhorter (Abdul Alkalimat); political scientist William Strickland; professor of English and African American Literature Stephen Henderson; and Jamaican Garvey scholar Robert Hill, among others. Together, they made IBW a place of Black intellectual ferment in the Atlanta University Center complex that likely hadn't been seen in a historically Negro college and university setting since the Howard University of the 1930s — the Howard University of Ralph Bunche, Rayford W. Logan, E. Franklin Frazier, and others.

At the top of IBW's agenda was the future of Black Studies and the nature and future direction of the new "Black history" as contrasted with the old "Negro history." I spent the academic year struggling with these questions on a daily basis — frequently seven days a week and ten-to-twelve hours a day. The problems we didn't solve during the day, we took home with us at night, frequently with other staff members or out-of-town guests who helped make our home an extension of the seminar/conference room at IBW. We saw these issues as life and death matters and struggled over them intellectually as if our entire future was dependent on their resolution. We believed they were.

During the summer of 1971, I managed a month-long summer research seminar (SRS) for graduate students from several colleges and universities across the nation. The SRS brought some of the leading Black intellectuals in the world to the Institute — St. Clair Drake, George Beckford, Edward Brathwaite, and C.L.R. James — to mention only a few. Most of them were from the Caribbean and many were or had been affiliated with the University of the West Indies. They brought with them a global perspective on the Black experience and a more Marxist-centered paradigmatic framework than I had ever encountered in my previous studies. The combination of the African-American centered experiences and discourse at the Institute that year and the global perspective provided by the SRS did it for me. Though I had arrived in Atlanta with no plans/commitments to return to Berkeley, the IBW experience convinced me that there was a vocation, a calling, for me in this developing field of Black studies. I returned to Berkeley from Atlanta, having discovered a path to the truth about my and Black people's heritage and a sense of mission and vocation.

Dr. Billingsley's five-year tenure at Howard University was marked by significant enhancement of the University's liberal arts, humanities, and social science programs, especially a restructuring of those elements of the curricula around the Black experience. Andy went on to become President of Morgan State College, and during his tenure there he led the effort to upgrade it to university status. Intellectually, he has continued to build on his foundational work on Black families, interpreting them from the perspective of Blacks' own realities rather than viewing them as pathological reflections of Euro-American families.

I completed my course work for the Ph.D. and took my oral exams in 1974. I accepted the position of Program Director at the IBW and served as its Executive Director for five-plus years, exploring ways in which scholarship on the Black experience could be placed at the service of Blacks' struggle for freedom and human dignity. After a three-year stint at the National Endowment of the Humanities, I became Director of the Schomburg Center for Research in Black Culture. My degree work at Berkeley, my work at the Institute of the Black World, and my fundraising-related work at the National Endowment for the Humanities were my strongest qualifications for the position. My only prior experience working in a library had been as a page in my undergraduate school library 25 years earlier.

From left to right: Howard University President James Cheek, with Amy Billingsley and Andrew Billingsley, 1970. *Photo provided by the Cheek Family Estate.*

PART III

INSTITUTION BUILDING AT HOWARD UNIVERSITY, 1970-1975

"Dr. Billingsley, ... performed one of the most auspicious administrative tasks ever in the history of Black higher education by recruiting a generation of scholars to come to Howard University."

Chapter 5

Dr. Andrew Billingsley: Creating the Black University at Howard

Ronald Walters, Ph.D. *

In 1969, one of the most astute decisions of Howard's 37-year-old president, Dr. James Cheek, was to name Dr. Andrew Billingsley, nearly 10 years his senior, as Vice President for Academic Affairs. Obviously, he wanted someone with the experience and commitment to Black education who could respond to the demands of students for the kind of Afrocentric education that would characterize a liberated institution and would assist the Black community in moving toward that state.

Dr. Billingsley's role as an administrator in this circumstance was born in the cauldron of the struggle for Black Studies at the University of California at Berkeley in the late 1960s. In 1969, the African-American Student Union presented a proposal to Chancellor Robert Heyns. That August, he appointed Dr. Billingsley as Assistant Chancellor to review the proposal and design a Black Studies department. Billingsley submitted his review to the Dean of the College of Arts and Letters, Walker Knight, who took it up with his Executive Committee; but they were unable to decide whether Black Studies should be a department or a program. The reaction to the demand of the African American Student Union in 1969 launched one of the first boycotts demanding a Black Studies department in the country, which led to a nationally recognized conflict between the Berkeley students, the Board of Regents, and Governor Ronald Reagan. This action, and others by Berkeley students soon after, set off a wave of student protests and demands for Black Studies all over the country.

By early March, a Department of Ethnic Studies, not Black Studies, had been approved; and, in September Dr. Billingsley was appointed its Acting Director. In June of 1970, however, he resigned this position to become Vice President for Academic Affairs at Howard University.[26] No doubt part of his motivation was that the movement for Black higher education was reaching a new and important phase captured by a critical article by

35

Vincent Harding that appeared in the August 1970 issue of Ebony magazine on "The Black University."[27] Dr. Harding felt that the idea espoused by students as one of the powerful rationales for Black Studies was that they wanted, at long last, to break with the intellectual domination that Europeans exercised over the history and culture of peoples of African descent and to create institutions of education that engaged in the struggle to create a new world for them, even in the midst of the domestic colonial situations taking place where they lived.

There were no attitudes more typical in the posture of some of the faculty at Berkeley than those toward the retention of their hegemony over the teaching of African civilizations, as Professor Karen Miller cites about the resistant attitudes of Berkeley's Faculty Committee on African Studies and others who doubted the intellectual viability of a Department of Black Studies. They recommended such alternatives as insertion of courses into the already established curriculum, i.e., beginning a center for Afro-American Studies or, at the very least, a department headed by a distinguished social scientist such as Dr. Kenneth Clark or a historian such as Dr. John Hope Franklin, both of whom opposed Black Studies.[28]

Moreover, another important reason for Black Studies was found in a volume surveying the condition of Black students in White institutions of higher education, reviewed by R. David Cobbs Jr. of Duke University in the *Journal of Negro Education*. It found not only that some institutional leaders and faculty were threatened by Black students who had expressed their "Black awareness" and had begun to make demands upon them, but Cobbs' conclusion was that the essays in the volume led the reader "to view the black student's situation on the white campus as being similar to that of an alien."[29]

Harding was of the view that there "are hundreds of Black academics and other Black intellectuals scattered across the nation who are literally waiting to note in what places the call for the Black University will be taken seriously." Then he noted that Howard University was one of those places where a movement toward the Black University had begun.

President James Cheek believed in the concept of a Black University and defined it in his own words:

> It is in the national interest that there be institutions of higher learning that are recognized as being black, that are acknowledged as black, that are clearly identified with the black community and that are committed to using the resources that knowledge can provide to resolve issues and problems that relate to the conditions of Black America.[30]

Howard was truly a unique institution because of its history and its students, who were attracted to the University because of its heritage and its role in the production of the Black middle class. A study by the American

Council on Education collected data on two types among the 8,317 students in the freshman class of 1972: predominantly Black colleges (PBC) and (UN) universities nationally (UN). James Stanfield extracted from the data a sample of the 732 Howard freshman class for comparison. He found that the aspirations of Howard students far exceeded those of UN and PBC students in selecting high-status professional career fields such as doctors, lawyers, and others. Moreover, they also excelled in such personal objectives as "becoming an authority in my field" and "influencing social values."[31] These aspirations were matched by the emphasis of Cheek and Billingsley on achieving excellence and strengthening graduate and professional education specifically.

Dr. Harding was right about the willingness of many Black academics to work in Black institutions, and Dr. Cheek hired Dr. Billingsley, who performed one of the most auspicious administrative tasks ever in the history of Black higher education by recruiting a generation of scholars to come to Howard University. Some examples of the scholars and intellectuals whom he attracted are:

Jeff Donaldson - Chairman of the Department of Art

John Oliver Killens - Writer-in-Residence

Stephen Henderson - Director of the Institute for the Arts and Humanities

Sterling Brown - Eminent author and proponent of Black culture

Haki Madhubuti - Poet-in-Residence

Charles Harris - Dorector of the Howard University Press (formerly of Doubleday/Random House)

Charles A. Martin - Editor-in-Chief of the *Journal of Negro Education*

Trumpeter Donald Byrd - Director of the Jazz Studies Institute

Doug Glasgow - persuaded to leave UCLA to head the School of Social Work

Tony Brown - Founder of the School of Communications

Chike Onwuachi - the African Studies Department formerly of Fisk University

What is evident here is that, along with new faculty, came new programs and curricular developments that would be regarded as logical, such as a Jazz Institute or a Press, or others that would be vehicles for the creative outlet for faculty to contribute beyond the university into the community and the nation at large. Thus, many of those credited to the tenure of President Cheek, ultimately a great president who served Howard for twenty years, were a product of the work of Dr. Billingsley.

He was so successful in recruiting outstanding faculty to Howard that it came to be said that when college presidents saw him coming, they would try to "guard their faculty."[32] In fact, so many of Howard's new Black faculty members came from the University of Michigan, including recent graduates Don Coleman (Engineering), Lawrence Gary (Social Work), advanced faculty Archibald Singham (Political Science), William Ellis (Political Science) and those in other fields, that some wondered if there were any left behind.

Ironically, I had attended graduate school at Howard University in 1966-1968 while also a graduate student at American University, where I eventually obtained my M.A. in African Studies and my Ph.D. in International Studies. American University had allowed me to credit courses taken at Howard because they did not have courses at the graduate level in African Studies. My first job was at Syracuse University in 1968-69, where I was an Assistant Professor in the political science department in the Maxwell School and worked with students to conceive a Black Studies program. However, I left there to become the founding Chair of the Department of Black Studies at Brandeis University, where Andy Billingsley had received his Ph.D. in the Heller School.

Let me add that I was one of those who read the piece by Dr. Harding but justified my presence at Brandeis with the logic that Black students were emerging quickly at white institutions through the growth of enrollments and that some Black faculty had to be there to provide them with the educational services they needed. Dr. Billingsley came through Brandeis one day and visited the newly established department, proposing that I think about returning to the Washington, DC, area to work at Howard University. It became a more and more attractive offer as I came to understand that the Dean of Arts and Sciences at Brandeis, Dr. Peter Diamantopoulos, was not disposed to provide the kind of financial resources that would make the department first-rate.

Dr. Billingsley and I had that in common. His own view of Black Studies was as such:

> We must make sure that as we put blackness into the curriculum that we do it in a manner that is a move toward excellence. We don't want to cripple black students with a watered down curriculum that doesn't really speak to their needs. We have to be very hard-headed about scholarship. We can't be soft, call it black and just dismiss it like that, because we're going to be liberated by training our minds and then moving into the community.[33]

Seeming to take Billingsley at his word, Dr. Cheek said the following at the fall 1972 Howard convocation:

> Black Americans and this university community must value excellence in quality more than we have ever in the past. In our determination to celebrate [and] affirm the Black presence as an integral, legitimate and unavoidable expression of the American presence in

the world, we must be equally determined to make being Black synonymous with being excellent, to endow that which is Black with an unmatched quality, and to express a dedication and a devotion that will be the envy of all men everywhere.[34]

I agreed to come to Howard in the spring of 1971 as a professor; however, at the end of June at Brandeis, Billingsley asked me to consider becoming Chair of Howard's political science department. Although I did not want another administrative position so quickly, I was so intrigued by his plans to elevate the graduate social sciences at Howard to excellent level. Billingsley had set an ambitious project in place, believing that "what we are about will have a lasting effect on Black people's lives." Part of the plan, as it affected me, was to strengthen the graduate programs in the arts and sciences. In his words,

> we have to turn out the sociologists, urbanologists, the psychologists who can define our needs and set about the task of implementing our goals. No longer can we sit and let ourselves be defined by people whose experiences put them at a distance from us. We can no longer react to their definitions. We must be the professional experts on ourselves.[35]

Nevertheless, to the incoming faculty, the changes wrought were often unsettling in many instances and, in some cases, there was strong push-back from faculty and administrators who had been at Howard for many years and who opposed the concept of the Black University. There was general acceptance of these goals, however, especially by faculty, staff, and students who understood where Howard was in history.

Dr. Billingsley's leadership was strong in mentoring those whom he attracted to Howard, not only by his academic administration of their units but also by his personal touch. His quiet genius and intellectual brilliance attracted us, but he mentored us privately by hosting dinners at his house with his wife Amy and growing family. It was thrilling not only to meet many of the intellectual giants of our day there, but also to engage the problems of Howard and our community at his table. This was the core of the genesis of the Black University.

Dr. Cheek's and Dr. Billingsley's goals were ambitious because Howard was substantially beholden to the federal government for support and, although President Cheek's requests were equally ambitious, they received meager response: (1970-71 requested $13 million, received $2.5 million; 1971-72 requested $24 million, received $6 million; 1972-1973 requested $37 million, received $9 million; 1973-74 requested $80 million, received $60.7.[36]

Since the University did not receive enough federal funds to do what

39

it wished, it was clear that other sources must come into play, and Dr. Billingsley's arrival coincided with that of Dr. Ben Payton, former President of Benedict College, who became the director of the Ford Foundation's Black College Program and administered millions of dollars to those institutions. The aim of the Ford Foundation was to initiate a six-year program of funding with the goal of helping the minority institutions to achieve parity with other non-Black institutions. And, although part of the initiative was to provide direct fellowships to minority students and institutional support, it also wanted to strengthen the graduate education of students at selected institutions such as the Atlanta University Center and Howard University. Therefore, in 1970, Howard received $300,000, which increased substantially to $1,750,000 in 1971 and beyond, to support graduate education in the social sciences.[37]

Through this initiative aimed to strengthen graduate programs, Howard University was able to benefit enormously since the funding enabled Dr. Billingsley to allow departments to offer competitive salaries to incoming faculty comparable to those of major institutions and provide adequate graduate fellowships to students that enabled them to consider doing their graduate work at Howard. Through this program, I was able to take Howard's political science department from 10 to 25 faculty, hiring 15 Black faculty members — all with the Ph.D. The department also instituted new courses in Black Politics, strengthened other fields, and attracted a significant group of outstanding Black graduate students. A similar dynamic occurred in the departments of History, Economics, and Sociology, spawning a new era of significantly increased production of graduate degrees in these disciplines.

Conclusion

Andrew Billingsley resigned his post at Howard University in 1974 and became President of Morgan State University in 1975. I resigned as Chairman of the Department of Political Science, also in 1974, to become a research fellow in the Institute for Social Research at Howard, headed by Dr. Lawrence Gary, and to complete several books. Nevertheless, I returned to the chairmanship later and remained at Howard for 24 years. Thus, I can attest to the fact that the foundation built by Dr. Billingsley during the time he was there stood the test of excellence, and many of the goals established were achieved since outstanding faculty, such as sociologist Joyce Ladner, educational psychologist Harriet McAdoo, historian Joseph Harris, Eleanor Traylor in Literature, and others continued to come. But others who came also achieved national recognition that contributed to the University's goal of both excellence and Blackness such that the struggle for the Institution of the Black University remained an ever-present goal.

Dr. Ronald Walters passed away September 10, 2010 in Bethesda, Maryland.

Chapter 6

An Examination of Andrew Billingsley's Role in Building Academic Excellence at Howard University During the 1970s

Joyce A. Ladner, Ph.D.

I learned about Andrew Billingsley some 47 years ago. It was in 1968, when his seminal study, titled *Black Families in White America*, was published. I had finished my doctorate a year earlier on Black adolescent girls and was in the midst of writing my book, *Tomorrow's Tomorrow: The Black Woman*. Billingsley's book was invaluable to me, a young, untested scholar in the making who was trying to chart new territory in the field but who had no models to turn to until I read *Black Families in White America*.

Andy's work was important to me at this stage of my development, and it inspired me to contact him. I wrote to let him know that I admired his and Amy's path-breaking work, which grounded Black families by placing them in a historical perspective and which importantly debunked the prevailing theories that Black families were disorganized, deviant, and had little of value to offer the wider society.

It was not long after this communication with Andy that students at Howard University began to protest. Charles Hamilton's special coverage of Howard students' sit-in at the University provides a detailed view of the student activism on Howard's campus before President James Cheek and Dr. Andrew Billingsley arrived.[38] The students had sought a court injunction against Howard's attempt to remove them from the administration building, and they prevailed.

The students' demand that President Nabrit be ousted was agreed to, and later that year 36-year-old Dr. James E. Cheek was hired to be president, declaring that "A New Era" had come to Howard.

It was in 1969 that President Cheek called Dr. Billingsley and offered him the job of Dean of the School of Social Work. Billingsley said he turned down the offer but did accept Cheek's request to head a national commission to redesign the School of Social Work. The acting Dean at the time was Ira Gibbons. Billingsley invited me to be on this six-person commission. We met several times and produced a noteworthy report with recommendations.

In 1970, Andy and Amy decided to leave Berkeley, where he was an Associate Vice President, to accept an offer from noted historian Vincent Harding to become a Senior Fellow at the Institute of the Black World (IBW) in Atlanta. The Institute was initially the research arm of the newly founded Martin Luther King Jr. Center for Social Change in Atlanta. In 1969, I joined the Institute's seven other senior fellows — historians Vincent Harding, Lerone Bennett and Sterling Stuckey; Chet Davis in education; Steve Henderson in poetry; and Bill Strickland in political science — I was the lone sociologist in the group. Andy, in turn, recruited several of his graduate students from the University of California at Berkeley, where he was Assistant Chancellor for Academic Affairs, to go with him to the Institute. They included Doug Davidson, George Napper, and Howard and Jualynne Dodson.

Andy said he and his family were driving from Berkeley to Atlanta and had stopped off at a Black family conference at the Aspen Institute in Colorado when he received a call from Dr. Cheek. He said, "My Vice President has resigned, and I need you. I am offering you the job." Andy said he explained to Cheek that he had already accepted an offer to become a Senior Fellow at IBW. He did agree to get back in touch with him when he arrived in Atlanta, however Andy and Amy Billingsley, later joined by Vincent and Rosemarie Harding, all flew to Washington to meet with Dr. Cheek. Vincent thought it was an offer Andy should not turn down, and he strongly urged him to take the job. Andy agreed, and that is how Andrew Billingsley came to Howard University, which proved to be one of his best decisions, and that as he led some of the most consequential academic changes in the University's history.

Billingsley came to Howard University in 1970, a year following the appointment of Dr. James E. Cheek as the University's President. Andy Billingsley was the right Vice President at the right time. The University was ripe for change. Student demonstrations had put Howard front-and-center in the media and on Capitol Hill. Alumni and other supporters, who were unaccustomed to students taking over the administration building, were calling for the ouster of Cheek's predecessor . Afro hairstyles, dashikis, and raised fists were all challenges to authority. Howard was supposed to be a different kind of place — a place where propriety, good manners, organized succession, and, most of all, seasoned faculty and administrators waited their turns.

When President Cheek arrived at Howard, he brought with him youth and high expectations. At 36 years old, he also cast aside the old "Howard way" and introduced the idea that youth and inexperience should be given a chance. His administration's theme, "A New Direction," signaled not only a break with the past but also a vigorous and bold new Howard University — and there was no better time to reorganize Howard than in 1969.

When Dr. Cheek hired Dr. Andrew Billingsley to the position of Vice President of Academic Affairs in 1970, Billingsley was faced with at least two major challenges: replace an aging faculty and create a new, vigorous academic enterprise that was consistent with Cheek's "A New Direction" theme. Given the change in demographics, Howard's academic leadership was undergoing a natural order of succession with an aging faculty. Some of the deans and faculty had been at the University since the 1930s. For example, E. Franklin Frazier in Sociology, and Abe Harris in Economics retired about the same time as Dr. Cheek took over. As Howard history professor Dr. Michael Winston said, "It was a time of great innovation and ferment."

The University moved with all deliberate speed, which greatly accelerated the enterprise. Dr. Cheek went to the U. S. Congress to request additional funding for the University's federal appropriation, and it was doubled in two years. This sudden infusion of funds brought with it a tremendous challenge because, under federal rules, monies had to be obligated the year they were appropriated. What to do with this tremendous amount of new resources? Cheek established a close relationship with then-Secretary of Health, Education, and Welfare Elliot Richardson, a moderate Republican. He agreed to expand Howard's academic budget for academic programs if Cheek could obtain additional funding from the Ford and Carnegie foundations. With the help of Billingsley, Cheek was successful.

Cheek challenged Billingsley to recruit new faculty (often young people) and give them significant responsibilities. He also told Billingsley not to allow salary concerns to prevent him from hiring someone. Billingsley said, "An example of Cheek's 'hire-young-people' policy was when he appointed 40-year-old Carlton Alexis to the newly created position of Vice President of Health Affairs, much to the consternation of the medical school faculty."

Andy told me that he viewed his role as that of recruiting new Black faculty and creating new Ph.D. programs in sociology, economics, political science, education and human development, and history. He was deeply troubled by the fact that neither E. Franklin Frazier, Ralph Bunche, nor other distinguished Ph.D. scholars had not produced quality doctoral students to continue their Howard legacy. With this as one of Andy's high priorities, he appointed me to chair the Ph.D. Committee. He worked with current faculty, including historian Lorraine Williams and economist Frank Davis, and young professors Clarence Lee, Martha Cobb, Jeanne Marie Miller, and Tony Brown, the latter of whom became the founding Dean of the School of Communications. Most notably, he also brought the eminent scholar Sterling Brown back from retirement.

It was here that Andrew Billingsley's role and contributions are most evident because it was up to him to operationalize or breathe life into the "A New Direction" theme in that core part of the University: teaching and research. In an unprecedented move, Dr. Billingsley recruited young department chairs and deans who had not risen through the ranks. Jeff Donaldson became Chair of the art department and brought with him the artistic concept and fellow artists from OBAC or Organization of Black American Culture, which had originated in Chicago. Ron Walters was appointed Chair of the political science department, and he set about infusing that curriculum with Black politics and all that it entails.

I joined Robert Staples and Ralph Gomes in the Department of Sociology and Anthropology. Staples was writing about the Black family, and I had just published my first book, *Tomorrow's Tomorrow: The Black Woman.*

Billingsley hired Douglas Glasgow from UCLA to be the new Dean of the School of Social Work. Glasgow's book, *The Black Underclass,* would have a strong influence on the social work curriculum. The faculty adopted "the Black perspective" as the foundation of the School's curriculum. Professors John and Harriette McAdoo also joined the faculty from Michigan State University.

Percy Pierre was already heading the School of Engineering, and he was granted support to recruit nine new faculty members for his School. One of those people was an electrical engineer named Eugene Deloatch. He also recruited Don Coleman from the University of Michigan in the field of computer systems engineering. These are but some of the young professors Andy recruited to fulfill the students' demands for a different curriculum.

The University became a combination of a living laboratory and an outpost of the Civil Rights Movement. Most of all, it was a place where we — idealistic, highly trained, bright young people — came to launch careers steeped in wanting not only to do well but also to do good. Some of us had come from the Civil Rights Movement, while others were steeped in the Black cultural revolution and were creating new ways to infuse Black culture into the preschool curriculum such as creating manhood programs for little Black boys.

Not content to stop with faculty recruitment, Dr. Billingsley also created three new institutes. These were the Institutes of Arts and Humanities, led by former Morehouse College professor and prominent poet, Steve Henderson; the Institute for Urban Affairs, whom he hired Michigan grad

Lawrence Gary to head; and the Institute for Higher Education, headed by Chicago-trained attorney Kenneth Tollett. Other important changes included Billingsley's transfer of Dr. Michael Winston from his faculty position in the Department History to the head of the University's Moorland-Spingarn Center, when he was just 32 years old. Billingsley also established the Howard University Press by recruiting the highly esteemed publisher Charles Harris from Random House to build the Press from the bottom up.

Academic programs are the spine or rather, the soul of a university. Andrew Billingsley was the right person at the right time for Howard. He was a strong academic leader because, in addition to his own productivity, he not only had a vision of what he wanted Howard's academic programs to be but also a grasp of the kinds of academic programs needed to strengthen the University's offerings.

I asked Andy what he considered to be his legacy at Howard University. He said, "faithfulness to scholarship, academic rigor, and building students from undergraduates to Ph.D.s."

Andy was a lot more than a Vice President at Howard. How do we take the measure of a person? How do we define the worth and value in the endeavors Andy undertook? Do we compare them to those of his peers—in this case, in other institutions of higher learning? Vince Lombardi said, "The measure of who we are is what we do with what we have." Andy did not have unlimited resources, but he managed to recruit some of the best young people available with what he had.

Andy was also a very supportive academic leader, as in "The test of a strong leader is not where he stands in moments of comfort and convenience, but where he stands at times of challenge and controversy." Andy stood with his faculty and supported their efforts. He was committed to doing his part to assist the University to carry on and build on its historic legacy grounded in academic excellence. He was, as I stated earlier, the right Vice President for Academic Affairs at the right time, and his contributions are firmly planted in Howard University's history, the fruits of which are still in existence today.

Andy was one of those men you always wanted in the trenches with you. If you went to battle, you wanted him beside you because you knew his courage would not falter and his commitment would not waver. Great fighters take the responsibility and do everything possible to win the game. He, however was an ordinary man who did extraordinary things. That's what made him great. His academic productivity will continue beyond his life through his works.

Chapter 7

The James Cheek–Andrew Billingsley Connection in the Expansion of the Doctoral Program at Howard University

Charles Jarmon, Ph.D. and Ralph Gomes, Ph.D.

Dr. Ralph Gomes and I have been colleagues at Howard University since 1978. When I arrived at Howard in 1978, Ralph was an Associate Professor and had served as acting Chair of the Department of Sociology and Anthropology. Gomes' appointment at Howard in 1970 was a result of the recruitment initiative that was undertaken by Professor Andrew Billingsley to accomplish President James Cheek's mandate to expand the University's doctoral program. At the time that I was appointed to the University in 1978, Andy had already left to serve as President of Morgan State University. He had accomplished his mission at Howard and was providing new leadership at Morgan. My earlier contact with him was through our mutual professional associations in the field of sociology; but, as most of my colleagues in sociology, I was familiar with his widely known classic work on the Black family, *The Black Family in White America,* which was published in 1968.

We could add much to this brief narrative about Andy's contributions to Howard during the time that he served in his role as one of our vice presidents. We will limit our comments primarily to the Graduate Program in the Arts and Sciences, with special reference to the Department of Sociology and Anthropology, where we are most familiar with the changes he helped to bring about. His substantial contribution to the broader areas of the Graduate Program is evident in the presentations of other colleagues contained in other chapters of this volume. While there was substantial transformation occurred in the overall graduate program at Howard during the time Andy was here, the effect of what he accomplished is still a part of what we do at the University today. With this understanding, the remarks here by Professor Gomes and me are about the changes that took place primarily in the Department of Sociology and Anthropology; however, the discussions we provide of the changes that occurred there are relevant to other disciplines in the Graduate Program.

A Brief Description of the Master of Arts Program in Sociology and Anthropology

The graduate program in the sociology department was created at Howard University in 1934, which was 39 years after the first undergraduate course was taught in the Department in 1895 by the noted scholar and mathematician, Kelly Miller. In 1934, E. Franklin Frazier had been influenced to leave Fisk University to establish a Master of Arts degree program in sociology at Howard University. Frazier, who would become one of the leading scholars in sociology, had no interest in expanding the sociology program beyond the Master of Arts degree. After his death in 1966, his successor and chairman of the Department, G. Franklin Edwards, continued the traditional "Chicago School" approach to the study of sociology that Frazier had established. Further, Edwards did not pursue the establishment of a doctoral program in sociology. It was only after the expansion of the graduate program under James Cheek and Andrew Billingsley that the Department was able to think seriously about establishing a doctoral program.

In 1970, President Cheek recruited Billingsley from the University of California at Berkeley, where he was serving as the Assistant Chancellor for Academic Affairs and was assigned to implement that University's new policies for incorporating Black Studies, Chicano Studies, and Ethnic Studies into its academic program. Professor Billingsley accepted the Howard offer, which would provide him with a much larger stage from which to implement his ideas about providing instruction that would be broad enough to incorporate into the academy the rising demands for Black Studies, African Studies, and Chicano Studies. Additionally, he would be able to create opportunities for Black students to acquire graduate degrees in areas where they were underrepresented. This was a pivotal period in Andy's career, both as a scholar and as a nationally recognized leader in the movement for establishing Black Studies. In the former instance, he had just recently published his noted book, *Black Families in White America*.

Arguments for a Doctoral Program in Sociology at the Beginning of the 1970s

Several arguments supported the need to establish a doctoral program at the beginning of the 1970s. First, in the closing years of the decade of the 1960s, there were an increasing number of Black students who were interested in and capable of pursuing a doctoral degree in sociology, thanks to the heightened awareness of the problems of race and class in America. Second, Howard's limited graduate program which only which offered a

Master of Arts degree could not accommodate these students; and third, such a program would not be attractive to many of the top Black scholars desiring to teach in departments with doctoral programs. It was clear that a doctoral program in sociology at Howard University would be a response to a national need for increased numbers of trained Black scholars with doctoral degrees. The magnitude of this problem was compelling, and Howard's Sociology Department pursued means to rectify this condition in the year that Andrew Billingsley became Vice President for Academic Affairs.

The department submitted a successful proposal to the Ford Foundation to establish a doctoral program. The problem that they were trying to address was clear. At that time, Black sociologists with doctorates were trained at predominantly white institutions, and the majority who had already earned their doctoral degrees also worked at these institutions. This problem was not confined to the discipline of sociology. The pattern was the same in the other disciplines of the physical sciences, humanities, and education. For example, the Department's proposal introduced data which showed that, between the 1970-1974 school year period, non-Blacks were granted a total of 1,850 degrees. In this same period, Black Americans were granted only 72 doctoral degrees, representing three percent of the total degrees awarded (*Sociology at Howard University: From E. Franklin Frazier and Beyond*). As this problem existed in the other disciplines as well, President Cheek announced the following in his inaugural address just prior to Professor Billingsley's arrival: "The national interest dictates that there be at least one university in the land devoted... to the special issues which the legacy of the race has created. Howard is commanded to be such a university."

Dr. Andrew Billingsley's Mandate and Commitment to the Department of Sociology and His Role in the Appointment of New Faculty in the Periods 1971-72 and 1973-1974

Dr. Billingsley was and has continued to be a transformative educator and administrator. He understood the transformative power of education and the responsibility of Historically Black Colleges and Universities (HBCUs) to empower Blacks in order to change their lives, the community, and society. This was the charge he gave the Department of Sociology and Anthropology in 1971 when he made the decision to assist us in developing a Ph.D. program.

In the two years, 1971 and 1972, steps were taken to initiate the development of a Ph.D. program in sociology. One of the major steps made by Vice President Billingsley in conjunction with the Department was to add five new, dynamic faculty members in 1971. These included Dr. Joyce Ladner, Associate Professor; Dr. Robert Staples, Associate Professor; Dr. Ralph C. Gomes, Assistant Professor; Dr. Johnnie Daniel, Assistant Professor; and Dr. Joan Harris, Assistant Professor. These faculty members were to be the core staff for the development of a solid doctoral program. In Dr. Billingsley's consideration of these faculty appointments, the quality of academic skills in core areas was important. Attention was given to finding faculty members with methodological, statistical, and theoretical competence; teaching and research devoted to the issues facing Blacks and the Black community; potential to produce young Black scholars who would go on to become leaders in their communities; and the desire to help students move forward. These appointments contributed significantly to the improvement of both the undergraduate and graduate curricula, particularly to the development of the Ph.D. program.

Dr. Robert Staples and Dr. Joyce Ladner were already established scholars before their arrival. Dr. Staples came to Howard's sociology department with a long list of scholarly publications, including the highly acclaimed books, *The Black Family* and *Introduction to Black Sociology*. Similarly, Dr. Ladner already had a list of significant publications, including her pioneer sociological study of Black girls growing up in the city: *Tomorrow's Tomorrow*. In her second pioneering book, *The Death of White Sociology*, she took aim at the hegemony of the "social science fiction" basis of Euro-American sociological theory and analyses. Dr. Ladner brought to the Department her experiences of being a scholar-activist through her membership in the Student Nonviolent Coordinating Committee which influenced her scholarship and research.

The alternative approach offered by Ladner, Staples, and the younger faculty sought a reconsideration of our approach to sociology — that is, of its sociological theories and methodologies. Their purpose was to provide a more comprehensive and inclusive perspective on Black life and culture in the United States. Senior faculty not only opposed altering the curriculum, they also opposed the development of a Ph.D. program. They argued that Howard's Department of Sociology and Anthropology should confine itself to developing a stellar M.A. degree program using the "establishment" sociology curriculum.

In the two years from 1973 to1974, professors Joyce Ladner and Robert Staples left the University on a one-year leave of absence. Dr. Ladner did not return because of her recent marriage and relocation. Dr. Staples did not return because of familial obligations. Their departures seriously affected the curricular development in the new Ph.D. program. After the departure of Ladner and Staples, Dr. Billingsley and Dr. Owens, who was then the Dean of the College of Arts and Sciences, appointed Dr. Ralph Gomes as the acting Chair of the Department with instructions to "jump start" the development of a proposal for a Ph.D. program in sociology.

The cadre of young faculty under the leadership of Dr. Gomes developed and submitted a proposal for the establishment of a Ph.D. degree in the Department, which was approved by the University's Board of Trustees, subject to the availability of funds to support it. With guidance and assistance from Dr. Billingsley, Gomes and his young cadre of turks submitted a funding proposal to the Ford Foundation and were awarded $1.5 million for over a three-year period. When the grant term ended, President Cheek and Dr. Billingsley negotiated with the Congressional Appropriations Committee to have subsequent funding added to the University's budget to demonstrate commitment to maintaining the Ph.D. program in sociology. Thanks to Dr. Billingsley's support, our budget increased.

The younger faculty won the war to establish the Ph.D. program in 1974; however, they lost the battle for developing a comprehensive curriculum despite Dr. Billingsley's success in recruiting additional young faculty to carry out that objective. Despite the push by the young sociologists of the Department, who called for modification of Eurocentric theory and methodology that would be uniquely suited for studying the social and cultural experiences of Black people under their peculiar circumstances in America and the Diaspora, the program reflected an "establishment" sociological pedagogy. The curriculum in sociology reflected standards of traditional methods and pedagogy, and members of the Department taught from methods and theories that reflected conventional approaches. However, this was offset, thanks to the assistance of Dr. Billingsley, by a budget increase that allowed the Department to hire new faculty and increase its number of specializations, which converged around five areas of specialization: urban sociology, intergroup relations, social control and deviance, social organization, and social psychology.

Over the past decade, inadequate financial support from the administration, reduction in the number of faculty members, and decisions by the Graduate School have had an impact on the programs that were created under Dr. Billingsley's period as Vice President for Academic Affairs. The Department, which at one period had had as many as seven specializations, has had to reduce its number of specializations to three areas: social inequality (race, class, ethnic, and gender relations), criminology, and medical sociology. This reduction reflected the need to maximize the use of decreasing resources with respect to both financial allocations and a decreasing number of faculty members. It has been remarkable that the Department has continued to be strong. Unfortunately, the anthropology component was eliminated from the Department.

Dr. Billingsley and the Ford Foundation Grant

The mandate for change in the Department, beyond expanding our faculty and increasing faculty productivity, required additional office space. Through the efforts of Dr. Billingsley and a Ford Foundation grant, we were able to reduce the overcrowded condition present in our faculty offices, where two and three faculty colleagues shared the same office, organized their research, and provided student advisement. This grant also provided resources for establishing a Social Science Statistical Laboratory in the basement of Douglass Hall, which enhanced faculty research and promoted the opportunities for graduate student involvement in empirical research under the advisement of their professors. This type of infrastructural development was key to the Department's growth, while at the same time promoting opportunities for interdisciplinary research between the social sciences.

A Glimpse of Dr. Andrew Billingsley's Impact on the Graduate Program in the College of Arts and Sciences; Ph.D. Degrees Awarded between 1970 and 1980

In the year prior to Dr. Cheek's arrival as President in 1968, Howard's Graduate Program produced 10 Ph.D. graduates in five departments and no department produced more than three doctorates. They were confined to the limited areas of the physical sciences and included chemistry, physics, zoology, and pharmacology. The only exception was the Department of English, which produced one Ph.D. graduate that year. Over the following decade, the annual production of Ph.D. degree recipients would expand exponentially from 10 to 51, with the number of departments producing doctoral degrees increasing from 5 to 22.

When Professor Billingsley arrived at Howard in 1970, only three departments awarded doctoral degrees in the humanities and the social sciences. They were the English department in the division of the humanities and the departments of African Studies and Political Science in the division of the social sciences. Twenty-eight graduate students were awarded Ph.D. degrees. Seventeen of the 28 (61 percent) were awarded by two departments, with 9 of them graduating from the English department and the remaining 8 graduating from the departments of African Studies and Political Science.

By 1974, the year Professor Billingsley left the University, the greatest gains in Ph.D. degrees awarded were in the areas of the humanities and the social sciences. The Department of African Studies and the Department of History had made the greatest gains in producing Ph.D. graduates. At the time of Dr. Billingsley's arrival at the University, African Studies had awarded only one doctoral degree; the Department of History had not yet awarded a doctoral degree. Within a five-year period, the number of Ph.D. graduates produced by the two departments increased to 18 in African Studies and 16 in the Department of History, respectively.

Dr. Billingsley's influence on Howard's Graduate Program continues, despite his departure for Morgan State University in 1974. For many of the programs, he had established the leadership during their infancy in his four years at Howard. They later began to produce doctoral students after his departure from the University. In this period, the most productive department in awarding doctoral degrees was the Department of Political Science, with 39 doctorates awarded between 1975 and 1980. The departments of African Studies and Psychology each awarded 21 Ph.D. degrees. At a level of production below these top producers of doctoral students, the Department of History awarded 17 doctoral degrees and the Department of English awarded 14. The next group of departments, ranking in descending order of the number of doctoral degrees awarded, were the Department of Communications, 10; the Department of Economics, nine; and the Department of Human Ecology, 8. The departments with the fewest doctoral degrees awarded during this period included the Department of Education, 5; the Department of Sociology and Anthropology, 3; and the Department of Social Work, 3. Several departments had not awarded doctoral degrees.

All the above departments have since become major producers of the nation's Black doctoral students. Despite its slow beginning, the Department of Sociology and Anthropology now ranks number 100 among departments producing doctoral degrees in the United States. We will always remember Professor Billingsley as the scholar chosen by Dr. James Cheek to move Howard University forward into a new social and cultural period that was essentially uncharted during the turbulent period of the 1970s.

Dr. Clifford Muse of the Moorland-Spingarn Research Center at Howard University was immensely helpful in supporting our efforts to retrieve the data on the number Ph.D. degrees awarded between 1970 and 1980.

Dr. Andrew Billingsley, Vice President of Academic Affairs at Howard University, 1974..

Chapter 8

New Developments in English Studies at Howard During the 1970s

Eleanor W. Traylor, Ph.D.

My senior college professor, Undine Smith Moore, while at Fisk University, wrote a chorale with organ, brass, woodwind, tympany, and everything else that could sound. The simple, resplendent lyric of the chorale sings:

> LORD, we give Thanks to Thee
> – for these thy servants –
> Hallelujah! Amen.

To that, I submit the proposal that English studies at Howard before, during, and since Andrew Billingsley's definitive vice presidency in the decade of the 1970s has maintained a language and a mission consistent with the intellectual and spiritual vitality of his project.

About 10 years prior to Billingsley's arrival, a poet publishing in *Dassien,* the young Howard poet's journal, had stunned a fractured academic community with these confident, resolute lines:

> My blackness is the beauty of this land,
> My blackness
> Tender strong, wounded and wise...
> And all my love a strong cathedral...
> My blackness is the beauty of this land.[39]

Our poet, Lance Jeffers, who came to teach Freshman English at Howard, was prophetically writing the birth certificate and the epitaph for a generation of young, teacherly scholar-artists, he among them. Some of them, such as Clyde Taylor, have become among the most recognized names in literary and humanistic scholarship, and some have been described by their students in this way:

> ...the young faculty, folks at the beginning of their careers...were closer to us in age and outlook. I can remember a number who encouraged, argued with, or counseled us as the occasion required, thereby

enriching in numerous ways our intellectual development.

My freshman English teacher I've never forgotten. She was an instructor and a challenging teacher who was really down with black literature and our people's culture. But this teacher was unusual in one other important respect: she was young, stylish, and really fine. Her name was Toni Morrison. She and her tall walking partner, another young, equally fine and elegant sister named Eleanor Traylor, would turn heads as they walked across the quadrangle.

"Wowie, who be them two fly sisters, mah man?" So naturally, their sections were always overenrolled with ardent young Howard men. Who arrived in class to discover with some dismay that the young women were also smart and very serious teachers.[40]

This memory, recorded in *Ready for Revolution: The Life and Struggles of Stokely Carmichael [Kwame Toure]* with Ekwuene Michael Thelwell, commingles with the memory of an age outlined in that book to reveal why the epic and cosmic imaginary of Lance Jeffers is key to understanding a generation who, with Howard's legendary seniors — "an array of excellent scholars…dedicated teachers…many of them progressive" — would become the teachers and co-participants both of Civil Rights activists and Black Arts progenitors. Jeffers also inscribed, in powerfully figurative language, the relationship between the junior and senior faculty and the direction their course of study would take in a poem called "Black Soul of the Land":

I saw an old black man walk down the road,
a Georgia country road.
I stopped and asked where the nearest town might lie
where I could find a meal.
I might have driven on then to the town nearby
but I stayed to talk to the old black man
and read the future in his eyes.

His face was leathered, lean, and strong,
gashed with struggle scars.
His eyes were piercing, weary, red,
but in the old grief-soul that stared
through his eyes at me
and in the humble frame bent with humiliation and age,
there stood a secret manhood tough and tall
that circumstance and crackers could not kill:

A secret spine unbent within a spine,
a secret source of steel,
a secret sturdy, rugged love,
a secret crouching hate,
a secret knife within his hand,
a secret bullet in his eye.

> Give me your spine, old man, old man,
> give me your rugged hate,
> give me your sturdy oak-tree love,
> give me your source of steel.
> Teach me to sing so that the song may be mine
> "Keep your hands on the plow: hold on!"
> One day the nation's soul shall turn black like yours
> and America shall cease to be its name[41]

Even the most sophisticated among us saw the senior faculty at Howard as paragons of humanhood and the smartest people alive. In English, Sterling Brown's *Negro Caravan* had changed the literary map of the country, and his premise that a great literary tradition rests upon a great folk tradition is the winning aesthetic argument of the day. Arthur P. Davis's *Cavalcade* opposed a theory of literature that denies contextualization. He too won.

Of course, these views and students' views of self-determination radically opposed a mode of being inscribed in the curricula of American and international institutions of higher education. Our students saw that curricula as an educational mission to civilize young Negroes fresh from the cotton fields. It was to render us "cultural," that is, polite and safe in word, thought, deed, and appearance so that ultimately superior white America might, in its benevolence, one blessed day accept the Negro."[42] None of us instructed students to take over the administration building; nevertheless, history happened. Any Google search will offer this information:

> During the sixties, even before students on white campuses demonstrated against the Vietnam War, students on black campuses raised the issue of whether their institutions of higher learning were "relevant" to the needs of the black community. In the forefront of this movement was Howard University in Washington, DC, then known as the "Harvard for blacks."

In 1968, two months before Martin Luther King's assassination, students seized the administration building in a dispute over the right of the campus newspaper to criticize the policies of the University president. The demands soon widened. Students demanded that the University establish a Department of Afro-American History and Culture. They wanted a new University president appointed. And, they wanted courses, that allowed them to reach out into the working-class community around Howard.[43]

By 1970, Gregory Rigsby, then an Assistant Professor at Howard, writing in *The Journal of Negro Education*, could flatly state: "Black Studies is a fact of life on American college campuses."[44]

During Andrew Billingsley's vice presidency, the voice of the Department of English intensified. By then, a Howard poet was heard throughout the land:

> Calling black people
> Calling all black people, man, woman, child
> Wherever you are, calling you, urgent, come on in.[45]
> …We want a black poem. And a Black World.
> Let the world be a Black Poem
> And Let All Black People Speak this Poem
> Silently
> Or Loud[46]

The listening world heard the voice of LeRoi Jones, by then known as Imamu Amiri Baraka, who claimed Toni Morrison as his teacher. Morrison, herself a Howard student-cum-teacher, published her first work of fiction *The Bluest Eye* — a novel that corroborates Billingsley's scientific study of *Black Families in White America*.

Scholarship flourished in the Department during his tenure:

- The Department hired Haki R. Madhubuti, signal Black Arts poet, linguist, and pedagogical theorist.
- A landmark dissertation historicizing "Negritude," that all-important movement of identity anticipating Diasporic Studies, was published by Dr. Gregory Rigsby.
- An unprecedented prosodic study of African American poetry appeared in newly hired Professor Stephen Henderson's *Understanding the New Black Poetry: Black Speech and Black Music as Poetic Reference*.
- The earliest book-length scholarship on LeRoi Jones becoming Amiri Baraka was published by Professor Theodore Hudson.
- More than 60 reviews of Black plays and articles on Black theater and playwrights for Hoyt Fuller's *Black World* alone, notwithstanding other scholarly publications by Dr. Jeanne Marie Miller, highlighted the Department's resonant scholarship.

Since then, the Department yet maintains a language and a mission consistent with the intellectual and spiritual vitality and development of Black scholars, devoted, in the words of Dr. DuBois, to "the possession and conquest of all knowledge." As poet Tony Medina, now Associate Professor in the Department of English, assuming the voice of Bob Marley, has put it:

> Each note I play
> Each song I sing
> Freedom coming
> From my guitar string[47]

On Saturday, May 7, 2016, when the President of the United States specifically addressed the Howard University community, the Department of English presented three candidates with the Ph.D. degree, further fulfilling

Dr. Billingsley's vision and our goal: to continue the professorial generations that serve our students. My own life has been centered by the processional tie that binds me to him. By that tie, I rejoice in a succession of young scholars whose pedagogy and scholarship, such as that of the present Chair of the Department of English, magnify Billingsley's excellence.

"[Billingsley] indicated that Howard's strength and promise were due to people such as Dr. Williams who were 'able, hard-working, dedicated, highly committed to excellence' and to advancing 'the University's mission.'"

Chapter 9

Lorraine Williams, the Ford Foundation, and the Rapid Expansion of Graduate Studies in History at Howard University in the 1970s

Edna Greene Medford, Ph.D.

In an era when STEM programs are regarded by many as the one sure road to progress for the nation and prosperity for the individual, one recalls with *some* degree of nostalgia an earlier time, when the humanities and the social sciences were regarded similarly. Our national obsession with competing effectively on the world stage in the areas of science, technology, engineering, and math is understandable on some level, but it feels unwise to those of us who believe that the humanity of humankind emanates from and is reflected in the arts—in great musical compositions, in inspiring literature, in sculpting and painting, in theatre. And it is the task of the disciplines such as history, sociology, economics, and the like to chronicle, study, and understand our collective experiences. In the not so distant past, scholars, administrators, and the funders of academic programs shared the belief that the promotion of these disciplines as well as the pursuit of science and technology strengthened us as a nation.

At no time was this truer than during the early 1970s at Howard University. The period of Dr. Andrew Billingsley's tenure as Vice President for Academic Affairs at Howard coincided with the unprecedented expansion of graduate education in the departments of History and Political Science. In July 1971, the University received 1.75 million dollars from the Ford Foundation to strengthen programs in these two departments, where the record of scholarship and teaching was already stellar. In History, Chair Lorraine Williams lost little time before putting her department's share (roughly $875,000) to good use. The funds supported a wide range of academic and administrative initiatives including curriculum development, faculty expansion, graduate student funding, faculty research, the hiring of additional support staff, and the refurbishing of the physical space on the third floor of Douglass Hall, where the department resided. By the end of Dr. Billingsley's tenure as Vice President and Dr. Williams's term as Chair, the graduate program in history was well on its way to becoming a campus jewel.

Dr. Williams assumed the position of chair of the history department in March 1970. In the fall of that year, the Department received modest assistance from a Ford Foundation grant that had been awarded to the social sciences division for the purpose of enhancing its undergraduate programs. Plans for strengthening that component were well underway when the much more substantial award designated for the graduate program arrived one year later.

Recognizing faculty acquisition as a priority, Dr. Williams sought to expand the academic staff by hiring additional members of the faculty in all categories. Three positions had been filled the previous year with the support of the Ford grant for the undergraduate program. This new funding enabled Dr. Williams to add 10 additional faculty positions—3 at the professor level, 2 at the associate professor, and 4 at the lecturer level. Rayford Logan, at that time Professor Emeritus, returned to the Department as Distinguished Professor of History. The hiring of lecturers allowed senior professors to take on greater responsibilities for the newly expanded graduate program.

With sufficient faculty in place, Dr. Williams led the effort to improve the curriculum. Faculty met frequently to discuss the best ways to enhance the program, keeping both broad coverage and academic rigor in mind. After much discussion and deliberation, the department decided to add four new courses, which included Interdisciplinary Approaches to History, History of Puerto Rico, Black International Protest Movements, and Independent Study.

Dr. Williams and the Department simultaneously launched an effort to recruit graduate students who would benefit from the new program. Designated faculty undertook recruitment trips and interacted with prospective students at conferences, drawing financial support for such activities from the Ford Foundation grant. The Foundation also enabled the department to offer a total of 16 fellowships and assistantships. This was 11 more than had been awarded the previous year. Each student received $5,000, a generous amount for the times.

The size of the faculty and student travel budget more than tripled during this period, thus enabling greater numbers to attend and participate in conferences and other professional meetings. The funds also enabled several faculty members to conduct research. Eight projects benefited from funding in 1971-72, with a focus on subjects that ranged from the study of the African presence in Peruvian society to Great Britain and slavery in East Africa to the Pan-African Movement.

As the graduate program expanded, Dr. Williams and Vice President Billingsley recognized the increased workload should be rewarded with adequate remuneration. The eight graduate faculty members who taught in the graduate program received merit increases; and the Chair's salary, which was based on an 11-month pay period, increased to 12 months to reflect the actual yearly commitment to administration.

Dr. Williams made full use of the $8,000 allocated in the grant for the purchase of books and other library materials. A Social Science Reading Room was established for History and Political Science students in Founders Library; and the facility received funding for general renovations, office equipment, and bookcases.

Understandably, the greatly expanded graduate program necessitated additions to the support staff. The Department employed one full-time secretary and a clerk-typist during the 1970-71 academic year, with the salary of the latter position supplemented by the Chair's personal funds. In the following year, when the Ford Foundation grant for graduate education was awarded, the Department succeeded in securing the services of one administrative assistant, six secretaries, and a clerk-typist. Apparently, only one of the secretaries and the clerk-typist were funded by the University.

And finally, understanding that adequate physical facilities would be necessary when building a stellar graduate program, Dr. Williams used the Ford Foundation funds to refresh departmental spaces. She had all offices and classrooms painted and carpeted, air-conditioning installed, office equipment and furniture purchased, and new chairs and maps secured for graduate classrooms. A new seminar room was made available for graduate classes.

These changes and additions facilitated both teaching and research and enhanced the stature of the history department and, consequently, the reputation of the University. The results of Dr. Williams's and her faculty's efforts, made possible by the Ford Foundation grant and supported by Dr. Billingsley, are a reminder of the centrality of the discipline to graduate education at Howard then and serve as a foundation for a solid academic program today. Its success also reminds us that it takes committed and visionary leadership to build a program that endures over time.

I close my remarks with reference to Dr. Billingsley's comments regarding the central role Dr. Williams played in securing Ford Foundation funds to enhance History's graduate program. Near the end of her tenure as Chair and his time as Vice President for Academic Affairs, Dr. Billingsley praised her effort to develop proposals for continuation of the Ford Foundation grant. He expressed optimism that there would be sufficient funding to "enable us to move a few steps ahead toward our goal of developing here at Howard, the strongest graduate training and research programs to be found in any university of our size." He indicated that Howard's strength and promise were due to people such as Dr. Williams, who were "able, hard-working, dedicated, highly committed to excellence" and to advancing "the University's mission." He encouraged her to call on him to say a word on her behalf the next time she was "up for promotion." However, if she planned to leave the University, he threatened to "take back all the nice things" he had said about her.

There was never any reason to take back those words because Dr. Williams remained at Howard for the rest of her career, transitioning from Department Chair to Vice President for Academic Affairs herself. (And, of course, along the way she edited the *Journal of Negro History*). As Vice President, she continued the commitment to the social sciences that Dr. Billingsley had pursued before her and, in so doing, she ensured that the History program would endure. The Department remains strong today, a testament to her vision and tireless devotion.

References

Arnold, M.S & Allen N.P. (1995), "Andrew Billingsley, The Legacy of African American Families." *The Family Journal* 3, 77-85.

Bert-Goodley, T. B. (2006), "Oral Histories of Contemporary African American Social Work Pioneers." *Journal of Teaching in Social Work*, 26, 181-199.

Gary, L.E. & Leashore, B.R. "High Risk Statistics of Black Men." *Social Work*, 27, 54-58.

Holland, T.P & Kilpatrick, A.C. (1993) "Using Narrative Techniques to Enhance Multicultural Practice." *Journal of Social Work Education*, 29 (3), 302-308.

Khullar, D. (2016 April). "Letting Patients Tell Their Stories." *New York Times*, 4d.

Lindner, M.D., Vancea, A, Mei-Ching, C., & Chacko, G, (2016). "NIH Peers Reviews: Scored Reviews Criteria and Overall Impact. " *American Journal of Evaluation*, 37 (2), 228-249.

Milburn, N.G., Gary L.E., Brown, D.R. & Booth, J. (1991) "Conducting Epidemiologic Research in A Minority Community," *Journal of Community Psychology*, 19, 3-12.

Saleebey, D. (1994). "Culture Theory & Narrative: The Intersection of Meanings in Practice." *Social Work*, 39 (4), 351-59.

"When high school students realized that some of their smart friends were going to Howard, they also applied. This was an example of the saying, 'recruit the best and get the rest.'"

Chapter 10

Reflections on Howard Engineering in the 1970s

Percy A. Pierre, Ph.D.

D r. Andrew Billingsley has made many contributions to the advancement of scholarship on the Black condition in America. Most important are his contributions to the education of Black people, particularly at Howard University. The 1970s were a special time in the history of Howard University, a time when both Andy and I were there. I was Dean of the College of Engineering at Howard University from April 1971 to May 1977.

A quote from Ron Walters, a former colleague of mine at Howard, captures the relationship between Andy Billingsley and Howard in the 1970s. Ron said: "Dr. Cheek hired Dr. Billingsley to perform one of the most auspicious tasks in the history of Black education: to recruit a generation of Black scholars to come to Howard University." There were already outstanding Black scholars at Howard. One of them who comes to mind is Dr. Clifton Samuels in the Department of Electrical Engineering. Cliff had risen to a full professor position at Purdue University before coming to Howard. He recognized that he could not affect the needed changes by himself. He welcomed those of us who came later.

Andy's job was to attract a critical mass of outstanding scholars to Howard and to transform the academic culture of the University. The impact of this group of faculty went beyond Howard. Many of us continued our work with Black students after we left Howard.

I am extremely proud of this group of Black engineering faculty, who not only changed the College of Engineering at Howard but also impacted Black engineering education throughout the nation.

Andy's job of recruiting that cadre of scholars mandated by Cheek required vision. Dr. Cheek provided a vision that he called a "university of the first class." One of Dr. Cheek's favorite sayings was that "our reach should exceed our grasp." It took me a while to understand what he meant by that. I finally realized that he meant we should aspire to more than we expect to achieve. And in the 1970s, we did achieve a lot.

I remember calling Andy about a potential hire who had come to my attention; however, I did not have money for a position to hire him. His name was Neville Parker. Andy said, "Hire him." I told Andy, "There is something else you should know. When Neville was a graduate student at Cornell during the student uprisings of the 1960s, a picture of Neville appeared in a newspaper with some other Black students. He was wearing Black Panther garb and — carrying a rifle." Andy said, "Hire him!"

Neville was a scholar but also committed to the advancement of Black people. Neville played a key role in establishing the Urban Systems Engineering Program at Howard. He later taught in Africa, after which he went to City University of New York, where he led a large research center in transportation. At City College, he impacted thousands of Black students.

Another story: A few years later, some students were killed on the Southern University campus during student protests. Two Southern faculty members were accused by the President of Southern of aiding the protesters. He fired both of them. One of those faculty members, George Baker, was a student of mine when I taught at Southern. The other faculty member was in physics.

I went to Andy and asked for money and authorization to hire George. Andy said we should hire both of the faculty members. George came to Howard. The other faculty member went to Rutgers. Later, George went to Xavier University, where he led their 3/2* engineering program and graduated many Black engineers.

Having money to act on hiring opportunities made a big difference. The scholars we hoped to recruit had many options. Many received financial offers at other academic institutions that were greater than what Howard normally offered. One of the most important things Drs. Cheek and Billingsley did was to provide the funds to compete with the financial offers our candidates got from other universities. Without those funds, it would not happen. The fact that Howard had money was not a coincidence.

In 1970, President Cheek was appointed as a special advisor to President Richard Nixon for Black colleges. That occurred in the wake of the killings of Black students at Jackson State University. Thus, Dr. Cheek had good connections in the Nixon administration. At the time, Howard got most of its funding from the federal government. Dr. Cheek was able to increase that funding substantially throughout the 1970s.

I first met Dr. Cheek in the spring of 1970 when I invited him to speak to the White House Fellows. I was then a White House Fellow working in the Office of the President for Patrick Moynihan on the Urban Affairs Council. At that meeting, Dr. Cheek outlined the condition of Black colleges in general but also talked about his vision for Howard. That is when I first heard the term, "a university of the first class." I was convinced that Dr. Cheek would do great things for Howard.

In the fall of 1970, I heard that Howard was looking for a new Dean of Engineering. I wrote to Dr. Cheek expressing my interest in the job. A critical role in convincing me to actually take the job was played by M. Lucius Walker, who had gotten his Ph.D. in mechanical engineering at Carnegie Mellon. He was one of the first Blacks to get a Ph.D. in mechanical engineering. Like Cliff Samuel, he recognized that Howard engineering needed many more like him to effect the change that was necessary. Lucius was involved in almost everything I did at Howard. When I left Howard, he was named Dean of Engineering.

In April of 1971, at 32 years old, I began my position as Dean of Engineering and Professor of Electrical Engineering, having never come through the academic ranks. I had a lot to learn. A big part of my mandate, as told to me by both Drs. Cheek and Billingsley, was to hire other outstanding Black faculty, expand research activities, and start doctoral programs. So what did we do? During the 1970s, Howard started many new programs. Most were the first at an HBCU. Much of the impetus for these programs came out of a faculty retreat at Airlie House in Virginia in the summer of 1971. There, we developed a strategic plan for the College, which served as a guide for the rest of my tenure as Dean.

As Andy and I agreed, the first priority was strengthening research and starting graduate programs. While the faculty bought into the challenge of expanding research and starting doctoral programs, they disagreed that that was the first priority. They insisted there was a more urgent challenge: to improve the undergraduate programs, particularly the quality of the students we attracted.

Office of Student Services

At that time, of our 583 undergraduate students, half were international students. Most of the international students were Iranian students. We were not competing for the best Black high school students. The faculty felt that, if we were to recruit the best faculty, we also needed to recruit the best students.

Dr. Joseph Cannon was a new faculty member in the new Department of Chemical Engineering. He had just graduated from the University of Colorado and wanted to compete for the best students. We decided to go after the winners of the National Achievement Scholarship — a national scholarship program for Black students, run by the National Merit Scholarship program. It provided partial support for students. To compete, we needed to add to that scholarship. I decided to focus all of the unrestricted grant money the College received on scholarships. Joe Cannon chaired the recruitment committee for the entire college. He and his committee members visited high schools and communicated with prospective students.

The number of National Achievement winners we attracted was limited; however, in the process of competing for them, we attracted many other outstanding students. When high school students realized that some of their smart friends were going to Howard, they also applied. This was an example of the saying, "recruit the best and get the rest." Getting a critical mass of outstanding students also changed the culture in the classroom. Expectations were higher. We also established an Office of Student Services and hired a full time recruiter, Carmen Brocksmith.

Joe later served as chair of the Department of Chemical Engineering. A member of his committee was Jim Johnson, who focused on recruiting for Civil Engineering. Jim later became Dean of Engineering at Howard, succeeding Lucius Walker, and he served for many years.

Urban Systems Engineering

Having addressed the issue of undergraduate education, the second high priority discussed at the retreat was making engineering relevant to the urban problems we faced at that time. Dr. Don Coleman came to us in 1971 from the University of Michigan with a doctorate in Electrical Engineering and a concentration in computers. He was the first faculty member I hired with the explicit intention to do something about urban problems. Andy liked the idea of urban systems and was very supportive. He liked anything that had the word "urban" in it, but I am not sure he knew what we were talking about. At that time, the country was having serious urban problems. Many in the engineering profession were saying, "If we can go to the moon, why can't we solve the urban problem?" Many engineering schools responded to this challenge. Howard was one of them.

We decided to start a new master's program called Urban Systems Engineering. It was one of the first of its kind in the nation. It would apply the new discipline of systems engineering to urban problems such as transportation and housing. We received a major grant from the Alfred P. Sloan Foundation to start the program. We received another major grant from the Rockefeller Foundation to support the program. Several of the graduates of the Urban Systems program went on to get Ph.D.s. Two of them returned to Howard as faculty members. This was the first program of its kind at an HBCU.

While Urban Systems Engineering was appropriate for its time, our program, like those at other engineering schools, has since been folded into the more traditional engineering programs. Continuing his service to Howard, Don Coleman later served as Associate Provost and as Interim Provost at Howard.

Master's Degree in Computer Science

Howard University was the first HBCU to start a graduate program in computer science. Professor Wolsey Semple was a civil engineer who received his master's degree from the Massachusetts Institute of Technology. When he returned to Howard, he started a computer lab to serve the entire College of Engineering. He proposed, and the University approved, the start of a computer-science master's degree.

Doctorate in Mechanical Engineering

From the beginning, it was my intention to start doctoral programs in the College of Engineering. Andy kept reminding me that I had promised to do that. No other historically Black university had one at that time. The biggest issue with respect to starting doctoral programs was resources. We needed both faculty and an enhanced research infrastructure.

The mechanical engineering department was the first to propose a doctoral program, under the leadership of Charles Watkins, Chair of the Department. Watkins was a very active researcher, who did not need a lot of equipment to do his work. I was confident that he could manage a successful doctoral program, which was approved in 1976. It was the first doctoral program in engineering at a HBCU. One of his faculty members who worked on the proposal, Vascar G. Harris, later became Dean of Engineering at Tuskegee Institute. Dr. Charles Watkins was later appointed Dean of Engineering at the City College of New York.

Doctorate in Electrical Engineering

The next obvious candidate to start a doctoral program was the Department of Electrical Engineering. The impetus for this program was the creation of a solid-state electronics lab. This lab was created with the help of Rockwell International, in collaboration with Cornell University. It still exists and has brought tens of millions of dollars for research for Howard.

Eugene DeLoatch, then Chair of Electrical Engineering, led the development of the lab and the doctoral program. Gene went on to become the founding Dean of the College of Engineering at Morgan State University.

He is the co-founder of the Black Engineer of the Year Award. He also served as President of the American Association for Engineering Education, the national organization of engineering educators.

The proposal for the doctoral program in electrical engineering was written in 1976. The program began operation in 1977. The proposal listed 10 electrical engineering faculty members with Ph.D.s, more than enough to justify the proposal. Today, Howard is one of the major producers of African American doctorates in engineering in the country.

Elizabeth Catlett Sculpture: Art and Engineering

One of the things I am most proud of is the Elizabeth Catlett sculpture on the side of the chemical engineering building. If you walk down Sixth Street, you will see a piece of art by one of the most famous African American sculptors of the last 100 years: Elizabeth Catlett. For me, it highlights the fact that engineering is art. We do not call it art, we call it design. In both art and engineering, however, imagination is the most important thing.

In 1970, the EXXON Foundation gave Howard $600,000 to build a building for the new undergraduate chemical engineering program. Howard was the first of the engineering schools at historically Black universities to offer chemical engineering. The EXXON Foundation also approved a grant of $35,000 for a piece of art for the building. A solicitation was developed for the sculpture and sent to the most famous African American sculptors in the country. The students strongly preferred Elizabeth Catlett, who received her B.S. from Howard in 1935. She proposed a bronze relief showing two students reaching up in the midst of many engineering symbols. Catlett had the piece for the chemical engineering building cast in Mexico, and it was installed in May 1978.

National Minority Engineering Effort

While I was Dean of Engineering at Howard, I participated in several national activities designed to increase the number of minorities in engineering. Being in Washington, DC, and being at Howard, I was often the first one called to participate in such activities. One of the things I did was to co-chair a symposium at the National Academy of Engineering on Minorities in Engineering in the summer of 1973. That symposium was a catalyst to a coordinated national effort to increase minorities in engineering.

Shortly after the symposium, I received a call from the Vice President of the Alfred P. Sloan Foundation. As previously mentioned, I had received a large grant from the Sloan Foundation for the urban systems program. He did not mention what they wanted to discuss, but I thought that they might want to give us more money. When I arrived, I found out they had another agenda; they wanted to hire me to run their new Minorities in Engineering Program. I was not prepared for that, so told them I would get back to them. I went to see Andy and told him about the proposition. I told him I did not want to leave Howard, having been there only two years. On the other hand, I did not want to say no to an organization from which I might want to get more money.

I suggested that we make them a counter offer that they would have to turn down; hence, they would be saying no, not us. The counter offer was that I would take the job half-time but with some money coming to Howard. Andy told me to talk to Cheek. Cheek agreed with the strategy. When I called Sloan and made the proposal, they accepted. For the next two years, I commuted weekly between Washington, DC, and Rockefeller Center in New York. This effort was the catalyst for the creation of many organizations that are still working to increase minority engineers, including NACME, GEM, MESA, and others.

When I left Howard, I became the Assistant Secretary of the Army in charge of research development and acquisition. My budget was $12B. I was later made Acting Secretary of the Army, and then President of Prairie View A&M University. I am currently a professor at Michigan State University helping to produce more Black engineering doctoral students.

Conclusion

I am sure Andy and I would agree that we were privileged to be at Howard in the 1970s. We had a president committed to making Howard a first-class university. Equally as important, he had the ability to provide the funds to work on this goal. We were also blessed with outstanding people currently on the faculty and a surge of young Black Ph.D.s we recruited jointly. They were formed at the height of the Civil Rights Movement and were committed to contributing to Black education. Together, we have been able to impact tens of thousands of Black engineering students at Howard and elsewhere.

In coming to Howard, I realized at that particular time that Howard was what I called "opportunity-rich." In many ways, the stars were aligned for progress. The rest was hard work to convert those opportunities into reality.

Note: A 3/2 program allows undergraduate students to be admitted to an engineering program after three years of study in a non-engineering major. They receive degrees in engineering after two years of study in the engineering program.

"[Andy's] respect for the values of the researcher, and for collaboration and interdisciplinary research as the norm, provided an avenue for Howard University scholars to compete for external grants and not compete within Howard, where the resources were limited."

Chapter 11

Some Reflections on the Expansion of Research in the Social Sciences at Howard University in the 1970s: The Case of the Institute for Urban Affairs and Research

Lawrence E. Gary, Ph.D.

The Institute for Urban Affairs and Research

Established in 1972, the Institute for Urban Affairs and Research had an ongoing mission to broaden the involvement of Howard University in developing viable solutions to urban problems. Employing a non-traditional, but holistic, framework for improving the quality of life in urban communities, the Institute executed its charge through three major programmatic thrusts: education, research, and community service.

The Institute's educational components included: a) Urban Studies – a graduate degree program, which assisted the students in becoming effective social-change agents; b) University Without Walls — an innovative, alternative program of study leading to the baccalaureate degree; and c) Special Services for Disadvantaged Students — a program of supportive services for disadvantaged students to help them in their academic, social, and personal adjustment to college life.

The research activities of the Institute were primarily coordinated through the University's Mental Health Research and Development Center, which was established in 1974 through a developmental grant from the Center for Minority Group Mental Health Programs at the National Institute of Mental Health. Additional funding for research was obtained from the Ford Foundation, the Alcoa Corporation, the National Institute of Education, the Office of Education, the Bureau of Health Research Administration, the Law Enforcement Assistance Administration, and the Fund for the Improvement of Postsecondary Education. Some research projects were as follows: Unmarried Adolescent Fathers, Help-Seeking Among Black Males; Informal Support Networks Among Blacks; and Social Interventions in the Schools. The Institute also conducted faculty development workshops, which provided research and grantsmanship training for faculty members from predominantly Black colleges and universities.

The Institute also had community service programs such as the Community Action Program, the Child Abuse and Neglect Resource Center, the Family Life and Youth Task Force, and the Black Women Symposium, which was held each year in the spring. A series of workshops, seminars, conferences, technical assistance programs, and training programs were provided to community organizations, local governments, professional groups, and individuals. To execute its program of research, education, and community services, the Institute maintained a wide range of resources, as reflected in its staff and facilities. By the end of the 1970s, the staff of the Institute included more than 60 full- and part-time persons with degrees in areas ranging from psychology, social work, political science, sociology, history, education, and economics to law, communications, business, journalism, and fine arts.

Facilities and resources of the Institute included a computerized data-processing center; extensive reproduction equipment; a graphics arts laboratory; a research library housing a collection of more than 10,000 books, journals, and other publications; a learning resource center containing approximately 10,000 manuscripts, books, films, and tapes on social and behavioral issues, child abuse, and mental health; and a number of conference rooms for meetings, consultations, and workshops. The Institute also produced a variety of publications including books, directories, occasional papers, conference proceedings, resource guides, and final reports. The Institute's two newsletters, *Urban Research Review* and *RECAP*, were published quarterly.

Personal Narrative

My framework for generating lessons learned from Dr. Billingsley is organized around three narratives. I still remember with fondness Dr. Billingsley's phone call to me in 1971 at the University of Michigan telling me I needed to come to Howard University and build a viable professional career. I came to Howard in August 1971 and retired June 30, 2012, as Professor Emeritus. That's 41 years, and what a wonderful decision I made! I worked directly under Dr. Billingsely's supervision for three years, first as an Assistant Director, and then as Director of the Institute. He taught me so much about the culture of the academy.

When I joined the faculty at the University of Michigan in 1968, the Dean of my school invited me into his office for a conference and gave me a practice lecture on the need to plan for my retirement. He told me about investment options, why I must save ten percent of my salary, and the need to keep up with investment opportunities. I followed his advice for 40 years. When I first came to Howard University, there was much discussion by some officials on the process — i.e., who to trust and who not to trust, who to watch out for, what to expect from my enemies, and so forth. However, Dr. Billingsley consistently told me to focus on academic products such as writing proposals, conducting research, publishing articles, and working with community groups. His advice to me was similar to that given by our mentors at the University of Michigan. For example, Dr. Henry J. Meyer had said to me: "Make sure that you publish an article from your dissertation." Thank you, Dr. Billingsley, for your advice: "How to keep a focus on the product rather than the process." (Lesson 1.)When I joined the faculty at Howard, I did not realize it would take more than two months to get paid! My wife was expecting our first child; we had no health insurance. I had expected a joint appointment between social work and political science. That did not happen! Dr. Billingsley told me to be patient. During this time, my wife called the public schools of Ann Arbor and arranged for our family to be kept on her insurance plan. He taught me that, at a Black university, you have to have the patience of Job! Everything would work out in due time. That was the second lesson I learned from Dr. Billingsley: It is important to have patience in your professional career.

"How to select the right comparison group" was Lesson 3. Dr. Billingsley's coming from a Research I University (University of California at Berkeley) suggested that he had a keen understanding of the following: the complexities in the academy, the nature of competition, a range of abilities and talents, what constitutes academic rigor, the difference between research and training grants, and the challenges of initiating a serious program of social science research.

His experience as an academic administrator at Berkeley taught us how to use soft power rather than hard power to accomplish certain goals. His respect for the values of the researcher, and for collaboration and interdisciplinary research as the norm, provided an avenue for Howard University scholars to compete for external grants and not compete within Howard, where the resources were limited. The goal was to create a new reward system for those who obtained grants. Billingsley also shared with me the need to keep an eye on what my University of Michigan classmates were doing professionally and what scholars in my field and specialization were doing, and not to focus so much on what my colleagues at Howard were earning or doing.

When the Institute was established in 1972, Howard was classified as a Comprehensive University, based on the Carnegie standards for classifying colleges and universities. Dr. James Cheek and Dr. Billingsley had a goal to transform Howard from a Comprehensive University to a Research I University. Like most HBCU's, Howard had a teaching culture rather than a research culture based on the faculty handbook and teaching load. Dr. Cheek and Dr. Billingsley did not wish to compare Howard to other HBCUs, so they developed a comparison matrix of six or seven major universities such as Tulane, Temple, Emory, University of Chicago, and Vanderbilt. Howard was compared to these universities in terms of faculty salaries, endowment dollars, external research dollars, number of Ph.D. programs and commitment to graduate education, offerings and range of B.A./B.S. programs, and types of research centers and institutes.

As a result of this comparison with these universities, a decision was made to create a number of research centers and institutes at Howard. There was a desire to move Howard toward a research culture instead of a focus on teaching. This shift in focus did result in some tension under the leadership of Dr. Billingsley; however, we did learn how important it is to have the correct comparison groups.

Organizational Narrative

Much was learned from Dr. Billingsley regarding the organizational development of the Institute. Earlier, I described some of the activities of the Institute during the 1970s. There were many challenges and issues impacting a new organization at Howard, such as:

1. hostility from the "old guards" who were very protective of the old system of rewards and power;
2. mixing of old programs, such as Upward Bound with new programs such as Community Action;
3. having a graduate educational program such as the Master of Urban Studies, along with an undergraduate program such as University Without Walls;
4. having a very diverse staff in terms of disciplines, levels of education, ideologies, and skill sets;
5. limited space and financial resources; and
6. a few lawsuits and hearings.

Dr. Billingsley was an excellent resource for me as we addressed these challenges. Moreover, service learning was not a tradition at Howard in the 1970s, except for maybe in social work, medicine, or dentistry. Dr. Billingsley helped to introduce service learning for undergraduates at Howard through the Community Action Program, which was funded by the federal government. As I recall, we learned about an opportunity for a grant and had two days to write the proposal. Mr. C. Payne Lucas played a role in helping us to get funded from the Action Program. I thank you, Dr. Billingsley, for your close supervision and direction. I now can appreciate the beauty of being supervised by a strong, competent Black man. I also wish to thank my grandparents (Ed and Henrietta Gary), uncles (Uncle Clab, Uncle Lee, Uncle Bro), my mentors at Tuskegee Institute (Dr. C. G. Gomillian, Dr. Charles Hamilton, and Dr. Paul Puryear), and my mentors at the University of Michigan (Dr. Henry J. Meyer, Dr. Roger Linds, and Mrs. Patricia Neal) for preparing me to receive and appreciate the importance of being supervised.

Research and Publication Narrative

Dr. Andrew Billingsley should be celebrated for his outstanding contributions to the social science literature (Arnold Allen, 1995). His research on Black families, Black organizations, and the Black community in general helped to lay the foundation for our research strategy at the Institute and for my own program of research. At the Institute, we did a critical assessment of the social science literature on the Black community and identified the major deficiencies of this research (Gary and Leashore, 1982; Milburn, Gary, Brown, & Booth, 1991). We used these literature deficiencies about the Black community to guide our research agenda and our strategies for obtaining external funding. For example, we developed techniques for literature assessment that organized our thinking around theory, methods, and substantive research findings. Then, we linked these literature assessments to who was on review communities at various governmental agencies and who was on editorial boards of journals to the priority statements of various governmental agencies and trends in various fields of social science research. We had an outstanding staff of researchers whose credentials reflected a variety of disciplines and institutions of higher education.

As a result of these efforts and strategies, we were able to obtain major funding from governmental agencies and private foundations in the 1970s. We actually received several Research Project (R01) grants (Linder et al., 2016). Publications were one of the products of the Institute, and they were linked to our research findings. We published our research findings in a variety of outlets such as books, refereed journals, newsletters, chapters in books, and occasional papers. The following books were published during the 1970s:

- *Social Research and the Black Community: Selected Issues and Priorities,* 1974;

- *Crime and its Impact on the Black Community,* 1975;
- *Restructuring the Educational Process: A Black Perspective,* 1976;
- *The Black Church: A Community Resource,* 1977; and
- *Mental Health: A Challenge to the Black Community,* 1978.

Our research was also published in revered journals such as *Journal of Politics, Social Work, Public Health Reports, Adolescence,* and *American Journal of Public Health.*

We are thankful to Dr. Billingsley for his guidance in the areas of literature assessment and communications skills. He encouraged the Institute to have the right comparison group. We did not compare ourselves to the various departments and scholars at Howard. We compared ourselves to other research centers at Research I universities. His emphasis on communicating your ideas was reflected in his own writings. Dr. Billingsley is an excellent writer, editor, and communicator. I thank him for demonstrating why it is so important to have effective communication skills.

Conclusion

We in the Institute learned much from Dr. Andrew Billingsley. I have identified the following 10 lessons learned from him during the 1970s:

1. Keep a focus on the product rather than the process.
2. It is important to have patience in your professional career.
3. One should exercise care in selecting the right comparison group.
4. You must master the art of managing your emotions.
5. You must separate your personal identity from the organizational identity.
6. You must learn how to respond to unanticipated opportunities.
7. Twists of fate are a part of life — sometimes stuff happens; just let it go.
8. Supervision is a protective factor; it is necessary for being successful in life.
9. Critical assessment is an important guide for developing a research agenda and strategy.
10. The art of effective communication and collaboration is necessary for conducting meaningful research.

The entire staff of the Institute owes much to Dr. Billingsley's leadership. May his leadership and commitments to the Black community and the general society be an example of an enduring legacy.

"The promise of Billingsley's work in Black Family Studies, and other areas that would come to serve as the foundation for a new way of thinking about the world within the academy, was that we could generate methodologies that actually reflected how Africans responded to the conditions that beset all humans..."

Chapter 12

The State of African American Studies in the 1970s and Today, a National Perspective; or Black Studies Without the Black Radical Tradition

Joshua Myers, Ph.D.

"Hegemonic control of Black Studies is as important to capital as any other field of knowledge production."[48]

These words were sounded in 1999 by Cedric Robinson, perhaps the clearest thinker on the meaning of Black radicalism, on the idea that African people can self-determine ways of freeing themselves. He was pontificating upon the paradox of emptying this tradition into the academy, which was and remains to be a source of deep tension, one leading to a reincorporation of the very terms under which Black Studies was created. The students who so bravely knocked down these doors were not, in the recent words of John Bracey, "seeking to change the academy." They were about a deeper, broader "social transformation" that the universities were in fact inherently arrayed against.[49]

Understanding resistance to Black Studies would be aided by recognizing this fact. After all, universities seek to uphold the status quo. What happens when that status quo has not only generated a political environment that has stricken Black people from the respectable domains of citizenship, but also an intellectual condition that impugns their very ability to conceive and frame that reality? Resistance happens. But, then, it is often co-opted, such that today we have Black Studies without the Black radical tradition, despite the fact that the latter was never killed and perhaps can never be.

It is necessary to affirm — as recent thinkers have only recently and dejectedly begun to do — that what passes as Black Studies in today's academy represents an outward disavowal of the political and cultural foundations for knowing the world, which attended its appearance in late 1960s and early 1970s.[50] Retracing the idea of the Black University concept is perhaps the best evidence of this purposeful distancing. For where it is even remembered, the idea of the Black University premised on the notion that the world — that reality — might be better framed from our own political needs and cultural assumptions? It is dismissed as idealistic, as a relic of the 1960s. Reducing these politics to historical relics, museum pieces, and fodder for historians of Black Power becomes necessary to intellectually incarcerate those working "in the vineyard," limiting the possibilities of what Africana Studies could be.[51] And it has worked.

When I was asked to comment about some of the older foundations and new directions in the discipline for these proceedings, I thought about some of the depictions of Black Studies as a success story. These are abundant. But one of these recent histories specifically mentions our honoree, Andrew Billingsley, and, as such, might shed some light about how his words foreshadowed the issues we now face and how they predicted what might be possible in terms of the future of Black Studies. The text, Martha Biondi's *The Black Revolution on Campus*, tells the story of the Ford Foundation's Conference on Black Studies in 1969, which took place in idyllic Aspen, Colorado. According to her account, the issue that impeded these talks was centered on the question of who controls and who defines the discipline, as it seems Ford was not ready to cede control to Black radical thinkers.[52] But, this would not go unchallenged.

So it was that Andrew Billingsley composed a missive, upbraiding the leadership of the Foundation for not only attempting to define the discipline for Black folks but also for utilizing "American white ways of doing things."[53] Yet today, ironically, the "American white ways of doing things" has become hegemonic in departments claiming to do Black Studies, not only in terms of the organizational structure of the discipline, which perhaps could be forgiven, if not for the complete relinquishing of the grander vision of orienting knowledge from the intellectual and cultural domains of African thought. This is something we see demonstrated in the work of Andrew Billingsley, whose studies on the Black family begin with the central fact that Africans in America have identities that extend beyond their enslavement.[54] The promise of Billingsley's work in Black Family Studies, and other areas that would come to serve as the foundation for a new way of thinking about the world within the academy, was that we could generate methodologies that actually reflected how Africans responded to the conditions that beset all humans but uniquely faced Black folks in the age of modernity: the ability to exist on one's own terms, as sentient beings, and to reproduce life. Black Studies portended not only the *Death of White Sociology,* to evoke Joyce Ladner's edited volume, but the "Death of White Studies" (that is, every other discipline).[55] Black Studies continues, but these questions about methodology have been largely ignored or connected to different intellectual and political traditions.

Let us, as Biondi suggests, attribute the obsession with American whiteness in postmodernist and critical race theories to the faulty logic concerning the success and permanence of Black Studies in the academy. It is Black Studies' ability to affirm and extend the academy's overriding logic of American liberalism, no matter the underlying content, topical range, or methodology that marks it as stable, successful, *and* growing.[56] When Billingsley, as well as Vincent Harding, St. Clair Drake, and Roscoe Brown lodged their protest to the Ford Foundation over the question of control, in many ways they were quite prescient. For Black Studies, when defined (and funded) by any logic other than the Black Radical Tradition, can become whatever the academy wants it to be, which is more often than not against the interests from which it emerged.

So yes, Black Studies is growing. Yes, the train is moving. But like Du Bois's metaphor for the elimination of the Jim Crow car, some of us got aboard the train (i.e., America, in Du Bois's formulation), and never actually asked, "By the way, where is this train going?"[57] Instead of a radical knowledge foundation for thinking and studying the best ways in which to free ourselves, Black Studies, in many places, is simply the university's diversity initiative — a way to fulfill a mandate that somewhat obscures the deeply ingrained racial politics of the university —and of course, the state. Black Studies scholars have become academic stars, public intellectuals who ride the wave of celebrity while distancing themselves from the Bad Negroes or from anything resembling intellectual independence of the kind E. Franklin Frazier envisioned in 1962 in his "The Failure of the Negro Intellectual."[58] This kind of Black Studies — defined by its content, not its politics or its methodological orientation — is quite comfortable for the white academy (and on certain levels, HBCUs as well). This institutionalization has rendered Black Studies accessible from the highest levels of the American higher education totem pole to the lowest.

In 2013, nearly two thousand (1,777) institutions had "some form" of Black Studies. These were dispersed quite well regionally, though the institutional form — that is, whether or not they were departments, programs, or other kinds of units — varied widely.[59] In 2016, according to the National Council for Black Studies[60], there were 17 universities that offered a Ph.D. in Black Studies, with the first coming over 25 years ago at Temple University. (None are HBCUs. One thing that Biondi's work does correctly affirm is that HBCUs have always been spaces where Black Studies was not only possible but necessary and even characteristic to the unique intellectual traditions that have existed in these places. A larger concern is the ways in which HBCU leaders ignore or evade this unique tradition.)

Despite this expansion, graduate workers in the discipline have not fulfilled the mission of creating an intellectual space that would answer the question: *What distinguishes Black Studies Ph.D.s from any other field?* And then they have failed to leverage that answer into paradigmatic efficacy, in ways that would guide and train more generations under this particular ethos. (Isn't that what disciplines are supposed to do?). Finally, to date, journals such as the *Journal of Black Studies*, *The Black Scholar*, and the *Journal of African American Studies*, *The Journal of Pan-African Studies*, the *Western Journal of Black Studies* publish regularly, though one would be hard-pressed to establish much of an editorial or intellectual trajectory if one peruses their recent issues. Although these professional mechanisms have generated careers (and I am grateful that they have), we might ask again: *Was this the only mission?*

But there are questions we might ask beyond how many programs, departments, and graduate programs exist in the field; these numbers are as complicated as they are contested. The bigger questions are: *What kind of Black Studies exists in these places? Are they defined by their content or their methodology? Are they reflective of an erstwhile political tradition or a more innovative academic clearinghouse for "race" talk? Does Black Studies exist as the "academic extension of the Black Radical Tradition," to quote Greg Carr, or does it exist to contain, ignore, and evade it?61 Does it even realize that it is still alive and well?*

This is our litmus test. Anything less misremembers what the fight was about. For those who seek to extend this tradition, Andrew Billingsley and his generation are the exemplars for whom our genius and political orientation is derived.

Chapter 13

Charles F. Harris and the Birth of the Howard University Press During the 1970s

Janell Walden Agyeman with *D. Kamili Anderson*

Like others in the book publishing industry, I was deeply moved by the news that Charles F. Harris Sr. had passed on December 16, 2015. It is a privilege to assist in recalling the origins and impact of the Howard University Press from its inception in 1971 and especially to comment at this time on Charles Harris's signal contributions to the founding and development of that extraordinary institution.

The remarks here have been informed by personal research and invaluable interviews with former staff and supporters including: Philip W. Petrie, Executive Editor during the earliest years of Howard University Press, who also has held editorial positions at several major book publishers and at *The Crisis* magazine; Fay C. Acker, former Senior Editor at the Press and most recently the Associate Dean of Andrew Rankin Memorial Chapel; D. Kamili Anderson, Public Affairs and Communications Specialist for the Howard University Libraries and the Moorland-Spingarn Research Library, who served as the final Director of the Press; Marie Dutton Brown, founder of Marie Brown Associates literary agency and a former editor at Doubleday Publishing Company, who served as an advisory board member for the Press as well as a faculty member of the Howard University Press Book Publishing Institute.

The 1970s was a decade of tremendous achievements and expansion for African Americans. The opportunities presented following the landmark Civil Rights legislation executed in the 1960s, and the continuing widespread campaigns for African American parity in employment, housing, health care, college admissions, and public education directly fed the fervent desire of many African Americans to pursue their noblest desires and contribute their best efforts in every arena of human endeavor. With the establishment of the Howard University Press, African American scholarly and literary authors whose work reflected the history and culture of African

Americans and our diasporic brethren, in particular, could now identify a new publishing outlet that sought out their work on a consistent basis.

The Howard University Press was the first university press founded by a Historically Black College or University to gain formal recognition and establish a consistent presence in the publishing industry. Until its close in the first decade of the 21st century, it was a bright light among the few Black-owned book publishers in this country and easily distinguished from other academic presses — attracting submissions and producing books written by many leading Black scholars and intellectuals of the era, including many Howard University faculty members. We Press employees thought of our work there as "transforming, a high calling," to quote Fay C. Acker. "We understood that the Press was a substantial part of the Howard University mission to lead the way to a more just, vibrant, inclusive future where the voices of all, especially the marginalized, are heard," she once told me.

"Howard works for change, and you know Charles [Harris] was about shaking things up, getting the story told," she added.

The Context for Creation of the Howard University Press

To accentuate the role the Press assumed from its founding and for considerable years beyond, it is important to understand the publishing climate of that era, which was decidedly unlike the contemporary landscape—at least as far as Black authors were concerned. Two major trends are immediately evident in today's book publishing dynamic. In one, traditionally published titles produced by the older, legacy companies are frequently "written" by celebrities whose popularity and widespread media visibility guarantee vast audiences, who are expected to purchase large quantities of the books. In the other, many thousands of independently published (also known as self-published) volumes are produced by individuals who have chosen to forego the traditional publishing route and produce their works utilizing the relative ease of electronic publishing arrangements. Today, Black writers are frequently published in generic literature forms such as commercial women's fiction and urban fiction, among others. Arguably, less prominently published novels are literary fiction or historical fiction, which involves social commentary, political criticism, or a focus on the human condition and other substantial narrative nonfiction based on scholarship.

This is a very different landscape from the 1970s and 1980s, when Howard University Press was conceived, at least as far as Black authors were concerned. Publishing itself was different then, in the sense that most of the published African American authors writing books for adult readership were considered either literary or scholarly writers. Black authors with promising ideas for books were generally commissioned to write volumes that were scholarly, stemming from their academic work, or literary in which topics of note could be explored within a framework of exquisite language and layers of thought and meaning. Typically, conferences where authors would initially present their work or join in vibrant discussions of concepts that could eventually form substantial volumes were magnets for editors, publishers, and Black intellectuals. Marie Dutton Brown recalls that Howard University itself was the site for numerous such meetings during the 1970s, some of which she attended.

The Press's birth was enthusiastically greeted as an exciting publishing outlet offering wider opportunities for scholars and literary writers of narrative nonfiction, in particular, to receive thoughtful consideration and possible publication. A launch luncheon held to announce the new publisher, held in Washington, DC, at one of the premier hotels, cemented this message: Howard University Press was a serious contender and deserved respect within the larger publishing community.

Once established, Howard University Press's mission did not change from season to season. Black authors with the best ideas and concepts for original books, including scholars nurtured at Howard University, were consistently sought out and encouraged to submit their work for consideration; and the Press maintained a viable publishing program for more than 30 years.

The Impact of Charles F. Harris Upon the Howard University Press

Charles F. Harris was immensely well suited to his role as founding director of the Howard University Press. He was a lifelong advocate of literacy and a champion of equal opportunity and equal access to knowledge for all people, particularly those who had historically been denied it. His obituary in *The New York Times* on December 23, 2015, was appropriately entitled, "Charles F. Harris…Championed Black Writers." A reprint heading summarized that he "Led Effort to Publish Work by Black Writers." Throughout his publishing career, which started at Doubleday and Company in the mid-1950s, he sought opportunities to include voices of marginalized writers whose work reflected the sensibilities and historical perspective of their ethnic and cultural communities. He led the Press from 1971 through the mid-1980s, when he returned to the trade publishing arena.

Early in his publishing career, Harris appears to have committed himself to creating opportunities for African American writers and others to publish fiction and nonfiction detailing African Americans' contributions to American culture and society. His consciousness on this point surely was influenced by prior life experiences. As a youth, he continued a family tradition of delivering local newspapers. He also was a graduate of Virginia State College (now Virginia State University) and an Army veteran. A story told by Philip W. Petrie is instructive on this point. Years before, Petrie first met Harris at a party Langston Hughes threw in Harris's honor, after Hughes's good friend Arna Bontemps reported that Harris had just been hired as the first Black editor at Doubleday Publishing Company. Langston Hughes wanted to ensure that Harris knew Black writers welcomed him and would look to him for support in the days ahead. After learning that Petrie was a fellow college graduate with similar interests, Harris recruited him to enter publishing and to join him when he took another editorial position at John Wiley & Sons, Inc. Harris later recruited Petrie to serve as Executive Editor of the newly-created Howard University Press.

From his beginnings in the publishing industry and throughout his career at the Howard University Press, Charles Harris's work, as expressed in a *Times* obituary, defied the notion that writing by African American authors, or that aimed at African American readers, "belonged to a niche market that was—at worst, inconsequential and at best narrow and unprofitable." In addition to his Doubleday tenure, where he founded Zenith Books, the first publishing house to create multicultural books for middle-grade readers (ages 10 to 13), he also worked at John Wiley and Sons; at Dodd, Mead; and at Random House before he was recruited to help establish a university press at Howard. Given my sense of the history of African Americans in publishing, I can think of no one better qualified than Charles Harris to have commanded the founding director post. I suggest today he possessed tremendous practical and professional experience for the job as well as a clear and expansive vision that underscored his achievement there.

The Press is Launched

From the start, the Press was established upon a solid foundation of professional excellence. Acquisitions were made by its board of directors,which certified the scholarly quality of the books published through a peer review process. The Press also exceeded the minimum requirement of the Association of American University Publishers that it employ "at least three full-time equivalent employees, including a director who reported to a vice-presidential level officer of the University who held "both fiscal and academic authority." In this manner, coupled with the frequency of books produced, the Press earned regular membership in the Association of American University Publishers, the premier membership organization representing nonprofit university presses and scholarly publishers. The Press also was a consistent presence at the leading professional and scholarly meetings, where its books were exhibited and its editors met writers with promising ideas. These meetings included the Modern Language Association, the Association for the Study of African American Life and History, the American Library Association, and the American Booksellers' Association, later known as Book Expo America.

Charles Harris brought the best of his considerable business acumen to the task. His acumen was based upon his astute understanding of commercial publishing dynamics and a vast network of contacts amassed throughout his career. He brokered major agreements with R. R. Donnelley & Sons for print solutions and with The Johns Hopkins University Press for book distribution and fulfillment operations, to ensure the success of the Howard University Press program.

Charles Harris advocated a publishing vision that celebrated scholarly works of seminal importance to the academy, particularly Afro-American Studies departments and academic programs in the humanities and social sciences, but he and the board of directors expected this organization to differ from the other university presses in distinctive ways. A brief look at its literary output confirms that this venture certainly charted new territory. Among the earliest titles published that established the Press's academic bona fides, all published in 1974, were: *A Poetic Equation*, a book of conversations between Margaret Walker Alexander and Nikki Giovanni, distinguished Black poets of different generations; Houston A. Baker, Jr.'s *Singers of Daybreak: Studies in Black American Literature* which defied the "Eurocentric" notion that Black literature is didactic in seven critical essays; *Bid the Vassal Soar: Interpretive Essays on the Life and Poetry of Phillis Wheatley (ca. 1753-1784) and George Moses Horton (ca. 1797-1883)* by M. A. Richmond, which quickly established that its definition of "worthy" publications was not limited solely to those produced by Black writers; *From the Dark Tower: Afro-American Writers 1900-1960* by Arthur P. Davis, an anthology developed from the work of a legendary Howard University professor whose tenure spanned the WWII years to the end of the Civil Rights Movement, 1944-1980.

In 1982, *Mental Health and People of Color: Curriculum Development and Change,* edited by Jay C. Chunn, Patricia J. Dunston, and Fariyal Ross-Sheriff, was noteworthy for its groundbreaking scholarship. In a 1984 interview with *The New York Times*, Harris said he expected it to "revolutionize the field" of mental health practice since it argued that "the traditional methods of treating mental illness may not fit people who come out of the Black background."

This vision included a strategy that was a forerunner of a practice widely employed in university press circles today. Howard University Press sought to broaden its influence and sales by actively courting the interest and support of professionals and lay readers outside the academy who desired access to marginalized voices and perspectives.

Thus, Harris empowered the Press staff to acquire and republish critically acclaimed, noteworthy scholarship and literary fiction of particular interest to African American and other marginalized communities of readers that had gone out of print, presumably because sales did not meet initial expectations, but whose ideas and expression merited reexamination. One result was the launch of the "Library of Contemporary Literature," a series of trade paperback reprints by acclaimed authors, including Paule Marshall, Junius Edwards, Barry Beckham, William Melvin Kelley, George Davis, Kristen Hunter Lattany, David Parks, and John Oliver Killens. All titles were released with new introductions from scholars of note. The Press saw their republication as a ripe opportunity to provide high-quality literature produced by African American authors with another chance to reach their potential readership.

This effort attempted to bring to public attention significant works of scholarship from abroad, resulting in the Press' republication of *How Europe Underdeveloped Africa* by Walter Rodney, a work originally published in Britain that became the firm's bestselling title; in addition to *Toward the Decolonization of African Literature* by Chinweizu, Onwuchekwa Jemie, and Ihechukwu Madubuike, which was originally published in Nigeria.

Similarly remarkable was the release of *Sweet Flypaper of Life*, a stunning photo-essay volume with photos by Guggenheim Award-winning photographer Roy DeCarava with text by Langston Hughes. It was republished to the delight of established fans who could no longer find this remarkable commentary on Black life in Harlem, first published in 1955, and introduced to a wide, new readership in 1984.

Because its approach to publishing differed significantly from most other houses of its day, Howard University Press was sought out by many writers who struggled for recognition in a publishing climate that too often was indifferent to their work. For example, the late, award-winning author of books for children, Walter Dean Myers, submitted one of his first novels to the Press. Since our mission did not allow the Press to produce books for young readers, I was tasked with rejecting his thoroughly engaging manuscript.

Opportunities to take on projects traditional publishers would dismiss but that complemented its mission enabled the Press to publish *Aiiieeeee!*

An Anthology of Asian-American Writers among its inaugural titles in 1974. Frank Chin, one of the four editors of this Pan-Asian effort that included selections from Chinese-, Japanese- and Filipino-American writers, is quoted:

> The blacks were the first to take us serious and sustained the spirit of many Asian American writers….[I]t wasn't surprising to us that Howard University Press understood us and set out to publish our book with their first list. They liked our English we spoke [sic] and didn't accuse us of unwholesome literary devices.[62]

Aiiieeeee! was notable for its inclusion of work that did not reflect the popular stereotypes of Asian Americans. It was a groundbreaking effort on the part of writers of color to define themselves on their own terms. "It helped to establish Asian American Literature as a field."

Charles Harris understood the importance of growing the ranks of African Americans within the publishing industry so that knowledgeable and skilled advocates for diverse perspectives are present and productive. In 1980, with a $61,000 grant from Time, Inc., he oversaw the creation of the Howard University Press Book Publishing Institute, the first publishing procedures course established by an African American institution.

In accordance with the University's policy, this was an equal opportunity program, and it enrolled a predominantly but not exclusively Black student body. The Institute provided students access to information about the book publishing industry and opportunities to enter it, which had not been systematically extended to African American college graduates so that they might consider and pursue careers in this powerful knowledge industry, which persists in employing miniscule numbers of African Americans and other minorities. Scholarship assistance was solicited annually and various publishers contributed funds to help defray tuition costs for deserving students. Additionally, efforts were made to match Institute graduates with job opportunities within the publishing industry. Several Institute graduates were hired by publishers, including the Howard University Press, in editorial, marketing and sales positions. These graduates include: Malaika Adero, who served in editorial positions at New American Library, Amistad Press, and Simon & Schuster, is now a publishing consultant heading Adero's Literary Tribe/ALT; D. Kamili Anderson,who joined the Howard University Press to provide publicity and promotions assistance and ultimately became its last Director; Regina Brooks, who has held editorial positions at major publishers and is the founder and lead agent for Serendipity Literary Agency; Michael Flamini, who is an Executive Editor at St. Martin's Press; Michael Nelson, who once handled sales and marketing support for the Howard University Press; Avis Taylor, who was once Administrator of the

Howard University Press Book Publishing Institute; and Christopher Terry, who was a member of the marketing team at the American University in Cairo Press for a number of years.

I once had the opportunity to share with Charles Harris and the Institute's students the profound impact that a dynamic, mission-oriented publishing professional can have upon readers who, by definition, agree to engage their minds with writing that can inform and entertain, some-times simultaneously. Long ago, when I was a middle-school student look-ing for information on which to base a speech topic, "Why I am Proud to Be a Negro," I discovered *A Glorious Age in Africa,* edited by Daniel Chu and Elliott Skinner, in the local library. This book became the basis of my award-winning speech. It also happened to have been among the first titles published under the Zenith Books imprint at the Doubleday Publishing Company. I was astounded so many years later to realize that my employer at Howard University Press, Charles Harris, was the founding editor of the Zenith line, which was the first attempt to create nonfiction, multicultural books for middle-grade students. I did not realize the connection until the start of my second year as Administrator of the Howard University Press Book Publishing Institute. As I noted when introducing Charles Harris to the class, I was deeply grateful for the impact his early professional contri-butions had made on my early academic performance. I also underscored for Institute students the tremendous influence that effectively published books can make upon minds prepared to receive and digest new information.

Conclusion

The inspired creation of Howard University Press during the administration of President James E. Cheek and ably facilitated by Dr. Andrew Billingsley, who orchestrated the many elements needed to establish the Press, was a signal achievement for the University. Its impact far exceeded the physical boundaries of the campus and those of us who helped develop and produce its books and related educational program as well as those who read and were informed by the nearly 100 books it produced. In significant part, the successful establishment of the Press can be attributed to the recruitment of Charles F. Harris Sr., a brilliant, articulate, determined, and committed visionary who helped to project Howard University as a thought leader within and beyond the academy. He was the right leader at the right time, and he had a huge impact through his work to shape the character and im-pact of the Howard University Press.

References

"Charles F. Harris, 81, Dies; Led Effort to Publish Work by Black Writers". http://www.nytimes.com/2015/12/23/books/charles-f-harris-81-dies-led-effort-to-publish-work-by-black-writers.html?_r=0

"Publishing: Booksellers' Convention" by Edwin McDowell, http://www.nytimes.com/1984/05/15/arts.publishing-booksellers-convention.html

Membership Guidelines for the American Association of University Publishers. http://www.aaupnet.org/aaup-members/becoming-a-member/guidelines-for-membership

"[Billingsley] passed to me across his desk a book that he was completing by a senior faculty member at Howard University. The book was The Destruction of Black Civilization *by Dr. Chancellor Williams. He asked if I had read it, I said no, and that I was unaware of the text or its author."*

Chapter 14

Confronting Blackness: Howard University, The Institute for the Arts and Humanities, and Stephen E. Henderson

Haki Madhubuti, Ph.D.

How absurd it is then, to assume, as some critics do, that a Black University would exist in a vacuum, when the question of identity — the question of blackness — is more than a matter of pigmentation, when it is ultimately a moral and philosophical position....In other words, one finally wills to be black....My firm belief is that by willing to be black in that philosophical sense, our schools can make a greater contribution to our personal well-being and to the world at large than by any other means that I can presently see.[1]

What does it mean to be Black? This was the defining question of the 1960s and is also at the intersection of today's struggles and studies. Few who have not experienced the multiple movements for Civil (Human) Rights, Black Power in all areas of human activity, Black Politics, and the Black Arts can truly appreciate the many Black minds — women and men working 24/7/365, most without serious compensation, peer recognition, academic support, rewards, or a plain "thank you", I know this because I was there and have shared such experiences with many of those talented, selfless, remarkable women and men.

During my short tenure as a poet, publisher, editor, essayist, and educator, primarily in higher education for over 42 years, I have seen, experienced, and suffered. As the journalist/activist Lou Palmer would often state, "This is enough to turn a Negro Black." I've had a unique opportunity to work with some amazing people — scholars, educators, poets, fiction writers, literary nonfiction writers, musicians, actors, visual artists, choreographers/dancers, and others. The beauty of interacting with most of these women and men is that I was young enough and open enough to literally soak in their shared knowledge. How does one really process and articulate such on-the-job education when the "job" is actually building and liberating one's own life? What I mean is, I was not born into what I have become. I am me as a direct result of reading and studying thousands of carefully selected books and having artistic, collegial, and familiar contact with hundreds of creative women and men. They saw something in my eyes, language mannerisms, posture, and political and cultural activism that I took for granted.

To put it simply, Black art saved my life and gave me a life. My confrontation with art, with foreign knowledges (most things outside the Black community) within the creative side of wellness and growth, all equipped me with another way of looking at and working in the world. Without the mentoring, love of extended familyhood, and works of Richard Wright, Paul Robeson, Carter G. Woodson, W. E. B. Du Bois, Malcolm X, Margaret and Charles Burroughs, Dudley Randall, Hoyt W. Fuller, Barbara Ann Sizemore, Gwendolyn Brooks, Carol D. Lee, and countless others, I would not be writing this today (see *YellowBlack: The First Twenty-One Years of a Poet's Life*).

At the complex age of 28, I found myself on the faculty of Howard University, the preeminent Black university in the United States if not the world. Howard University in the 1970s was the only Black research university in the nation whose history is one that would inspire anyone looking for a challenge as a student or professor. I clearly remember lying about attending Howard University at 18, in my short life as an on-the-road-magazine-subscriptions salesman. My sales pitch was that I was working my way through Howard University, thereby legitimizing and aiding me in my goal of selling *Ebony, Jet, LIFE, Time, Reader's Digest, Post,* and other magazines — it worked. Having read Sterling A. Brown and Alain Locke and others of Howard University also paid off.

Fast forward to the summer of 1970, after Black rebellions in Detroit, Chicago, Los Angeles, Cleveland, and most urban enclaves, where multitudes of Black people — then called Negroes — lived, worked, and planned for a better life, I received a call from the office of Dr. Andrew Billingsley, the nationally respected social scientist and author of *Black Families in White America* (1968), who was at that time Provost and Vice President for Academic Affairs at Howard University. He shared with me his idea of starting a new institute that would seek to answer some of the life-giving and life-saving questions that I (a young poet) and millions of others in this nation and the world were asking about the development, future, station, and advancement of Black people or African Americans — that is, people of African ancestry.

Dr. Billingsley stated that the University was starting a new initiative, the Institute for the Arts and Humanities, and wanted to know if I would come in and talk to him about joining the faculty and helping with this new venture. I said yes, and within a week I was sitting in his office talking to the man, scholar, activist, educator, writer, and deep thinker on the condition of Black people in the United States and elsewhere. His concerns, which I heard in his voice and saw in his face, were most certainly due to the deadly climate of the 1960s, where the new direction for our people was coming from. He passed to me across his desk a book that he was completing by a senior faculty member at Howard University. The book was *The Destruction of Black Civilization*[2] by Dr. Chancellor Williams. He asked if I had read it, I said no and that I was unaware of the text or its author. Returning to our conversation, he stated that Dr. Stephen Henderson, one of the co-founders of the Institute of the Black World along with Dr. Vincent Harding and Chair of the English Department at Morehouse College, would be the new Director of Howard's Institute for the Arts and Humanities (IAH). He asked if I knew Stephen Henderson, and I answered yes — and no. I will come back to this later.

Provost Billingsley wanted to receive an answer immediately to the University's very generous offer. In making an offer, I'm sure he was aware of my teaching history at Columbia College Chicago, Cornell University, and the University of Illinois–Chicago, where I was currently employed. I was not looking for a job, but for a mission. My title would be Poet-in-Residence, along with the great fiction writer John O. Killens, the designated fiction Writer-in-Residence. I would be assigned to the English Department, where I would teach two courses: one in Black literature and the other in creative writing, along with my responsibilities at IAH. I had only one request that was non-negotiable. He and others of the planning committee were well aware of my founding of Third World Press (1967) and co-founding of the Institute of Positive Education (1969), along with its K-3 school. There were other components, but the Press and school were the most critical. My request was to commute each week between Washington, DC, and Chicago, arriving on Tuesday and returning to Chicago Thursday evening or Friday morning. Obviously, there would be weekends that would require me to remain in DC for special programming at IAH.

His response was not unexpected. "Young man, don't you realize that we have full professors and others who have worked most of their professional lives here and understand that their first responsibility is to this University?" I answered yes, however, earlier that year, I had read Alvin Toffler's *Future Shock*. He had written about professors fulfilling more than one appointment at two or more major universities, and had noted that they were accommodated. While teaching at Cornell University (from 1968 to1969), I observed that they allowed that practice among some of their top faculty members. Dr. Billingsley's answer was a firm no! I thanked him for the offer and my first trip to Washington, DC, got up to excuse myself, and left. Before I exited the administration building, his secretary rushed toward me and asked me to return. Dr. Billingsley commented on my negotiating skills for being such a young man and stated that, along with my salary, he was able to find a weekly stipend for air travel between the two cities for three years. However, he stated, in no uncertain terms, I had to have an apartment in the area. I said yes, signed the contract, and started working at my dream university in the fall of 1970. I stayed until 1978, using DC as my second home, which also enabled me to fruitfully contribute to the Institute for the Arts and Humanities and travel extensively nationally and internationally while completing five books of poetry and essays.

Stephen E. Henderson

I first encountered the work of Dr. Henderson in the pages of *Negro Digest/ Black World* magazine in its March 1968 issue on the subject of the Black university. I was serving on the faculty of the University of Illinois–Chicago as its first Black Poet-in-Residence. Black students along with Black faculty, staff, and workers were fighting to start a Black Studies department there. That issue of *Negro Digest/Black World* was instrumental in providing intellectual and cultural ammunition for our fight. There were articles by Gerald McWorter (Abdul Alkalimat), Nathan Hare, Darwin Turner, Vincent Harding, and a powerful essay, "The Black University: Toward Its Realization," by Stephen E. Henderson, in which he comments on faculty, curriculum, and research for a potential Black university.

I first met Dr. Henderson in 1968 at a conference at the University of Wisconsin–Madison, where he and professor Mercer Cook were the key presenters in a symposium titled "Anger and Beyond: The Black Writer and a World in Revolution." I was still Don L. Lee, and at that time living in Chicago. I was invited in to read my poetry at the gathering on August 8 and 9. After my poetry reading, I was able to interact with Dr. Henderson about the paper he delivered, which formed the basis for his essay, "Survival Motion: A Study of the Black Writer and the Black Revolution in America." It was the second part of the book he and Mercer Cook had authored, titled *The Militant Black Writer: In Africa and the United States* (1969). Henderson, as a poet, scholar, and cultural worker, had his analytical mind attached to the underside of the Black community. His understanding of the blues, Black poetic form, and the all-encompassing role that Black music plays among African people from birth to death was critical in his analysis. He writes early in his essay about the importance of Blackness, Black poetry, and Black writing:

> To write Black poetry is an act of survival, of regeneration, of love. Black writers do not write for white people and refuse to be judged by them. They write for Black people and they write about their blackness, and out of their blackness, rejecting anyone and anything that stands in the way of self-knowledge and self-celebration. They know that to assert blackness into America is to be "militant," to be dangerous, to be subversive, to be revolutionary, and they know this in a way that even the Harlem Renaissance did not. The poets and the playwrights are especially articulate and especially relevant and speak directly to the people. (Cook and Henderson, 1965)

Our second meeting was at the Institute of the Black World (IBW) and the King Center's official opening in January 1970. "A Celebration of Blackness" was the inviting calling card of the newly minted IBW. Included in the celebration was Katherine Dunham's dance troupe. The great poet fiction writer, scholar, and teacher, Margaret Walker Alexander, gave the keynote, and I read poetry. It was a celebration like few others. Dr. Vincent Harding of Spelman College and Morehouse College's Stephen Henderson, co-founders of IBW, were truly brothers-in-arms (both served in the military for two years), in ideas, and in commitment (both men taught at predominantly Black colleges); and each had a long view of the Black world (both graduating to the rank of respected, advanced scholars). Dr. William Strickland joined the founders later and helped to make IBW into a world-class think tank that focused primarily on Black themes. My continued association with Henderson, Harding, Strickland, and Howard Dodson (soon to become IBW's symposium coordinator) was through Third World Press publishing three of their "Black papers": Lerone Bennett Jr.'s "The Challenge of Blackness," Margaret Walker Alexander's "How I Wrote Jubilee," and St. Clair Drake's "The Redemption of Black Africa and Black Religion."

My third and most lasting meeting with Dr. Henderson came when he joined the faculty at Howard University in 1971 and assumed a double appointment in the departments of African American Studies and English. In 1973, along with Andrew Billingsley, John O. Killens, Sterling A. Brown, myself, and others, Henderson became the founding Director of the Institute for the Arts and Humanities at Howard University. His stature as a scholar and critic was growing nationally due to his publishing of his ground-breaking study, *Understanding the New Black Poetry: Black Speech & Black Music as Poetic References*. With this book, Henderson had become a part of the intellectual conversation around the legitimacy of the work of the Black Arts poets and others. As a scholar, he not only embraced our work but was in a cultural and intellectual league in our fight against a corrupt political and literary stranglehold that tried to direct, control, and take ownership of our revolutionary voices. In his overview, he writes clearly, with little nuance or ambiguity, about his mission and enlightened view of his study:

> Black poetry in the United States has been widely misunderstood, misinterpreted and undervalued for a variety of reasons—aesthetic, cultural and political—especially by white critics; but with the exception of the work of a few established figures, it has also been suspect by many Black academicians whose literary judgments are self-consciously "objective" and whose cultural values, while avowedly "American," are essentially European. This poetry has also been misrepresented in a number of anthologies, not only the so-called integrated ones, but also in some which are exclusively Black. I shall not designate any of these, for my intent is not polemical. Besides, there are many reasons why an anthology may not be "representative." The central problem, however, is one of selection. (Henderson 1973, 3)

Dr. Henderson's synthesis of the leading Black poets and their ideas immediately put him in the company of other Black critics and writers who were not colorblinded by "integration" and white nonsense talk. They were Hoyt W. Fuller, Addison Gayle Jr., Carolyn Fowler, Richard Long, Mary Helen Washington, Darwin T. Turner, Larry Neal, Eleanor W. Traylor, Houston A. Baker, Eugenia Collier, David Llorens, and others on the Black side of life.

Dr. Henderson's directorship of IHA was professional, collegial, extended-family-like, direct, and in-your-face fair, with a 24/7 open-door policy to his office. He and we programmed to our strengths. It was John O. Killens who helped initiate our national writer's conferences based upon the work he had done at Fisk University. Most of the scholarly literary symposiums were chaired by Dr. Henderson. I, as a poet, activist, and organizer, developed a relationship with local poets and people in struggle. In 1971, Dr. Henderson suggested that I become more experimental in my course offerings, so I developed and taught a course titled "Worldview: Toward a New Consciousness." This was an offering that explored and conducted a deep examination of the relationship between Black literature, Black music, Black visual art, and Black politics. I also took my classes on trips outside the university to local Black venues such as bookstores, art galleries, and live music and poetry events. Over the years, the course and the IAH programs attracted brothers and sisters, students, and non-students from the surrounding areas and beyond.

I also was able, due to my youth (and over-the-top activism) to develop working relationships with advanced students at Howard and other universities, and with young artists and other people in the Black community. Back then, Washington, DC, was known and celebrated as "Chocolate City". In fact, I recorded two albums: *Rise, Vision, Comin'* (1973) and *Medasi* (1976) with the Afrikan Liberation Arts Ensemble, under the able direction of a master musician/composer, Agyei Akoto. One of the benefits of teaching at Howard University was that there were many stars on faculty whose talents we liberally drew upon. They were elder poet/scholar Sterling A. Brown; historian Chancellor Williams; Black Arts visual artist Jeff Donaldson, who was also a founder of AFRO-COBRA and one of the creators of the internationally referenced "Wall of Respect"; internationally acclaimed filmmaker Haile Gerima (*Sankofa*); political scientist extraordinaire Ronald Walters; international *Down Beat*-acclaimed trumpet player/composer Donald Byrd; rising biographer and writer Paula Giddings; visionary sociologist Joyce Ladner, respected editor Charles Harris; and, of course, our own John O. Killens and many others. Howard University and its Institute for the Arts and Humanities was the place to be in the 1970s. Numerous Black writers and thinkers (C. L. R. James and Aimé Césaire), visual artists, and musicians of the Black Arts Movement (BAM) made it a point to visit us — invited or not — during the eight years I was there.

In concluding this too-short retrospective, I must say a few words about Steve's (as he ordered us to call him) poetry. He was always in search of answers in his scholarship and creative work. Black with a capital 'B' denoted culture, identity, direction, and location in his writing. He was a fine poet. During the IAH years, he seldom published poems; however, he privately shared his work with me. As mentioned earlier, our bond as poets and brothers existed before Howard University.

My first and lasting impression of Brother Steve is that he was as serious about Black people, Black consciousness, and Black poetry as a first love. Our discussions took on a new urgency as he was completing his master work, *Understanding the New Black Poetry*. He had featured me and other Black Arts poets in his co-authored book, *The Militant Black Writer* (1969), but would give me out-size evaluation, recognition, and credit as one of the prime movers of the Black Arts Movement.

Looking back on his poetry, one of his major poems is his five-part narrative entitled, "The Game Changer." This poem is a fighting poem: "Unlike any other pebble thrown in the well / This one has a bombshell story to tell." The poem's speaker, Sam, appears

> Anchored at the base
> Sam's climb straight up mountain face
> Fingers bloody bone
> Dripping down mountain stone face
> Ledge appears in front of cave...

We must imagine throughout this five-part narrative poem that Sam is a stand-in for Steve Henderson himself, who continuously changes frequency throughout the poem and has "Elevated DNA / beyond parted Red Sea." He ends this magnificent piece with the following stanza:

Next, Now, North
Yet, Yellow, Yin or Yang
Guarding, Gate, Gargantuan
Fearlessly, Facing, Fiend
Sam's, Saber, Shines
Winding Willing, Wind
Battle, Began, Between
Cutting, Crisply, Clean
Limber, Legs, Leap
Knowing, Knowledge, Knight
Neck, Negate, Next
Dropping, Double, Doors

There would not have been a successful IAH without the loving touch of Stephen E. Henderson. As an unassuming, great, and insightful artist and scholar, he guided us and pulled from us the best we had to offer. My final words are:

Steve was Blackbone consciousness,
never to spit, pee or speak false words into the southern wind.
he was quiet hurricane staring down floods & fire
he hated winter forest of snow and killer rainwords
his weapons of language & blues significations, Blackness within the Black
saw us before we knew us, defined a mission,
worked a miracle.

Bibliography

Cook, Mercer. Henderson, Stephen E. *The Militant Black Writer: In Africa and the United States.* Wisconsin: The University of Wisconsin Press, 1969.

Henderson, Stephen E. *Understanding the New Black Poetry: Black Speech & Black Music As Poetic Reference.* New York: William Morrow & Company, Inc., 1973.

Negro Digest/Black World. Illinois: A Johnson Publication, March 1968.

White, Derrick E. *The Challenge of Blackness: The Institute of the Black World and Political Activism in the 1970s.* Florida: The University Press of Florida. 2011.

[1] Excerpt taken from Henderson's essay, "The Black University: Toward Its Realization" published in the March 1968 issue of Negro Digest/Black World magazine.

[2] Third World Press published The Destruction of Black Civilization in 1974. Chancellor William's seminal work is still in print.

Left to right: Baltimore Mayor William Donald Schaefer, Andrew Billingsley, Morgan State University President, and Earl Graves, MSU Alumnus and Founder/Publisher of *Black Enterprise* magazine, 1980.

PART IV

INSTITUTION BUILDING AT MORGAN STATE UNIVERSITY, 1975-1985

"The nation had begun to take seriously the Black revolution ushered in by student revolts all over the country, and institutions of higher education were leading the way. Of all the invitations proffered, I selected Morgan State in Baltimore."

Chapter 15

Building a Great University: The Morgan Years, 1975 – 1985

Andrew Billingsley, Ph.D.
and Bathsheba Bryant-Tarpeh, Ph.D.

B y January 1975, I had finally determined that the time had come for me to return to my research, writing, and teaching. The question was where? My first choice was to spend two years at the Center for Scholars, a think-tank at Stanford University. That would enable me to complete a first draft of my *The Other Side of Slavery* book. Unfortunately, the Stanford Center was full for the next two years. They would be pleased to take me after that. Meanwhile, I was bowled over by the numerous invitations to consider the presidency of several colleges and universities both Black and white.

The nation had begun to take seriously the Black revolution ushered in by student revolts all over the country, and institutions of higher education were leading the way. Of all the invitations proffered, I selected Morgan State in Baltimore. Other institutions whose presidency I was approached to consider included the following: Grinnell College, Iowa; Antioch College, Ohio; Governors State University, Illinois; Kentucky State University; Virginia State College; Norfolk State College; Detroit City College; and College in New Jersey. President King V. Cheek had been candid about the problems at Morgan. They had received inadequate and unequal funding by the governor and the legislature along with all the other Black colleges in the State. (Thirty years later in a case brought by the alumni of Black colleges, federal judge would declare a history of such funding unequal and order restitution). A strong factor was the support for Morgan by the Black citizens of Baltimore. Many of the Black school teachers and other civic leaders had studied at Morgan or their relatives had done so. Also, the small Black delegation in the legislature was strongly supportive of Morgan and the other Black institutions and, most had studied at Morgan. Cheek pointed out that the *Afro-American* newspaper and the descendants of Carl Murphy were also supportive.

I recognized the significance of the granting of university status to Morgan State College by the state legislature on its funding. I thought that it would generate new state funding; and if I were willing to spend substantial time at Morgan, there would be the opportunity to build another Howard, another strong Black university. That was the compelling challenge that drove my decision more than any other. It was also important that I had the support of the chairperson of the Morgan State presidential search committee and of the distinguished attorney Frank Decosta, son of the even more distinguished educator, Dr. Frank Decosta Sr. He had spoken with his sister, Miriam Decosta Willis, a faculty member at Howard, who had worked closely with me on several projects. She gave him a good report. He invited me to come for an interview. The search committee had been in operation for several months since King Cheek's departure, and although the search committee was close to making a selection, he asked them to delay until I could be interviewed. Attorney Decosta was even more positive than King Cheek about the enormous potential of building a new University at Morgan.

I submitted my resume. An interview was scheduled. Amy and our daughter Angela drove with me to Baltimore. The committee met in the headquarters of the *Afro-American* newspapers. The newspaper and its staff and owners were strong supporters of Morgan and of the university's mandate. Decosta, though not a member of the new Morgan State University board of trustees, would remain among the strongest supporters of me and my family at the University and in the community.

Sometime in February 1975, Amy, Angela, and I drove to Baltimore for the interview. The next day, Decosta called to say that the search committee and the full Board of Trustees of State Colleges had approved my election as president of Morgan State College. I should plan to begin as soon as possible, but not later than April 1, even if at first on a part-time basis. Governor Marvin Mandel signed the legislation creating Morgan State University, and I automatically became its President.

Given the favorable outcome of the meeting, Amy invited the President's cabinet to come to dinner at our home in Washington, DC, so that we could get acquainted and they could give me some informal briefings on Morgan. My acclimation was helped by Interim President Frazier. He was most gracious to me during the several weeks of transition. He took me to a meeting of the entire faculty and staff. They greeted both Amy and me most warmly.

It was an exciting new beginning. I was 49 years old; and with the experience at two major universities under my belt (Berkeley and Howard), I was eagerly looking forward to leading in the creation of a new one. I was prepared to leave Howard, and I was open to this apparent opportunity to build another Howard, another Black university, up the highway in Baltimore. Still, it helped to have the cautious entreaties of Vincent Harding, King V. Cheek, Congressman Parren Mitchell and especially the chair of the presidential search committee (the distinguished Attorney Frank Decosta, who would be one of my strongest supporters and friend to my family during my 10 years at Morgan). I was elected the last President of Morgan State College on May 17, 1975, by the Board of Trustees; and appointed to be the first president of Morgan State University by its (new) Board of Regents on July 1, 1975.

My address to the trustees, college, and community representatives entitled, "Strides Toward Excellence," was delivered on May 17, 1975. It should be noted that I claimed the mantle handed down from Thomas Jefferson, Martin Luther King Jr., and Dr. Martin Jenkins in my convocation address on July 3, 1975, entitled, "Reflections on the Birth of Morgan State University," In that address, I set forth my perspective as the new President of Morgan State University.

Later that year, when we all gathered in the governor's office to witness his signing of the Morgan State University Bill — Senate Bill 527, "The Welcome Bill," named for State Senator Verda Welcome, who had introduced the bill and pushed it through to passage — I was appalled when Governor Mandel turned to Senator Welcome and said, "Now, Verda, there is no money in this bill. I told you that the budget was tight this year. There will be no new money added to the Morgan budget. You all will have to operate on the same budget Morgan had last year." Senator Welcome was not fazed. "I know that Governor," she replied, "but you know it takes more to run a University than it does a college. And when times are better, I know you're gonna do right by Morgan State University." She was optimistic. Governor Mandel seemed to be the only person in the room not excited about the birth of this new university in the state's system. We would get no new funds to build a university for three long years until Governor Mandel was in jail and Lt. Governor Blair Lee, as Acting Governor, was persuaded to add a million dollars to Morgan's budget to begin the University's expansion. (However, his allocation was less than half of our proposed budget, which had already been reduced by the State Board of Higher Education). But, despite the absence of state funding, there was still excitement at Morgan and in the city of Baltimore. However, it had become clear that to mount a university, we would need to press for federal funds and private funds.

New Urban Programs

We worked hard over the next two-and-a-half years preparing an array of new programs. Since these new programs would be part of our academic affairs offerings, my Vice President for Academic Affairs, Dr. Horace Judson, played a lead role. Since the expansion would be primarily at the graduate level, as befitting a university, Dr. Clara Adams, my first Dean of Graduate Programs, worked indefatigability with faculties in selected departments to elevate appropriate subjects to the graduate level. Indispensable to my leadership team was Dr. Wright L. Lassiter, a genius at compiling the financial aspects of our plan, and, Dr. Maurice Wilson, my pivotal first Director of Institutional Research. It was with considerable excitement at Morgan that the Verda Welcome Bill had been passed by the legislature and signed into law by Governor Marvin Mandel in 1975, but would take some two-and-a-half years before it would be appropriated. Even so, the new graduate degree programs would take another year to become operative.

Our program and budget request consisted of 12 programs for which we had received the approval of the State Board of Higher Education; still, we had to argue hard before the House and the Senate budget committees. We knew that the legislature could not increase the governor's budget, but it would certainly delete or reduce items in the budget. At that early time in Morgan's expansion, the budget committees in both the House and the Senate consisted of members from districts outside Baltimore, and they were uniformly hostile to the Morgan budget. Senator Clarence Blount from Baltimore, a Morgan graduate and member of the Senate Budget Committee, was enormously helpful.

The dozen programs I sought to be instituted were the following:

1. Advanced degree planning staff and facilities — some legislatures were hostile toward this item. They asked: why did we need new funds and staff? Had not these new programs already been planned? We were successful in defending all these items.

2. Doctoral Program in Educational Leadership — this would be Morgan's first Ph.D. program and the leading edge of what would become an array of such programs. Dozens of educational leaders in the city and the state with master's degrees could now pursue the terminal degree without leaving the state. We began the program in fall 1978 with five new faculty and 15 doctoral students. Our first graduate from this program was Elzee C. Gladden, a highly respected, innovative principal with 37 years experience in the Baltimore City Public Schools. When he marched across the stage

three years later to receive at my hand the first doctorate to be awarded in the over 100-year history of Morgan, the whole house came to a standing ovation.

Morgan was a strong college, and it became a strong doctoral-granting institution. However, lacking state and federal funds to support its success, the doctoral programs at Morgan grew slowly. When I spoke recently with Dr. Clara Adams, we reflected on these early years of hard labor and took pride in the way doctoral study at Morgan has emerged.

All of the members of the President's Cabinet, most of the faculty, and I at Morgan had earned Ph.D. degrees at major universities in the nation. We knew that in order to avoid the danger of being a university in name only, we had to add doctoral offerings to the Morgan program. Although a number of departments were strong enough that a few faculty additions would prepare them to offer doctoral studies, we selected education, sociology, social work, and public administration for our initial doctoral offerings. Education was the most ready, with a strong faculty and strong master's degree programs already. I came to Morgan buoyed by the success I had at Howard in expanding Ph.D. programs — even in departments with fairly strong faculties but that offered only the master's degree such as history, sociology, political science and economics (see Part III).

Concomitant with doctoral degree programs, we also knew that research was the *sine qua non* of major universities. We struggled mightily to get state support for these initiatives, and although a number of these initial offerings struggled somewhat through the years to reach and maintain the integrity of doctoral education at the highest level, their successes confirmed the wisdom of our initial conceptions and we now observe the plethora of Ph.D. programs at Morgan some 30 years since.

While at Morgan, I spearheaded the creation of several institutes including the Institute for Urban Research (IUR). These institutes, though not part of academic departments, had their own staff or budgetary resources, as well as potential for obtaining grant funds from external resources. National government agencies and private foundations (i.e., Ford, Carnegie, Mellon) constituted major resources for faculty and graduate student research funding. The IUR has been enormously resourceful in receiving support for family, student, and community research. Over the years, it has had sterling leadership. It fit securely into Morgan's urban mission. My first appointment for Director of the Institute's Center for Urban Research was from the University of Missouri, and he had been one of the early exponents of digital facility. At one point, my favorite research assistant, Robert Hill, came to spend 10 years further strengthening the Institute after I had departed Morgan.

My 10 years at Morgan (1975-1985) were filled with challenges galore. My family largely enjoyed the experience, benefitted from it, and moved on in their lives and careers. My wife Amy, who had a master's degree in psychology, went back to school and earned a master's degree in business administration (MBA) at the University of Baltimore. She then became branch manager at the First National Bank and moved on up in her career including high-level government service. After two years at Baltimore City High School, we enrolled our children in boarding schools in Massachusetts. They were well prepared by their upbringing and did well in school. After high school, we encouraged them to study at a small historically Black college for their undergraduate studies and later attend large universities for graduate work. After visiting several schools, Angela chose Talladega College in Alabama, then Howard University to study business, computer science, and math. Bonita chose Spelman College in Atlanta, Georgia, and then University of Missouri for graduate studies in communications, followed by a long and rewarding career in public information.

Upon my retirement from the presidency at Morgan, I renewed my interest in research and scholarship. The Morgan Board of Regents awarded me a one-year leave with pay and a contract to return to Morgan afterward as Professor of Sociology with tenure. During my 10 years as President, I had put my scholarship on hold. It was the only 10-year period in my 50 years of university work at five universities that I had not written a single book or a single scholarly article. I was able to keep my mind working beyond university administration by delivering papers at the University, in the community, and elsewhere; however, my longing for the deeper elements of scholarship gave way to university building. I fought numerous battles — winning most of them, but losing quite a few. To refurbish my scholarly work, I accepted an invitation from the University of California at Berkeley to become a visiting Scholar-in-Residence for a term. I taught one course on the family and dug into research work in preparation for writing a second edition of my historic Black family book, which had begun and evolved at UC Berkeley some two decades earlier. Amy and I enjoyed being back in Berkeley with our old friends Harry Specht and Harriet Morrison, along with Tom and Ginger Alexander.

At Christmas time, Angela and Bonita flew out to join us for a celebration of the good old times which, even though pleasant beyond measure, were a little bit "yesterday." I also spent a semester as Visiting Scholar at the Fordham University School of Social Work with Jim Dumpson and other familiar scholars.

Looking back at my Morgan years, I can state that we won some battles and lost some. On the winning side, we count (1) The new university-level graduate programs, including the first Ph.D. programs; the M.S. in Architecture, Landscape Architecture and City Planning MBA program; the new radio station (WEAA) under the inspiration of future Congressman Kweisi M'Fume; working with student government leadership including Peter Harvey, who would go on to be elected Attorney General of New Jersey; and expanding support for the MSU Choir under Director Nathan Carter and his assistant Eric Conway. The engineering school climbed from its origins with the aid of Congressman Clarence Mitchell. There was also an increase in the percentage of faculty with the terminal Ph.D. degree from 35 percent on my arrival to 65 percent at my departure, thanks to the continued expansion of the Fulbright Scholar's Program under Dr. Sandye McIntyre II, and the erection of new science facilities and the first new student housing in a generation.

The list of failures is also impressive. First, I was never able to get the support of the Governor for Morgan's budget or for the capital budget, except for the time when Governor Mandel was in jail and Lt. Governor Blair Lee gave us the first funds to start graduate programs. Towards this end, when the long and fierce fight for the School of Engineering landed on Governor Hughes's desk with the vigorous support of Clarence Mitchell Jr. and the Baltimore community, he was persuaded to sign the budget. This occurred only after a second new School of Engineering was authorized simultaneously at the predominantly white University of Maryland, Baltimore County. Years after my departure, I marveled at the fact that Morgan's President was gifted with two Democratic governors, who had both been mayors of Baltimore and were both familiar with and supportive of Morgan. Governors Donald Schaefer and Martin O'Malley, each of whom served two four-year terms, finally gave substantial and fair amounts to Morgan's budget.

Another failure was related to my efforts to keep the Morgan enrollment climbing steadily. We faced hard economic times during that period, and Morgan's student enrollment declined despite our best efforts. When that happened, the state government cut back Morgan's basic budget and cut back the number of faculty. I well remember the days and nights with Dr. Wright Lassiter, my Vice President for Finance, and Dr. Horace Judson, Vice President for Academic Affairs, struggling to manipulate the budget. We mandated deep cuts elsewhere to keep from dismissing faculty and refrained from filling vacancies or giving promotions. Combined with that debacle, state authorities denied our repeated requests to raise Morgan faculty salaries to levels equal to their counterparts at white universities. To add insult to injury, we were allowed to hire new faculty for the new university programs at competitive faculty salaries, yet the existing faculty members who had helped us design those new programs were denied faculty raises. In retrospect, I believe that if I were on the faculty at that time, I would have lodged a vote of no-confidence in the President; there were no provisions for holding the governor accountable.

Looking back at my time at Morgan, I'm reminded of a song made famous by Frank Sinatra:

> Mistakes, I made a few
> But then again too few to mention
> I did what I had to do
> And saw it through without exemption
> And to think, I did all that and may I say
> Not in a shy way
> Oh, no, oh no not me
> I did it my way.

Finally, in the spirit of Langston Hughes in his "Mother to Son" poem:

> We kept the lights on
> We kept the doors open
> We kept the Morgan spirit alive
> and laid the groundwork
> so that in the fullness of time
> our successors could build the magnificent
> Morgan State University that it is today.

Chapter 16

Morgan State University and the Urban Mission

Wornie Reed, Ph.D.

A ndrew Billingsley's academic contributions go beyond his seminal scholarly work on the Black family, his work on the Black church, and related scholarship. He made significant contributions to the urban mission of universities in general and scholars in particular. For nine years, from 1975 to 1984, Billingsley served as President of Morgan State University. During his presidency, there were several major developments at the school, including the transformation of Morgan to university status and its designation as Maryland's "urban university". This involved the establishment of five academic divisions: the College of Arts and Sciences, the School of Education, the School of Urban Studies, the School of Business and Management, and the School of Graduate Studies. This brief paper is about the meaning and impact of adopting the urban mission for the university.

Maryland's Urban University

Under Billingsley's tenure, Morgan State was designated as Maryland's urban university. This was a major step for the University as it joined a national movement in higher education — the assumption of an urban mission for urban universities, similar to the mission of the land-grant universities, which tended to be located away from urban areas. At Morgan State, it took the forms of establishing a doctoral program in urban education, the Institute for Urban Research, and the Urban Commission.

Morgan's Urban Mission

Establishing Morgan State as Maryland's urban university addressed the issue of the future viability of the University by providing an ongoing *raison d'etre*. This was especially important because of another development that had been occurring over the preceding couple of decades: the building of campuses of the predominantly white state university system in areas where historically Black colleges and universities were already established. The local example was the University of Maryland/Baltimore County (UMBC), which opened across town from Morgan State in 1966. This, of course, had a negative impact on Morgan. Its enrollment dropped significantly in the 1970s as the college enrollment of African American students shifted to UMBC and other places. Such schools were being established in several places across the South in the 1960s, including Montgomery, Alabama, and Nashville, Tennessee. Individuals associated with Alabama State and Tennessee State Universities sued their two home states, however, and the federal court halted the expansion of the University of Tennessee into Nashville.

The other key move in securing the designation of Morgan State as Maryland's urban university occurred when Morgan joined the movement among universities in major urban areas to declare an urban mission for these schools. This urban mission was to be comparable to the missions of land-grant universities, which were established to provide at least two major services: to educate the sons and daughters of their constituents, who were often farmers; and to help those farmers in addressing their problems, which concerned growing better crops. Similarly, urban universities accepted the mission of educating the sons and daughters of their constituents — namely, people in cities — and helping those cities with their problems, the many problems of urban areas.

The Morrill Acts of 1862 and 1890 funded educational institutions by granting federally controlled land to the states to develop or sell to raise funds to establish "land-grant" colleges. The original mission of these institutions was to teach agriculture, military tactics, and the mechanic arts, as well as classical studies so that members of the working classes could obtain a liberal, practical education. A key component of the land-grant system is the agricultural experiment station program, designed to pass along new information to farmers, especially in the areas of soil minerals and plant growth.

In the late 1970s, thirteen public urban universities in major metropolitan areas of the United States formed the "Urban 13," a research-sharing association. These institutions were the University of Alabama at Birmingham, the University of Cincinnati, Cleveland State University, Florida Agricultural & Mechanical University, Georgia State University, the University of Missouri-Kansas City, the University of New Orleans, the City College of New York, the University of Pittsburgh, Portland State University, and the University of Houston. The leaders of these institutions assumed that their schools needed to take leadership roles in their respective urban areas. They reasoned that the rapidly growing urban centers were driving our economic, cultural, and political futures, and that the public institutions in those centers should be the engines behind that growth.

The informal "Urban 13" continually added members to their group, and in 1998 established the formal Great Cities Universities organization, which evolved into the Coalition of Urban-Serving Universities. This consisted of 27 institutions across the country, including Morgan State University. This coalition focuses on Congress and has liaisons with several federal agencies. The Coalition sees itself as addressing three areas of central importance to cities and residents:[63]

Human Capital: addresses the need for training of urban teachers and students at each stage along the educational pipeline;

Strengthening Communities: emphasizes building the capacity of the institutions to engage with their communities on social policy and economic development and

Urban Health: focuses on ameliorating urban health disparities in cities through university-community partnerships, with attention toward increasing the number of urban health professionals.

Billingsley's operationalization of the urban mission at Morgan State led to the establishment of the Baltimore Urban Development Commission, the doctoral program in educational leadership, and the Institute for Urban Research (IUR).

Urban Development Commission

The Baltimore Urban Development Commission was an umbrella-type organization co-led by Morgan State and the Mayor's office; its director was the director of the Institute for Urban Research. This commission encouraged and assisted the development and implementation of various community projects by other organizations and agencies. While the Commission did not carry out projects itself, it was clearly an expression of the leadership role the University was taking in community development.

Urban Education

The doctoral program in educational leadership was the first doctoral program at Morgan State. Aimed at preparing persons for leadership positions in urban school systems, the program produced its first graduate in 1983.

Institute for Urban Research (IUR)

A key aspect of the urban mission is to provide research and technical assistance on issues in urban areas. By establishing the Institute for Urban Research, Billingsley took a strong approach to the urban mission. He did this very well, establishing a full-scale center with appropriate resources.

For example, fully developed in the early 1980s, IUR had 13 full-time staff persons and a couple of part-time research assistants.[64] The staff included seven Ph.D. positions — the director and six research scientists, with each research scientist expected to teach one course in addition to their research duties. The staffing included six clerical staff persons.

The Institute was established in 1979 under provisions of the Maryland State Legislature to conduct basic and applied research on problems relevant to and affecting urban communities. The creation of the Institute reflected both the need for an organized research effort as well as the sense that such an endeavor could best be undertaken within the framework of Morgan State University's comprehensive urban foci.

The urban environment is highly diversified. Issues and problems produced in this setting are often the result of complex interactions that characterize contemporary urban life. In this context, any specific academic discipline is limited in its usefulness in addressing the diverse problems present in the urban environment. Thus, attempts to systematically examine urban issues and propose alternatives can benefit substantially from multidisciplinary efforts. The structure of IUR readily provided for such interdisciplinary team work.

Research Program. The research program of the Institute was designed to fulfill the broad urban mission of the University and specific program objectives. The three specific areas of research emphasis at IUR during the early 1980s were:

- the urban community
- the urban family
- gerontology

The Institute's research on the urban community had both local and national components. The local component consisted of studies and analyses that had primary relevance to the Baltimore metropolitan area. Primary data as well as relevant secondary data on local issues were collected and analyzed. The national component focused on urban issues and problems affecting Blacks and other minorities. This effort consisted of research on such topics as unemployment, crime, housing, and medical care.

The Institute's research focus on the urban family had a special emphasis on Black families. Problems such as single parenthood, teenage pregnancy, and access to child care facilities were some of the specific issues addressed at IUR.

The gerontology focus of the Institute's activities involved research on such issues as older persons' access to social services, national health care policy and the aged, and the sociopsychological aspects of aging.

In addition to the three main focal areas described above, the Institute

conducted research in several other fields, including the following areas:
- criminal justice
- transportation
- immigration policy
- social history
- fertility trends

Selected IUR Research Projects. The following is a list and summary of some of the Institute's research projects to illustrate the kinds of work done at IUR.

- *A Test of the Value of Expected Out-Of-Pocket Cost Savings as an Incentive for Changing Beneficiary Choice Behavior* (Funded by the Health Care Financing Administration). This project was designed to develop basic knowledge of how elderly health care consumers obtain and process information and how they balance various factors in making decisions under Medicare. It also tested the degree to which a significant number of beneficiaries can be motivated (by exposure to expected out-of-pocket costs) to act as cost-conscious buyers, thus putting pressure on providers to increase the rates at which physicians would accept the Medicare fee schedule.

- *An Evaluation of Clinical Supervision Procedures Selected County Driving While Intoxicated (DWI) Programs in Maryland* (Funded by the Maryland Department of Transportation). This was an evaluation of a program in which clients with drinking-while-driving behavior were provided with treatment and education.

- *An Evaluation and Analysis of the Summer Youth Employment Program* (Funded by the US Department of Labor). Monitoring activities were conducted for the regional offices of the Office of Youth Programs of the US Department of Labor. These monitoring efforts consisted of worksite visits, personal and group interviews with the Summer Youth Employment Program participants and supervisors, validation of time and attendance records, and review of policies and payroll procedures at the worksites.

- *The Economic Status and Labor Force Integration of Recent Haitian Immigrants in Miami, FL (*Funded by the US Department of Labor). This study was a comprehensive investigation of the socioeconomic status of recent undocumented Haitian entrants in the US. Specifically, the study sought to examine several interrelated issues: underlying causes for undocumented Haitian immigration, demographic and economic characteristics of the entrants; labor market experiences and problems in the US, and entrant participation in public benefit and service programs. Findings pointed to the need for policies concerning the immigration status of the entrants and for job training programs to increase their employability.

- *Evaluation of Pedestrian Safety* (Funded by the Maryland Department of Transportation). This evaluation of pedestrian safety programs operated by Baltimore City and Baltimore County was based on extensive examinations of various activities under the programs as well as detailed analyses of pedestrian-related accident data furnished by the Maryland Accident Reporting System for the years 1978, 1979, and 1980. The results suggested the need for a number of countermeasures aimed at reducing pedestrian accidents. These included emphasis on the in-depth study of spots or localities having high occurrences of pedestrian-related accidents as well as comprehensive and integrative efforts by various agencies and groups aimed at preventing pedestrian-related accidents.

- *Black-White Differences in Income, Occupation, and Unemployment: An Analysis of Current Populations Survey Data, 1968-1980* (Funded by the US Department of Labor). Using the Current Populations Survey data, the study examined the Black-white differences in income, employment, and occupation during the period 1968 through 1980. These findings showed that neither the Civil Rights legislations of the mid-1960s nor the economic growth of the 1960s and the 1970s led to significant improvement in the relative socioeconomic positions of African Americans.

- *Data Analysis and Enhancement Project* (Funded by the Maryland Department of Transportation). This project evaluated the Data Analysis and Reporting Technique for the Maryland Department of Transportation and provided analyses of data on factors associated with automobile accidents. The results were used in attempts to reduce the number and severity of accidents in the state of Maryland

- *Socioeconomic Effects of National Energy Programs on Minorities* (Funded by the Department of Energy). Primary survey data regarding energy use and energy-related attitudes of low-income and minority households were collected from a sample of Baltimore City residents. Implications for national energy policies and for alternative community-based strategies were discussed based upon the findings in the study.

- *The Role of the Black Media in Disaster Reporting to the Black Community: A Study of Message Transmission and Community Response* (Funded by the National Science Foundation). This study examined the influences of Black-owned media and organizations in disaster preparedness for Black communities and the responsiveness of individuals in those communities. The study site was Mobile, Alabama, a heavily Black-populated city with several Black-owned media, and the site of Hurricane Frederick on September 12, 1979. Owners and managers of Black-owned and white-owned radio stations and newspapers were interviewed.

A content analysis of newspaper articles and radio station logs was conducted, and 200 disaster victims were interviewed to obtain information on message reception and information utilization with respect to the hurricane.

- *OFDWI Programs in Maryland* (Funded by the Maryland Department of Transportation). This study evaluated county-sponsored DWI programs in the state of Maryland. Specifically, the study examined several program components on a statewide basis. These included program staff and administration, the client referral system, diagnosis and processing, client program attendance and attrition, curriculum and DWI course content, operational budgets, program evaluation procedures, and interactions between programs and other external agencies. DWI programs in 23 Maryland counties and Baltimore City were involved in the study.
- *McLean Hunter Cable TV Survey* (Funded by McLean Hunter Corporation). The purpose of this project was to secure data from a random sample of some 600 heads of households residing within the city limits of Baltimore and to conduct a comparative study of other un-penetrated urban areas on the marketability of cable television in Baltimore and other cities.
- *Black-White Differences in Housing Quality': An Analysis of Trends and Differentials* (Funded by the US Department of Housing and Urban Development). This study examined trends and differentials by race in housing quality using 1960 Census data and the Annual Housing Survey data for 1974, 1976, and 1978. Using more appropriate analytical techniques than had been used in previous research on this issue, the study found that although Blacks as well as whites had substantial overall improvements in housing quality over the period examined, there was no substantial decline in racial disparity.
- *Baltimore Area Study.* Probably the most significant study done at IUR was the Baltimore area study, significant because it exemplified the urban mission objectives. Requested by a committee of the Baltimore United Way, this study collected information and data on the experiences and attitudes of Baltimore City residents on various community issues including employment, health, crime, and housing. The volume produced by this project was used by the United Way as background information for the planning of some of its projects and, for several years, it was also used by the Baltimore Urban League to inform its work.

Assessment of the Status of African Americans

Though this review is principally about Andrew Billingsley's forward-looking leadership at Morgan State, I will also discuss briefly his significant assistance with the project, "Assessment of the Status of African Americans," as it represents an extension and elaboration of the work at IUR. In 1984, with $2 million in funding from foundations, the National Research Council (NRC) of the National Academy of Sciences began a study to report on the status of Blacks from 1940 to the present and on the future status of Blacks in the United States.

The NRC study, which was billed as an update of the Gunnar Myrdal-led study, *An American Dilemma*, faced severe criticisms along the way. Many critics complained about the limited involvement of African American scholars in the conceptualization, planning, and development of the project. They noted that many African Americans who were prominent in some of the areas under study were conspicuously omitted from the study panels.

Critics of the NRC study were concerned about the ramifications of a major study of African Americans in the ideological climate of the 1980s. There had been a dismantling of the Great Society programs and a cease-fire in the War on Poverty. Some critics were concerned that a major study by a prestigious academic organization like the NRC might serve to validate the 1980s trends toward limiting the role of government in addressing the ills of society, especially those concerning race. Furthermore, these critics contended that NRC study groups, though including a number of persons with commitment to principles of equality and fairness, included a significant number of scholars who ruled out both the historical oppression of African Americans and contemporary racial discrimination as major influences in the existing conditions of African American communities.

As a result of these concerns and considerations, in the spring of 1987, after having moved to UMass/Boston to develop the William Monroe Trotter Institute in 1985, I initiated the Assessment of the Status of African Americans project. Thirty-five scholars were organized into study groups, one for each of six topics: education; employment, income, and occupations; political participation and the administration of justice; social and cultural change; health and medical care; and the family. An additional 26 scholars provided original papers to the project. The study groups were established to analyze the status of African Americans in each of the topical areas in anticipation of the results and analyses of the NRC's study.

Four books were produced from this project, including the book, *Research on the African American Family: A Holistic Perspective*. Working with Robert Hill, Billingsley led the family study group that produced this book, with Robert Hill doing the lead writing. In my view, this book is a codification of the approach to studying Black families using the social systems approach that Billingsley discussed in his seminal book, *Black Families in White America*, back in 1968.

These authors noted that the conventional perspective accepted by large numbers of social scientists and policymakers is the deficit model, which attributes most of the problems of Black families to internal deficiencies or pathologies. They contend that the causes and nature of the current crises among Black families can be better understood — and addressed — if a holistic perspective is employed. This perspective leads to systematic examinations of the separate and combined effects of societal trends; social policies; and factors at the community, family, and individual levels.

At Morgan State University, Billingsley set in place a means by which a university could accomplish its urban mission, with the implicit understanding that these important community issues must be addressed. In his work with the Assessment of the Status Americans project, he showed how we can, and should, go about that work on one key aspect of African American life: the family. Thus, his impact on community-relevant scholarship exceeds his own personal scholarship.

Attendees at the "40th Anniversary of Black Studies" symposium at the University of Maryland, College Park: Jim Turner, Acie Byrd, Bob Hill, Joyce Ladner, Fran Wilson, Lynn Bolles, Ron Walters, Andrew Billingsley, Sharon Harley, Charles Henry (2009).

PART V

A RETURN TO SCHOLARSHIP AT THE UNIVERSITY OF MARYLAND, COLLEGE PARK AND THE UNIVERSITY OF SOUTH CAROLINA

"As I was completing a three-year term as Acting Chair, Dr. Billingsley and I met for the first time. I shared with him the impact his writings on Black families had had on my career trajectory."

Chapter 17

Dr. Andrew Billingsley: Mentor, Colleague, Friend

Roger H. Rubin, Ph.D.

In 1968, I was a doctoral student in child development and family relationships in the College of Human Development at the Pennsylvania State University. Having completed a master of science degree in this department with a master's thesis titled, "Matricentric Family Structure and the Self-Attitudes of Negro Children," I decided to continue a similar theme for my doctoral dissertation. A campus visit by a Black minister from a rural Pennsylvania town provided me with the opportunity to have access to a unique population. The town was in reasonable driving distance from campus. Residents included a large population of African Americans, brought from the Southland to labor in the local silicon mines.

Unusual for a northern rural area to have a significant Black population, this locale was further attractive for its numerous adolescents. It was for the needs of this youthful group that the minister had traveled to Penn State to request educational tutoring for his disadvantaged young in a racially polarized town. As a graduate assistant in a course entitled "Families and Communities," I was assigned to bring undergraduate students for tutorial purposes to the town. Two years of this responsibility gave me an intimate acquaintance with dozens of Black adolescents, as I shared experiences with them on their streets, homes, and educational institutions.

It was at the beginning of this experience that Andrew Billingsley published *Black Families in White America*. I was profoundly influenced by the theoretical framework and context of this work, as it reflected my sociological background and sympathy for structural-functional analysis of social problems. The final product of my association with this community was my dissertation, "Family Structure and Peer Group Affiliation as Related to Attitudes about Male-Female Relations among Black Youth." Eighty-five subjects— 46 males and 39 females— who comprised almost the entire population of unmarried, unengaged, Black youth from ages 13 through

20, participated. Little did I know at the time that Dr. Billingsley would become a member of my academic family, my colleague, and lifetime friend.

By 1986, I had served 14 years as a member of the faculty in the Department of Family Studies (now Family Science) and occasional Acting Chair at the University of Maryland, College Park. It was in that year that Andrew Billingsley arrived on campus as a senior-level sociologist providing academic guidance to several programs. As I was completing a three-year term as Acting Chair, Dr. Billingsley and I met for the first time. I shared with him the impact his writings on Black families had had on my career trajectory.

My first academic appointment was at the University of Tennessee at Knoxville in 1970, where I was given the honor and challenge of teaching the Black Families course. I assigned Dr. Billingsley's book and was gratified by the ensuing success of this offering. He inquired about applying for the permanent department chairmanship and whether I was pursuing the position. I encouraged him to apply, as I would be much more excited about serving under his leadership than my own. The outcome was a success, and he served as Chair of Family Studies for over a decade. Dr. Billingsley expressed particular interest in my dissertation and wondered what had happened to the adolescents I had studied 20 years earlier. Together, we returned to the town for several days of interviews using old name files from my collective notes. Much to our pleasure, we found considerable upward mobility, largely due to military service and the opening of jobs at the nearby prison. The fellowship we shared on this excursion provided a bond of mutual respect and opportunity for future academic projects.

In 1993, Andrew Billingsley published the sequel to *Black Families in White America,* titled *Climbing Jacob's Ladder.* An updated look at African American families over many centuries, this acclaimed work was completed during his tenure as department chair. Administrative relief was provided by me, appointed as acting chair. This event exposed me further to Billingsley's research techniques and scholarly discipline. It also provided me with insights into his leadership skills in forming a diverse team of supportive staff who devoted themselves to the man and his project. This would prove invaluable to the next step in Billingsley's contributions to sociological advances in family studies. *Climbing Jacob's Ladder* unquestionably established Billingsley among the finest scholars to ever study Black family life.

This recognition culminated in the awarding by the Ford Foundation of a grant to study the impact of the Black church on family formation, adaptation, and resiliency. Possibly among the most critical institutions in the Black community, the church and its religious directives had never been so extensively researched. Answering questions about the exact consequences of church policies, programs, and social values were examined. The product of this enormous task was the 1999 publication of *Mighty Like a River: The Black Church and Social Reform*. I was honored to have been selected among the scholars researching and interpreting the significance of this material. Billingsley assigned me the opportunity to evaluate and write on the subject of the Black church and its relationship to Black youth. This resulted in the publication of two journal articles and a monograph: Rubin, R. H., Billingsley, A., & Caldwell, C. H. (1994). "The Black Church and Adolescent Sexuality." *National Journal of Sociology*, 8, 131-148; Rubin, R. H., Billingsley, A., & Caldwell, C. H. (1994). "The Role of the Black Church in Working with Black adolescents." *Adolescence*, 29, 251-266; and Rubin, R. H., Billingsley, A.,& Caldwell, C. H. (1995). "The Black Church and Youth-at-Risk for Incarceration." Monograph on Youth in the 1990's, 4, 61-74. Preceding the publication of these papers in Pittsburgh, presentation was made at the 1992 meeting of the Association of Black Sociologists.

On April 16, 1998, the Department of Family Studies of the University of Maryland and the Consortium of Universities of the Washington Metropolitan Area presented a forum, to celebrate the diversity and strengths of African American families and to honor Dr. Andrew Billingsley. I served as co-chair of the forum which brought together Drs. Harriette Pipes McAdoo, Robert Hill, Ron Walters, Tony Whitehead, Suzanne Randolph, Cleopatra Howard Caldwell, Peggye Dilworth-Anderson, and David C. Driskell — all recognized scholars in their own right. I was deeply moved by the knowledge that the man who had so positively influenced my career received the accolades of his peers.

More recently, I attended a symposium in celebration of the 90th birthday of Andrew Billingsley at Howard University. I wrote in the program that Dr. Billingsley's interpersonal skills and scholarship provided a model for learning worthy of emulation and respect. It was an honor to share in celebrating his lifetime achievements and contributions to the enrichment and advancement of the social sciences. It is especially rewarding for me to call such a gentleman my mentor, colleague, and friend. Oh, and my wedding attendee in 1994!

Finally, age seems to be no deterrent to Andrew Billingsley. His interest in Robert Smalls, born into slavery, who became a Union hero during the Civil War by stealing a Confederate ship from Charleston and delivering it to Union lines, is the latest of his book publications. Smalls went on to become a United States Senator from South Carolina during Reconstruction. I recently visited Robert Small's gravesite in Beaufort, South Carolina. I learned from the locals that, partially due to Billingsley's book, Smalls is being rediscovered by a new generation. How fortunate I have been to have Andrew Billingsley in my life.

"Dr. Billingsley gracefully captured the essence of an enslaved body with an enlightened mind and unbridled spirit becoming a celebrated war hero, consummate public servant, and unheralded statesman. He delved deeply into the private musings and public persona of a genuine American hero."

Chapter 18

Dr. Andrew Billingsley's Scholarship on Robert Smalls Teaches Important Lessons about This Consequential South Carolinian

Congressman James E. Clyburn (D-SC), Assistant Democratic Leader in the US House of Representatives

"Freedom." That was the one-word answer Robert Smalls gave to President Abraham Lincoln when the Commander-in-Chief asked him why he risked everything to commandeer the Confederate warship, the *Planter*, and deliver it to Union forces in the waters surrounding Charleston, South Carolina. Freedom was the motivation of heroism and the cause of his life, and Smalls envisioned a strong public education system as the implement and the guardian of that cause.

In his 2007 book, *Yearning to Breathe Free*, Dr. Andrew Billingsley chronicled the life and legacy of the gentleman I perceive to be the most consequential South Carolinian in our state's history and one of my personal heroes, Congressman Robert Smalls. His life began in bondage on April 5, 1839, and it featured dramatic heroism in the Civil War and revealed visionary leadership in the post-war years. Yet, this consequential life would remain hidden from our awareness were it not for the diligence of many and the scholarship of a few like Dr. Billingsley.

The South Carolina history books I grew up with contained no mention, not even in the footnotes, of Robert Smalls and his extraordinary contributions to our state's history. But, I had a few teachers who dared to step outside of their comfort zones and dared to inform us of who and what we were.

In recent years, leaders of our military have recognized this hero of the Civil War. The United States Navy has named an Illinois training camp in his honor, and the U.S. Army christened a transport cargo ship the *Major General Robert Smalls*. I was greatly honored to have been invited to speak at its launching and was pleased to participate. South Carolina, however, has done little to honor or remember this significant figure. Robert Smalls should rank among the most honored and revered South Carolinians, but he does not, and I daresay that it is simply because of the color of his skin.

Smalls gained his freedom in one of history's most dramatic heroic acts. Because of the inhumanity of man and the cruelty of the institution of slavery, he was uneducated. By the grace of God almighty and personal ingenuity, however, he was highly intelligent and greatly motivated. That intelligence and motivation equipped him with the wherewithal to escape from slavery, abscond with a Confederate ship, and pilot it safely into the arms of freedom. His knowledge of the waters around the Sea Islands of South Carolina and a "yearning to breathe free" tremendously aided the Union forces in 17 engagements in that key area in the war. His contributions were rewarded rather handsomely, socially and financially.

After the war, Smalls entered the political arena and achieved much success, with public education topping his agenda. Education has been, and still is, the foremost ingredient for dignity and the most crucial ladder for social and economic mobility for all Americans. Its pursuit had been reserved for the elite, and African Americans—for 10 generations—had been denied such by law. Robert Smalls thrust himself into the vanguard of that effort in the 19th century.

Although he had not been allowed to be schooled himself, Smalls founded a school for Black children in 1867. He authored the resolution at the 1868 Constitutional Convention mandating that South Carolina provide a free and compulsory public school system for all, becoming the first state in the United States to do so. He also published a newspaper, the Beaufort *Southern Standard*, starting in 1872. Smalls was one of only two people to participate in both the 1868 Constitutional Convention, which made him a full-fledged citizen, and the 1895 Constitutional Convention, which reduced him to second-class citizenship.

Robert Smalls died in 1915 of natural causes in his birthplace of Beaufort, South Carolina—ironically, that was the year Dr. Carter G. Woodson founded the "Association for the Study of Negro Life and History, currently known as the Association for the Study of African American Life and History (ASALH). He died having retained some of the wealth he had accumulated but having lost much of the dignity he had earned. He died having been falsely accused and convicted of a crime of which he was not guilty. He died having seen the post-Civil War gains of former slaves reversed by two crucial Supreme Court decisions, *Cruikshank* in 1872 and *Plessy* in 1896, which established and solidified the Jim Crow system of racial segregation and legalized discrimination against African Americans.

Despite the fact that Robert Smalls' contributions to public education are grossly understated, the importance of a strong public education system to the success and advancement of all Americans cannot be overstated. As we continue our pursuit of "a more perfect union," strong public schools and adequate public education are central to the effort.

My foreword to Dr. Andrew Billingsley's *Yearning to Breathe Free* is a small contribution to his great, insightful treatise on the life and significant legacy of Robert Smalls. Dr. Billingsley gracefully captured the essence of an enslaved body with an enlightened mind and unbridled spirit, who became a celebrated war hero, consummate public servant, and unheralded statesman. He delved deeply into the private musings and public persona of a genuine American hero. I felt it my duty, as one of Smalls' successors here in the United States Congress, and the first African American to represent South Carolina in this august body since the dreadful post-Reconstruction era, to associate myself with Dr. Billingsley's scholarly and passionate work.

Andrew Billingsley, 2007, at a book signing for *Yearning to Breathe Free*, published by the University of South Carolina Press.

Chapter 19

Harriet Tubman in South Carolina: The Only American Woman to Lead an Army into Battle

Andrew Billingsley, Ph.D.

Introduction

On the morning of Monday, October 16, 2005, I was having breakfast at my house in Columbia, South Carolina, and reading the morning newspaper, *The State*. The headlines of the story read, "WORK COVERS SITE WHERE RAID FREED 700 SLAVES!"

The story, filed by senior staff writer Wayne Washington from rural Beaufort County, began as follows:

> Archaeologists have unearthed artifacts they believe pinpoint the location of a Combahee River ferry boat crossing used in a Civil War raid led by legendary abolitionist, Harriet Tubman.

Then, citing Tubman's legendary exploits on the Underground Railroad, Washington wrote:

> But no single act in Tubman's life would free more people than this Combahee River Raid. And yet in the state where it took place, its details are not widely known.

As the historian Jason Elerbee, who was part of the team of scholars who discovered and recognized the historical significance of this site, told Washington, "This is African American History, Women's History, Military History...and much more."

Washington, who did extensive and credible research for this story, marveled at Tubman's heroism; "Fourteen years after Tubman ran for her own freedom in 1849, here she was in 1863, aboard a U.S. warship named *John Adams*, leading a company of Black U.S. Army soldiers, probing deep into enemy territory, risking capture or worse if the Confederates all around her were roused too soon." The reporter continued, "And yet even in the state where it all took place its details are not widely known."

That article was written in 2005. Since that time, a great deal has become known in the state of South Carolina about the Combahee River ferry raid, and Harriet Tubman's role in scouting, planning, and leading it. Notably, since archaeologists have unearthed numerous additional artifacts from this site, several remarkable events have happened: (1) The South Carolina Department of Transportation widened the road considerably at US Highway 17 running across the spot at the Combahee River; (2) the department has also built a modern new steel bridge across the Combahee River at that spot; and (3) the South Carolina State Legislature, on the initiative of Reverend Kenneth Hodges, then a State Representative, passed a resolution designating that new bridge "The Harriet Tubman Bridge." Let us consider what and who brought Harriet Tubman from her home in Canada to Civil War South Carolina in the spring of 1862.

The Gathering Storms of War

The U.S. Civil War, which brought Harriet Tubman to South Carolina in spring of 1862, had been gathering for a very long time. It was averted once again by the Compromise of 1850, when the federal government sanctioned the practice of slavery in the southern states and Texas, and forbade slavery in the northwest territories. The same U.S. Congress, in the Kansas-Nebraska Act of 1854, which sanctioned slavery in those territories, overturned this compromise. Some scholars believe that act of national policy opened the floodgates of war. It was this action, which brought John Brown to prominence as a fierce and fearless fighter against slavery, that unleashed and led a raging and bloody war between the forces for and against slavery.

Then and for years afterwards, Brown could not rest and would not let the nation rest until his catastrophic demise in the aftermath of his armed attack on the federal arsenal at Harpers Ferry, Virginia, on October 16, 1859, and his execution on December 2, 1859.

Some scholars believe that John Brown's raid at Harpers Ferry, which was put down by Robert E. Lee of Virginia on order of the President and subsequently investigated by a U.S. Senate Committee headed by U.S. Senator Jefferson Davis of Mississippi, was the end of the road for negotiation and compromise. Not nearly as well known, even to this day, is that though Brown did not have many troops at Harpers Ferry, his admirers and supporters throughout the northern states were legion. Prominent among these was "The Secret Six," a group of wealthy white men in New York and Boston who provided financial support as well as personal logistical support for Brown's movement. Also prominent among John Brown's supporters leading to the Harpers Ferry Raid were Frederick Douglass and Harriet Tubman. It was Frederick Douglass, well connected and well acquainted with them both, who brought John Brown and Harriet Tubman together.

On April 7, 1858, Brown traveled to St. Catherines, Ontario, Canada, on the urging of Frederick Douglass, where he put up at a local hotel. He then sent a messenger to Tubman's home asking her to join him at his hotel, indicating that Frederick Douglass had recommended such a meeting. Tubman told the messenger she would be glad to meet with Brown. She asked him to go back to the hotel and ask Brown to come and meet her in her home on North Street in St. Catherines. She said, "Tell him that he will be quite safe here." She also wanted Brown to meet with a few of her friends, who were gathered at her home.

So, there, on April 7, 1858, at her home in Canada, a full year and a half before Brown's Harpers Ferry raid, Tubman and John Brown had their first face-to-face meeting. Harriet had invited her brothers and a few other carefully selected guests. It was a historic, fateful, and fulsome encounter. Brown was eloquent in his vision: his antipathy to slavery, his commitment to destroy it by armed struggle, and his specific plans for the armed attack and capture of the U.S. federal arsenal at Harpers Ferry. He pleaded for their support. Harriet Tubman signed on immediately. She would help him raise recruits for his army and help him raise funds for it as well. It became, between Tubman and Brown, a veritable mutual admiration society. She considered Brown the single white man in the U.S. she admired the most. John Brown addressed her as "General Tubman" and wrote to his son that Tubman was "the most of a man I ever met with."

The Port Royal Experiment

On November 6, 1861, Union forces landed at Port Royal Sound, in the Atlantic Ocean off the coast of South Carolina. These islands contained the richest of cotton and rice plantations, where slave labor made the white planters among the wealthiest in America. When Union forces landed, all the white planters and their families swiftly abandoned those islands, taking with them all the personal items they could carry. Those "abandoned lands" contained 10,000 Black people on 200 plantations, covering more than 60,000 acres.

The challenge for the Union was what to do with and for these people, now free, but utterly dependent and many in straits of desperation. The U.S. Army took over. The Army requested help from the Treasury Department. The Treasury Department appealed to northern abolitionists and other welfare agencies for help. Hundreds of civilian volunteers from the North poured into the area. They were teachers, medical personnel, college students, lawyers, business people, agricultural specialists and farmers, and a host of others. All who came to South Carolina under the label of "The Port Royal Experiment."

Prominent among these civilians was the educator and poet, Charlotte Forten from Philadelphia, who came to teach at the Penn School founded and headed by Philadelphia native, Laura Townsend. Harriet Tubman, on the other hand, came expressly to work with the military.

Harriet Tubman's Civil War

In January 1862, the abolitionist governor of Massachusetts, John A. Andrew, who knew Tubman very well, asked her to come and see him. She did. He persuaded her to go to South Carolina. This is the same Governor John Andrew who, a year later after Emancipation Proclamation in January 1863, would organize and send the 54th Massachusetts Infantry and its leader, Colonel Robert Shaw, to South Carolina as well. Later, in South Carolina, Tubman would have occasion to collaborate with this infantry and Colonel Shaw. (Indeed, she told friends later that she had made breakfast for Colonel Shaw just before he led his last and fatal raid.)

Meanwhile, Governor Andrew sent a message to General Rufus Saxton, then commander and military governor of the Federal Department of the South. The Governor wrote: "I am sending to you Harriet Tubman. A pioneer of the Underground Railroad. She will be valuable to you to serve as a spy, scout, and nurse when needed." The Governor added: "She would be a valuable person to operate within the enemies lines in procuring information and scouts."

Tubman arrived in Beaufort, South Carolina, in the spring of 1862 and reported directly to General Saxton. Saxton was a well known, strong abolitionist. He and Tubman got along very well.

In the first few months, her duties were not spectacular. She "nursed wounded soldiers, both Black and white, and worked at the Contraband Hospital." One scholar has written: "But Harriet Tubman had come to South Carolina to wage war on slavery. And, she would be given that opportunity by General David Hunter, Colonel Thomas Wentworth Higginson, and Colonel James Montgomery."

General Hunter's High Command

1. General David Hunter was the successor to General Rufus Saxton and head of a war council for his district. He had been appointed in the summer of 1862 to take command from General Saxton.
2. Tubman became a prominent member of this leadership team.
3. A third member of General Hunter's high command was 23-year-old Robert Smalls. Just three months out of slavery with no

formal education, Smalls was traveling with the elite. In the past three months, he had met and worked with accomplished men and women who represented institutions at the highest levels of society. It was already apparent that a major source of Smalls's achievement was his capacity to establish strong and trusting relationships with people who shared his commitment to freedom and were in positions to be of assistance to him.

In halting General David Hunter's efforts to recruit Black soldiers, Lincoln had reminded him that only Congress or the President had the authority to deal with slavery. There was a widespread assumption that, after two infractions of national policy, Hunter was about to be removed from his command. An important meeting between Admiral Du Pont and General Hunter occurred on May 29, 1862, after which Du Pont wrote his wife about the high regard he had for Hunter. Offering his support to Hunter, Du Pont also told the general of his high regard for Robert Smalls, who might be of some help to Hunter in this situation.

On August 9, 1862, three months after Hunter's emancipation initiatives had been canceled and three months after the seizure of the *Planter,* Smalls met General Hunter. It was the beginning of a long and fruitful relationship that lasted until after the war and even beyond Hunter's death. Hunter also invited to this meeting General Saxton and Reverend French.

At the meeting, General Hunter restated his belief that it was not only right but also a military necessity to enlist Blacks into the Union forces. Hunter had concluded that his military mission could not succeed without Black troops, and he doubted that the United States could win the war without them. The ranks of the white volunteers were thinning, and the enlistment of new white recruits had slowed to a trickle. Meanwhile, the Confederates were gaining strength from several major victories over the Union. There was a gathering consensus in the nation and in the military that President Lincoln had little chance of renomination and no chance of reelection in the upcoming November elections unless the Union forces could turn the tide against the Confederacy.

Hunter told Smalls that he had been authorized by Du Pont to send Smalls on a most important and delicate mission. He needed Smalls to go to Washington and perform another service for his country. Hunter's situation was desperate. Not only had the President and the Secretary of War called a halt to his efforts to recruit Black troops, but also, because of the Union defeat that very day at Bull Run and heavy losses in General George McClellan's peninsula campaign, Hunter had been ordered to send some of his dwindling numbers of white troops to Richmond.

Hunter wanted Smalls to speak with Secretary of War Edwin Stanton and other members of Lincoln's cabinet to convince them to authorize Hunter's enlistment of Black troops. Smalls was astonished but not intimidated. He was willing to do whatever was asked of him to advance the Union cause, but he wondered what he could possibly say to the officials that General Hunter and others had not already said.

Hunter reassured Smalls by reminding him of his capture of the *Planter* and of his success in getting the different factions in Port Royal to work together. Smalls's record in delivering the *Planter* would speak loudly in Washington, Hunter told him because it would demonstrate that Black men could make important contributions to the Union cause. There were two other things Hunter did to reassure Smalls. First, he gave Smalls a written statement to hand to Secretary Stanton requesting authorization for Hunter to enlist Black troops. Smalls could then elaborate on the request from his own experience and in his own way. Second, Hunter asked the Reverend French to accompany Smalls to Washington and introduce him to Secretary Stanton.

Smalls was ready to accept this mission. He knew that he had no other choice; he was a soldier and must obey an order no matter how impossible it might seem. Although apprehensive, he was honored to be given such a difficult task. He was also eager to undertake the mission because General Hunter had persuaded him that the War hung in the balance and, with it, any hope for the abolition of slavery. Being religious, Smalls undoubtedly felt sustained by the same ultimate force that sustained Moses when God commanded him to lead his people out of Egypt. Smalls requested a few days leave to spend in Beaufort with his family, during which his mother and his wife helped him pack and prepare for this journey.

On August 16, 1862, Smalls and French sailed from Hilton Head, South Carolina, aboard the steamer *Massachusetts,* bound for Washington, DC. On August 20, 1862, they met with the Secretary of War. Stanton was so impressed with Smalls that he arranged for Secretary of the Treasury Salmon P. Chase, the other strong abolitionist in Lincoln's cabinet, to meet with Smalls and French as well. French reported that Smalls regaled Secretary Chase with his story for nearly an hour. A few days later, Stanton ushered Smalls and French into a meeting with President Abraham Lincoln. Smalls proposed that if the President would authorize the enlistment of Black troops, he would personally recruit ten thousand Black men, "and they will be better soldiers than the present ones because they will be fighting for their freedom." President Lincoln was enthralled with Smalls' recitation on his capture of the *Planter*. At that time, the President was wrestling mightily with the question of admitting Black troops, having been urged to do so by Frederick Douglass and others. Lincoln expressed his appreciation to and admiration for Smalls, and a few days later complied with Smalls's request.

When Smalls and French returned to Beaufort, Smalls personally delivered to General Rufus Saxton an order from the President and the Secretary of War dated August 25, 1862, authorizing the enlistment of five-thousand African American troops, the first unit of Black troops officially admitted by Lincoln into the Union army. Smalls set about recruiting Blacks for this regiment. He volunteered for duty with the regiment, but Admiral Du Pont needed him for further service in the Navy. Though this regiment never reached its full strength, it functioned with distinction.

1. A fourth member of this military leadership team was Colonel Thomas Wentworth Higginson. He arrived November 24, 1862, to take command of the First South Carolina Regiment of Black Troops. This abolitionist had been sent to Hunter by Massachusetts abolitionist, Governor John Andrew. These two Black South Carolina Regiments, it will be noted, were established before the Emancipation Proclamation on the authority of General David Hunter, who knew what it would take to win the war. He was a friend and co-worker of Harriet Tubman in the abolitionist and Underground Railroad Movement. He, like Tubman, was a strong admirer and associate of John Brown.

Colonel Higginson's February 1, 1863, report to General Saxton gives an assessment of this regiment:

> Nobody knows anything about these men who has not seen them in battle. I find that I myself knew nothing. There is a fierce energy about them beyond anything of which I have read.
>
> No officer in this regiment now doubts that the key to the successful prosecution of this war lies in the unlimited employment of the Black troops. The superiority lies simply in the fact that they know the position of the country while white troops do not, and moreover they have peculiarities of temperament, position, and motive that belong to them alone. They show the resolution and the sagacity that a personal purpose gives. It would have been madness to attempt with the bravest white troops what I have successfully accomplished with the Black ones.

In forwarding Higginson's report to Stanton, General Saxton concluded: "No one knows better than the traitors now in arms against our government the great element of strength that the cause of liberty and the Union have in the hearts and muscles of these loyal Blacks. And finally, in my humble opinion, it would be no misapplication of the best energies of the Government should they now be directed toward the arming and disciplining of everyone that can be brought within our lines."

General Saxton, Secretary Stanton, and perhaps President Lincoln had every reason to be pleased with the order to enlist Black troops. Eventually some 285,000 Blacks were officially recruited into the U.S. Army. Some say that this particular resource provided the margin of victory for the Union.

1. In time, a fifth military leader was added to Hunter's War Council. He was Colonel James Montgomery. Montgomery arrived February 24, 1863, to take command of the Second South Carolina Regiment of Black Troops. Tubman was immediately attracted to him. He had heard of her from John Brown personally. Montgomery had fought along beside John Brown in Kansas. Montgomery would become Tubman's closest ally.

2. A sixth military leader in General Hunter's army was Colonel Robert Gould Shaw, who was also sent by Massachusetts Governor Andrew as Commander of the 54th Massachusetts Regiment. Tubman worked with him and served him breakfast on the last, fateful day of his life.

This military leadership team was now able and willing to (1) carry out President Lincoln's ultimate mission to save the Union. They were prepared to do so by (2) waging war on slavery. They had long known what Lincoln had finally come to know: the only way to accomplish these two missions was to add a third mission: (3) to admit Black troops to the U.S. Armed Forces. There was now, at long last, no other way to win the war.

Tubman's Pass

Now to underscore and affirm Tubman's place in General Hunter's estimation and in his leadership team. General Hunter issued a public pass to Tubman sometime in February 1863. It was to Tubman and addressed to all the officers under his command. It read as follows:

Pass the bearer, Harriet Tubman, to Beaufort and back to this place, and wherever she wishes to go; and give her free passage at all times on all Government Transports." This official pass continued: "Harriet Tubman was sent to me from Boston by Governor Andrew of Massachusetts, and is a valuable woman. She has permission, as a servant of the Government to purchase such provisions from the commissary as she may need.

We now know that Tubman was a certified member of General Hunter's leadership team right up there with Colonel Higginson and Colonel Montgomery and Captain Smalls and Colonel Shaw. She was also about to embark on this next phase of war, in which she would need and deserve all the support she could get from these military leaders and colleagues.

In spring of 1863, after Hunter's pass and Higginson's report to Hunter on the accomplishments of his Black troops, Harriet Tubman was handed a special assignment. This assignment would be the toughest she had yet faced during the Civil War in South Carolina and, indeed tougher, than her mission up North on the Underground Railroad. In the spring of 1863, despite the boost in Black enlistments after Emancipation Day on January 1, 1863, the war was not yet going well for the Union. Hunter had been asked to send some of his white troops to Richmond to bolster Union efforts to capture that city. Hunter needed to replenish his troops and vamp up Black recruitments. Enter Harriet Tubman. It would be the reason she had come to South Carolina: to wage war against slavery.

Colonel Montgomery asked Tubman to come see him at his Second South Carolina Black Regimental Headquarters. He told her that General Hunter had a special assignment for her. He wanted her to secretly scout out the vast area in Confederate-held territory along and beyond the Combahee River. General Hunter wanted to know the number and location of Confederate soldiers, guards, and pickets. Then, he wanted her to go beyond the river and determine where the Combahee ferry crossing was stationed and how it was being defended. Finally, Montgomery told Tubman that General Hunter also wanted her to check the location of the large plantations on the other side of the Combahee River. He wanted to know how many Black men were still on these plantations and how many would be willing to join the Union Army. He wanted to know whether any white men were still there. He wanted to know about storehouses of cotton and grain and other material that may be of use to the Union Army. Montgomery asked her to come back periodically and report her findings to him. Tubman lived a long time after the War. She lived to be 100 years old. She often told associates in the North that she was not afraid to undertake this assignment because the Lord, Frederick Douglass, and John Brown had convinced her that the only way to get rid of slavery was to fight and win the war, and she was now called to fight.

Colonel Montgomery confided to Tubman that General Hunter wanted to make a major military incursion into that area and needed her to scout out the area in preparation for this event. However, nothing in this assignment was new to her, except the fact that armed Confederate soldiers would be standing between her and her objective. Tubman was not daunted by the assignment. She knew it was something big. She also knew, the believing person she was, that this just might be the reason that her spiritual advisor and Massachusetts abolitionist, Governor Andrew, and Frederick Douglass had urged her to go to South Carolina in the first place. She no doubt had a sense that this might be her own John Brown moment. Not Harpers Ferry, Virginia, in October 1859, but Combahee River Ferry in South Carolina in June 1863.

Harriet accepted the assignment, of course, but not before asking a lot of questions and making two requests of Montgomery. First, she asked him to provide to her a small number of strong Black men whom she would train and supervise in carrying out this secret scouting assignment. Second, she asked to have a limited amount of funds to assist her in this undertaking. Both requests were granted. The names of the men have now become well known to us and to history. They were:

1. Isaac Hayward
2. Mott Blake
3. Gabriel Cahem
4. Sandy Sellers
5. George Chisholm
6. Solomon Gregory
7. Peter Burns
8. Charles Simmons
9. Samuel Hayward
10. Walter D. Plowden

One time, in about 2007, when I read this paper to an audience at the Tabernacle Baptist Church, one member of the audience, who did not speak up during the talk, approached me after, reporting that she was a descendant of Walter Plowden, who served in the war and settled in Beaufort County afterwards.

Several of the men in Tubman's group had lived on the plantations that were being targeted. Walter Plowden had the reputation of being able to row a boat up the Combahee River at night without being detected. (On the night of the actual invasion, he would be seated in the lead ship, along with Tubman and Colonel Montgomery, to help them steer clear of torpedoes that had been planted there by Confederate soldiers.)

Montgomery also gave Tubman one-hundred dollars to use as she saw fit during the spy mission. Apparently, some was used to reward her spy recruits and some to bribe persons on the plantations to give her information.

Tubman reported several times to Montgomery what she and her troops were finding. It is well known that Tubman could not read or write. Therefore, she reported to Montgomery orally and he wrote down what she told him. This frail Black woman was dictating to this white male Army Colonel, and he was taking dictations! It had to be in writing because the Union Army used these notes to make the battle plan. She collaborated with Montgomery in laying plans for the actual raid.

It has been reported that: "In the days leading up to the raid, when

Tubman and her men were scouting the territory, some Confederate soldiers guarding the territory were spooked. Several times, they thought they heard suspicious noises in the brush along the river, but each time they drew their arms and went to the site, nothing was there." Each time they reported these incidents to their leader, Confederate Army Captain James Lowndes. Finally, on May 26, 1863, just five days before the raid began, the Captain became so angry about the faulty reports that he fired off a special order to his men, threatening court martial for any soldier reporting another "groundless alarm." We now know, of course, that those alarms were not groundless. They were Tubman and her spies at work.

Then, on the late evening of June 1, 1863, around midnight, and on through the early morning of June 2nd, history was made along the Combahee River, running between Colleton County and Beaufort County, South Carolina.

Larson has recorded the raid as follows:

> On June 1, 1863, Tubman became the first woman to plan and execute an armed expedition during the Civil War. Acting as an advisor to Colonel Montgomery, Tubman led a raid from Port Royal to the interior, some twenty-five miles up the nearby Combahee River. Using communication networks that were the province of black mariners, Tubman's successful spy mission provided crucial details about rebel enforcements and heavily mined waters. Leaving under the cover of darkness, three U.S. Army warships: The John Adams, The Harriet A. Weed, and The Sentinel, moved slowly along the river carrying three hundred Black armed soldiers from the Second South Carolina Regiment and smaller contingent of white troops from the Third Rhode Island Battery. When The John Adams and Harriet Weed were about a quarter of a mile apart, Harriet Tubman stood with Colonel Montgomery and another officer in the lead boat, The John Adams, with Walter Plowden, the local scout who helped direct the ships around the mines. After locating many torpedoes the pilots of The John Adams, The Harriet Weed, and the Sentinel were able to navigate through the channels of the river without incident. Under Tubman's leadership, Montgomery and his small force made their way to the plantations where Tubman and her scouts had identified Confederate warehouses and stockpiles of rice and cotton.

At about dawn on June 2, 1863, with fog rolling slowly over the rice fields, Colonel Montgomery landed some of his Black troops, sending them into the fields and woods to rustle out any Confederates hiding in waiting and to warn the slaves, telling them to come to the river and join the Union. They set fire to several of the plantations — destroying homes, barns, rice mills, and steam engines — and they confiscated thousands of dollars worth of rice, corn, cotton, horses, and other farm animals. What they could not take with them, they destroyed. "We broke the sluice gates," the regiment's surgeon reported to *Harpers Weekly*, "and flooded the fields so that the present crop, which was growing beautifully, would be a total loss." The enslaved people — men, women, children and a few chickens — fled to the Union boats. Under Tubman's leadership, Montgomery made his way to the Combahee ferry, where he ordered the destruction of the pontoon bridge.

Montgomery ordered the whistles blown on the steamers, signaling to the area's enslaved people to abandon the plantations and fields and come aboard the ships. Overseers, plantation owners, and managers tried in vain to keep the slaves from running away. Though they brandished whips, guns, and pistols, their threats of punishment and even death were almost useless against the mass desertion.

The scene was extraordinary. Tubman said later that this scene reminded her of "the children of Israel coming out of Egypt."

Larson continued:

> "They all spent the night of June 2nd crowded together on board the three U.S. Army warships making their way back to Beaufort. A violent storm during the night made the passage uncomfortable, but by morning the sun was shining brightly." The refugees were led from the boats to a church in Beaufort (The Tabernacle Baptist Church), where they were housed temporarily while arrangements could be made for their settlements elsewhere. Montgomery delivered an address to them, which was followed by a speech from Tubman. 'The Black woman who led the raid,' a reporter from the *Wisconsin State Journal*, who witnessed the victorious return wrote, 'and under whose supervision it was originated and conducted. For sound sense and real native eloquence, her address would do honor to any man. It created quite a sensation'.

The Harriet Tubman Bridge

Now, some 143 years after the Combahee River raid, the state of South Carolina has begun to honor Harriet Tubman and her Black Union soldiers and spies in a major way. This has been due in no small measure to the labor of Reverend Kenneth Hodges, current pastor of the Tabernacle Baptist Church in Beaufort, where Tubman and Colonel Montgomery addressed the crowd at the end of the raid on June 3, 1863.

Reverend Hodges, a history buff, acclaimed photographer, and owner of Ly Benson's Art Gallery in Beaufort, also represented Beaufort County in the South Carolina State Legislature. Another Black preacher, Reverend Clementa C. Pinkney, who represented the adjoining Colleton County in the South Carolina State Senate, has also assisted him. Their efforts and the endorsement of the entire Legislative Black Caucus culminated in the following action: On February 16, 2006, both houses of the South Carolina state legislature passed a joint resolution directing the Department of Transportation to designate the new bridge across the Combahee River at US Highway 17 running south from Charleston to Savannah as "The Harriet Tubman Bridge" and to erect appropriate markers of signs at this bridge that contain the words: "The Harriet Tubman Bridge."

This was done. Then, on October 18, 2008, I had the distinct honor to be invited by Representative Kenneth Hodges to attend the official opening and dedication ceremonies for The Harriet Tubman Bridge.

Many ordinary people and dignitaries gathered at the memorial service at the new bridge. It was presided over by Reverend Kenneth Hodges. Catherine Clinton, author of the 2004 book, *Harriet Tubman: The Road to Freedom,* gave the event her commendation. Karen Hill, Executive Director of the Harriet Tubman Home and Museum in Auburn, New York, and Vivian Abdur-rahim, founder and Director of The Harriet Tubman Historical Society in Wilmington, Delaware, are leading a national effort to establish a National Day of Celebration to honor Tubman. Congressman James Clyburn, whose district covers the site, has proposed that the site be incorporated into the Gullah-Geechie Cultural Heritage Corridor, which would bring federal recognition. This has since been done. Michael Allen of the National Park Service gave the project his blessings. Author Catherine Clinton observed that, "building a bridge and naming it after Harriet Tubman shows it is honoring many histories, and by doing that is building a bridge to the future."

After the service, Reverend Hodges led us all in a ceremonial walk across this brand spanking new Harriet Tubman Bridge. I could not help reflecting on the fact that, for many years to come, South Carolina natives and the thousands of visitors from over the nation who find themselves driving down US Highway 17, running from Charleston, South Carolina, to Beaufort, South Carolina, Savannah, Georgia, and into northern Florida, will pass over this Harriet Tubman Bridge over the ancient Combahee River which, at its discovery in the early 18th century, was named "River Jordan." And won't that be something?

REFERENCES

Larson, Kate Clifford. *Harriet Tubman. Bound for the Promised Land.* New York: Random House, 2004.

Humez, Jean M. *Harriet Tubman. The Life and the Life Stories.* Madison, Wisconsin: University of Wisconsin Press, 2003.

"The Raid on Combahee," *The Charleston Mercury*, 19 June 1863.

"The Enemy Raid on the Banks of the Combahee," *The Charleston Mercury,* 4 June 1863.

King, Wilma. "Harriet Tubman: The Road to Freedom." *Journal of Southern History* 71, No.3 (August 1, 2005).

Paras, Andy. "Bridge Brings Focus on Tubman: Combahee River," *Post and Courier*, 18 October 2008.

Akerman, Meghann. "Bridge Renamed After Tubman," *The Beaufort Gazette*, 19 October 2008.

Washington, Wayne. "Work Covers Sight Where Raid Freed 700 Slaves," *The State*, 16 October 2005.

Chapter 20

Following Dr. Andrew Billingsley in Beaufort, South Carolina, Following Dolly Nash, Robert Smalls, and Harriet Tubman, 1997-2010

Reverend Kenneth F. Hodges

Little did I know when I became the pastor of Tabernacle Baptist Church in Beaufort, South Carolina, in October of 1995, that the gravesite and bust of Robert Smalls and the unique history of the South Carolina Low Country would attract noted scholar and historian Dr. Andrew Billingsley to Beaufort. I could never have imagined that, for over the next decade, I would find myself following Dr. Andrew Billingsley as he followed Dolly Nash, Robert Smalls, and Harriet Tubman.

Janet "Dolly" Nash, the great-granddaughter of Robert Smalls, kept Robert Smalls's memory alive as she vividly retold his life's story. Dolly lived in Cape May, New Jersey, part of the year and part of the year in Beaufort, South Carolina. In Beaufort, Dolly and her husband John lived in a cottage behind the Robert Smalls House on the very grounds where Robert Smalls was born. In Beaufort, Dolly could be found visiting the local churches; lecturing at the University of South Carolina, Beaufort; riding her bicycle; crabbing in the local creeks and walking the streets of Beaufort. She walked the very streets that Robert Smalls and Harriet Tubman once walked. As she walked she enthusiastically talked about "Grandpa." It would only be a matter of time before Dr. Andrew Billingsley would find his way to Beaufort, South Carolina. He could not help being drawn to the direct descendant and greatest fan of Robert Smalls as he contemplated writing a book on Robert Smalls and his families.

I first met Dr. Billingsley at the gravesite of Robert Smalls. Robert Smalls is buried in the cemetery of the Tabernacle Baptist Church. Dolly was sharing the stories of the life and times of Robert Smalls with Dr. Billingsley. She wanted him to stand where she often stood—at the graveside of her beloved Grandpa. Dolly pointed out the gravestone of Robert Smalls, his first wife Hannah, his second wife Annie, and his daughter Sarah. From the gravesite of Robert Smalls, they walked slowly to the bust of Smalls. Dr. Billingsley admiringly gazed at the bust, then read aloud the inscription engraved on the monument: "My people need no special defense, for the past history of them in this country proves them to be equal of any people anywhere. All they need is an equal chance in the battle of life."

Dolly invited me to join Dr. Billingsley and her as they returned to the cottage where she and her husband, John, lived. Dolly's cottage resembled a small museum. It displayed treasured pictures of Robert Smalls and her family, faded newspaper and magazine articles, and personal items that once belonged to Robert Smalls. Most of the items would be packed in boxes, plastic containers, and bags and loaded in the hatch of Dolly's pickup truck when she returned to Cape May.

With very little coaxing, Dr. Billingsley soon had Dolly retelling the fascinating stories of Robert Smalls. Dolly picked up a hand-drawn map illustrating the waterways around the Charleston harbor and began to tell the story of Robert Smalls's daring capture of the steamship *Planter*. She spoke of Smalls's vision, courage, leadership, and yearning for freedom. She told how Smalls, at age 23 and a slave, captured the Confederate warship, the *Planter,* and sailed away to freedom. With a bold leap of faith, Smalls freed not only himself but his wife Hannah, their four-year-old daughter Elizabeth their three-month-old Robert Jr., and others.

Because of the capture of the *Planter*, Smalls was recognized as the first hero of the Civil War. After the war, Smalls quickly entered politics and served in the South Carolina legislature, five terms in the U.S. Congress, and over 20 years as the collector of customs at the Port of Beaufort.

Dr. Billingsley's research and fascination with the life of Robert Smalls would bring him to Beaufort frequently. He often could be found, many times with Dolly, revisiting places affiliated with Robert Smalls. He visited the Mercy Cemetery where Smalls's oldest daughter, Elizabeth Lydia Smalls Bampfield, whom, Smalls brought away to freedom on the *Planter*, is buried next to her husband, Samuel J. Bampfield, and 7 of their 11 children. One of the Bampfield children is Janet Bampfield Davidson, Dolly's mother. Billingsley also frequented the Beaufort National Cemetery, where many Black soldiers that Smalls helped to recruit are buried. He often would return to the place where I first met him, at the Robert Smalls burial site in the Tabernacle Baptist Church Cemetery, to stand where Smalls lay.

Inspired by Dr. Billingsley and Dolly, I decided to establish the Robert Smalls Room at the gallery that I owned in Beaufort. I began compiling various articles, documents, and images related to Robert Smalls. Many of Dolly's collection were copied and photographed to be displayed.

The Robert Smalls Room at LyBensons' Gallery was opened on February 23, 2004. Dr. Billingsley, Dolly, and many descendants of Robert Smalls gathered for the opening and unveiling of a replica of the steamship *Planter*. Dr. Billingsley shared excerpts from the book that he was writing about Robert Smalls. Dolly retold the stories of her beloved Grandpa. Before Dolly completed her remarks, she turned to Dr. Billingsley and jokingly said, "I wonder if you will ever finish that book!" Dolly's trip to Beaufort for the opening of the Robert Smalls Room would be her final trip to Beaufort. Before leaving Beaufort to return to Cape May, Dolly informed one of her cousins and a close friend that cancer was all through her body. Dolly passed away on March 17, 2004, at the Burdette Tomlin Memorial Hospital in Cape May, New Jersey, after suffering from complications caused by cancer.

Hearing of Dolly's passing, I felt compelled to call Dr. Billingsley to see how he was handling the loss of his dear friend. When I began to talk about Dolly, I soon realized that he had not heard of her death. I then shared that Dolly passed away. After a period of silence, I offered a brief prayer.

Dolly and Dr. Billingsley were looking forward to attending the Christening of the *Major General Robert Smalls* logistical support vessel in Moss Point, Mississippi, on April 21, 2004. Dr. Billingsley, descendants of Robert Smalls, and many of us from the Beaufort community traveled to Mississippi for the christening ceremony. The christening ceremony was dedicated "In memory of Janet 'Dolly' Nash." Though the ceremony was a historic and jubilant event, Dolly's absence was felt.

Dr. Billingsley continued to advance the life and times of Robert Smalls through the Robert Smalls Lecture Series at the University of South Carolina. He completed the book, *Yearning to Breathe Free: Robert Smalls of South Carolina and His Families,* and dedicated it "To the memory of Janet 'Dolly' Nash and John 'Boot' Nash." Dr. Billingsley returned to the Robert Smalls Room at LyBensons, where he assembled with Dolly for the last time for a well-received book signing.

Dr. Billingsley was drawn to Beaufort to do research for the writing of his book on Robert Smalls. However, while doing his research on Smalls, he was compelled to begin the journey of following Harriet Tubman. He discovered that the very streets that Dolly and Robert Smalls traveled, Harriet Tubman traveled as well.

On November 7, 1861, a federal fleet commanded by Commodore Samuel Francis Du Pont, with a force of 12,000 men under General Thomas W. Sherman, attacked and easily took forts Walker and Beauregard which were located on opposite sides of the Beaufort River at the entrance of the Port Royal harbor. The town of Beaufort and the Sea Islands were evacuated by the majority of the white inhabitants who abandoned townhouses and plantations, leaving behind most of their slaves.

In March of 1862, many northern missionaries came to Beaufort and the Sea Islands to aid the nearly 10,000 newly freed slaves. In the spring of 1862, Harriet Tubman decided to come to the South Carolina Sea Islands to help alleviate the suffering of a people abruptly freed and in need of the basic necessities of life. In Beaufort, Harriet Tubman served the Union Army in many capacities. She served as a scout, spy, and nurse. She also ran an "eating house" in Beaufort. She established a "wash house", where she taught newly freed women to do washing, sewing, and baking for the Union soldiers so they could become self-sufficient.

She also assisted in the recruitment of Black soldiers. On June 2, 1863, Tubman helped to lead a Union raid on several plantations along the Combahee River that freed over 700 slaves. After the productive raid, 100 to 180 new recruits were added to the regiment. Dr. Billingsley often stood looking out over the Beaufort River, where Harriet Tubman boarded and got off one of the three steam-driven gunboats to begin and end the raid. He would sit in silent meditation in the church where historians believe that the newly freed slaves were housed and addressed by Harriet Tubman after the raid.

Following Dr. Billingsley as he followed Harriet Tubman inspired me to introduce legislation to name the new bridge that crosses the Combahee River the "Harriet Tubman Bridge." The bridge is where many of the freed slaves boarded gunboats after fleeing the plantations during the raid. When the new bridge was completed, the dedication ceremony for the Harriet Tubman Bridge was held on Saturday, October 18, 2008. Dr. Billingsley traveled from Columbia to be a part of the ceremony. He later stated that it was an event that he never would have missed.

Dr. Billingsley would frequently return to Beaufort. He most recently returned to give a lecture entitled, "Robert Smalls and Harriet Tubman During the Civil War in South Carolina." Dr. Billingsley overwhelmed the audience as he vividly retold the daring stories of the capture of the *Planter* and the Combahee River raid. He shared the many contributions of Robert Smalls and Harriet Tubman during a pivotal phase of the history of America.

The Robert Smalls gravesite is now a part of the National Park Service's Underground Network to Freedom program. A monument to honor Harriet Tubman for her services rendered in Beaufort during the Civil War is in the process of being built and will be placed on the campus where Robert Smalls is buried.

Recently, I stood where I first met Dr. Billingsley, at the gravesite of Robert Smalls. A walking-tour group passed the bust of Robert Smalls and the tour guide began to tell the stories of Robert Smalls, just as Dolly had told them to Dr. Billingsley when I first met him. The tour guide then continued to tell the story of the nearly three years Harriet Tubman spent in Beaufort during the Civil War, pointing out where her monument will be placed. I could not help but realize how fortunate I was to have the privilege of following Dr. Andrew Billingsley in Beaufort as he followed Dolly Nash, Robert Smalls, and Harriet Tubman.

"Dr. Billingsley's ability to be a bridge between the academy and the community is evident in his personal decision to become a member of one of the churches highlighted in Mighty Like a River."

Chapter 21

Andrew Billingsley: A Leader in Connecting the University and the Community

Patricia Motes, Ph.D.,
Ana Lopez-DeFede, Ph.D.,
and Sheila Heatley, M.B.A.

"If your actions inspire others to dream more, learn more, do more, and become more, you are a leader."
John Quincy Adams

Dr. Andrew Billingsley joined the Institute for Families in Society (IFS) at the University of South Carolina (USC) in 1996 as a visiting scholar with a one-year appointment which eventually lasted until 2010, with the exception of his one-year appointment as a Fulbright Scholar in Ghana at the University of Accra. He masterfully accomplished several goals: his scholarly responsibilities and the building of relationships with the staff and faculty of IFS; his research on Robert Smalls, an African American slave whose heroic deeds during the Civil War earned him freedom and national acclaim; his research on the Black Church; and his desire to establish university and community relations. In all of these endeavors, he brought attention and distinction to the University and to the state of South Carolina.

Dr. Billingsley published two important books during his 15-year tenure at the IFS: *Yearning to Breathe Free: Robert Smalls of South Carolina and His Families* and *Mighty Like a River: The Black Church and Social Reform*. From our different relationships with Dr. Billingsley, we witnessed how he made a difference at the IFS, at the University, in the community, and at the state level. We end our commentary with tributes on the importance of his role as a leader and mentor at IFS.

Connections with the Local Community

Not only did Dr. Billingsley bring attention and interest to the life of Robert Smalls within the University and the broader South Carolina community, he partnered with the African American Studies program to establish the Robert Smalls Lecture Series. Since 1997, this annual lecture series, which attracts diverse participation from across South Carolina, has brought notable African American scholars to campus to present and dialogue on issues relevant to the African American community. The annual lecture is designed to share cutting-edge research and scholarship in African American Studies with the University community but, more importantly, it is designed to share this cutting-edge research and scholarship with the general public.

Though his primary focus during that one-year appointment may have been on advancing his research and scholarship on Robert Smalls, Dr. Billingsley was also in the midst of finalizing a different book that focused on the Black Church. While working to complete the final details of that book, Dr. Billingsley found himself becoming immersed in the life and outreach of Black churches in his new home in Columbia, South Carolina. His book on the Black Church, *Mighty Like a River: The Black Church and Social Reform,* was anchored primarily by research on large churches in major metropolitan areas of the nation. Although he had completed fully the research for this book, attention to the role of churches in his new community compelled Dr. Billingsley to work with his publisher to allow him to include additional research on churches in Columbia and rural South Carolina.

Linking his completion of *Mighty Like a River* to ongoing community-based research at the Institute for Families in Society, Dr. Billingsley included details from a survey of Black ministers in three rural South Carolina communities that showcased their strong concern for social problems in the community and, simultaneously, the challenge of needed resources to initiate and/or sustain work to address such concerns.[65] In addition to highlighting efforts in rural communities, Dr. Billingsley also highlighted the efforts of three churches in the Columbia-capital city area. As Dr. Billingsley describes in his book, these three churches —Brookland Baptist, Bethel AME, and Bible Way of Atlas Road — are exemplars of activism and social reform in "smaller cities, towns, and communities."[66]

Dr. Billingsley's ability to be a bridge between the academy and the community is evident in his personal decision to become a member of one of the churches highlighted in *Mighty Like a River*. As a member of Brookland Baptist, he became immersed in the church ministries and community outreach programs. He served as an enthusiastic member of the Brookland Foundation board of directors (1998-2003), which has a mission to improve the lives of people by developing and promoting efforts to enhance their spiritual, emotional, physical, social, and economic well-being. He actively supported the Foundation's programs and initiatives. In support of the Foundation, while also providing a link back to his university scholarship, Dr. Billingsley held a book signing for *Mighty Like a River* at Brookland that raised funds for the work of the Brookland Foundation.

The Institute has continued its partnership with Brookland Baptist. One of the faculty members at IFS who is also a member of Brookland has worked to continue this university-community partnership. She has served as a director of the Foundation board, a member of its Health and Wellness Program, and a participant in other outreach entities of Brookland that support parenting and youth development. This linkage with Brookland resulted in the Foundation honoring an IFS professor in 2013 as a "Featured Survivor" at its annual Color Pink Breast Cancer Awareness Gala, which supports screening mammograms and educational programs.

Of special note, the USC retirement celebration events for Dr. Billingsley in 2010 were held on the campus of the University and also at the Brookland Conference Center. This was indeed a fitting way to honor Dr. Billingsley and his notable efforts to connect the community and the University. This two-day event brought together a range of leaders from small, community-based organizations with luminaries in the academy.

Statewide Connections and National Priorities

As one of the foremost scholars of the African American family, Dr. Billingsley's community service, research, and scholarship have had an ongoing focus on families, youth development, and racial disparities. In his early career as a social worker, he led youth service projects. One of his early and significant writings, *Children of the Storm: Black Children and American Child Welfare*, explored the failure of the nation's child welfare system in protecting and supporting Black children. His seminal publication, *Black Families in White America*, served as a required text in graduate social work and other human service programs. In fact, this text helped to shape the professional development of several of the faculty, staff, and leaders of IFS.

After completing his 1997-1998 tenure as a Fulbright Scholar in Ghana, Dr. Billingsley returned to the University of South Carolina as Senior Scholar in Residence at IFS and as a professor of sociology and African American Studies. Though many of the local efforts described above also facilitated statewide connections, Dr. Billingsley's return to USC allowed him to broaden his research and scholarship linkages. The following highlights provide a glimpse of three of his significant statewide efforts that also link to national priorities.

Dr. Billingsley, upon returning to the Institute for Families in Society, was focused on fatherhood. In partnership with the Sisters of Charity Foundation of South Carolina, IFS was providing technical assistance and research support that launched that foundation's first funding project, "Reducing Poverty through Father Engagement," known as the Fatherhood Initiative. Dr. Billingsley lent great support to the IFS team in support of this initiative. His and IFS's technical assistance and research support would later be instrumental in the Foundation's decision to create a formal infrastructure for its fatherhood work. In 2002, the Foundation established the South Carolina Center for Fathers and Families, a faith-based organization with a mission to develop and support statewide efforts in repairing and nurturing relationships between fathers and families. Dr. Billingsley would offer direction and support as a member of the Foundation's board of directors from 2008-2010, as the Center's fatherhood efforts expanded and impacted numerous South Carolina communities and beyond.

Having been involved for many years with the National Urban League as a scholar and advisor, Dr. Billingsley was readily embraced by the Columbia Urban League and its longtime leader, Mr. J. T. McLawhorn. In partnership with the Columbia Urban League, Dr. Billingsley was able to use his scholarship to encourage community action in support of social justice.

In 2000, Dr. Billingsley shared his research findings on the African American experience by discussing the roles of the church, the family, and the community in the Columbia Urban League's *The State of Black South Carolina: An Action Agenda for the Future,* an annual report on issues affecting the status of African Americans in South Carolina. Later in 2008, in partnership with Dr. Patricia Stone Motes and other colleagues at IFS, Dr. Billingsley helped to bring attention to the issue of racial disparities in South Carolina's juvenile justice system by sharing the findings from a series of statewide policy studies on the overrepresentation of minority youth in the juvenile justice system.

Dr. Billingsley's work with the Columbia Urban league provided him with an avenue to share his research and scholarship with state leaders and the broader community. Recognizing the scholarly contributions of Dr. Billingsley and his efforts to advocate for programs and policy to promote social justice in 2004, the Columbia Urban League presented him with the Whitney M. Young Award, which is given annually to someone who has worked to advance race relations and promote civility and equal opportunity in South Carolina.

Dr. Billingsley's research on Robert Smalls offered numerous statewide, regional, and national opportunities for him to connect his academic work to community efforts focused on racial disparities and social justice. The extraordinary contributions of Robert Smalls to the state of South Carolina were generally unknown by most in the state, with perhaps the exception of those in Beaufort, the home of Robert Smalls. Dr. Billingsley's research on Robert Smalls — shared in community forums, academic halls, museums, professional conferences, public schools, churches, festivals, and other venues — brought honor and recognition to Robert Smalls, and, in a unique way, helped foster an atmosphere to address issues of social justice and race relations. Indeed, as Congressman James Clyburn writes in his Foreword to *Yearning to Breathe Free: Robert Smalls of South Carolina and His Families,* "Robert Smalls should rank among the most honored and recognized South Carolinians, but he does not simply because of the color of his skin."[67]

In 2007, the South Carolina House of Representative adopted a resolution (H. 4042, May 2007)[68] recognizing and honoring Dr. Billingsley for the completion of his book on Robert Smalls. The citation notes that "the book chronicles the life of Robert Smalls, the 'audacious Civil War hero and visionary South Carolina statesman,' and 'places [his] heroic achievements, abiding commitment to his families, and his championship of universal public education against the backdrop of the changing fortunes of the larger Black community.' The resolution further notes that "Dr. Billingsley has enriched our understanding of a critical period in the history of our State and nation in his seminal new work."

Dr. Billingsley's professional standing as a university professor extends beyond South Carolina, as attested to in the resolution by South Carolina's House of Representatives. Preeminent as an African American sociologist, recognized as one of the foremost scholars of the African American family, retired from a distinguished academic career having served as Vice President for Academic Affairs at Howard University and President of Morgan State University, Dr. Billingsley's arrival at IFS was significant. It increased the University's community connections at national and international levels. Building on his established relationships, Dr. Billingsley used his scholarly work at IFS to bring attention to issues within South Carolina while also focusing on national priorities such as race relations and social justice. He used his work to strengthen the University and champion the community.

A Legacy of Mentorship at IFS

During his 14 years at the University, Dr. Billingsley was a force for social change. His personal and supportive embrace of others expanded his reach to further advance scholarship, community change, and an appreciation for the diversity of humanity. This certainly has been our experience here at the Institute for Families in Society.

Though some of us were impressed by the presence of the eminent Dr. Andrew Billingsley at IFS, there were others who knew nothing of his history.

In either instance, Dr. Billingsley offered himself as a thoughtful person interested in learning more about our priorities by asking questions and being available to offer support, if needed, to accomplish those priorities. He became a generous mentor to each of us. He valued us as individuals.

Sheila Heatley, who worked closely with Dr. Billingsley for nearly a decade providing administrative support for the development of the book on Robert Smalls, describes Dr. Billingsley as the "inspiration" for her growth as a professional. His reliance on her, along with his positive feedback for her efforts, gave her confidence that she could handle tasks she had not thought were within her capacity. She conducted library research, she found archival resources, she summarized research findings, and she attended conferences and took notes to support the book. She increased her comfort in meeting important people in both university and community settings. She attributes her work experiences with Dr. Billingsley as a major contributor to her decision to pursue a bachelor's degree and later to obtain her M.B.A. degree.

Dr. Billingsley was a consummate mentor and teacher. He taught undergraduate seminars in African American Studies. He supported master's theses and doctoral dissertations. For sure, Dr. Billingsley understood that these students offered the potential to move the University forward, to advance community development, and to engage in humanitarian scholarship. He worked closely with multiple students in the University's African American Studies, Social Work, Public Health, and Sociology departments.

Notable among Dr. Billingsley's student connections was Anton Gunn who, in 2000, was a graduate research assistant at IFS working to complete his M.S.W. degree. It was also in 2000 that Anton's younger brother was killed in a terrorist attack on the *USS Cole*. In the midst of grief, Anton continued his graduate studies. Dr. Billingsley proved to be a great supporter to Anton during this challenging period. Anton attributes the tragedy of the *USS Cole* bombing as "sparking his activism into electoral politics." Certainly, the support and encouragement of Dr. Billingsley was also important to his laying out a plan that successfully launched him into the political arena.

Anton became the first African American in history to represent District 79 in the South Carolina House of Representatives. Later, he would head the Office of External Affairs at the U.S. Department of Health and Human Services, where he played a pivotal role in the implementation of the Patient Protection and Affordable Care Act ("Obamacare"). Currently, Anton serves as Executive Director of Community Health Innovation and Chief Diversity Officer at the Medical University of South Carolina. Across all these leadership roles, Anton has continued to actively address issues of social justice. Such efforts fit perfectly with the mentorship influences of Dr. Andrew Billingsley.

Dr. Billingsley also supported and mentored faculty members. It was an easy task for him. He worked alongside us, he respected us, he affirmed our efforts, and, notably, he prodded us to examine alternatives. Dr. Motes, an IFS research professor and colleague of Dr. Billingsley, recounts the importance of his wise counsel and mentoring as she pursued different professional development opportunities in support of her career goals. Working jointly on projects, she appreciated his ability to share knowledge and give credit to each member of the team. His generosity as a professional, but more as a person, helped to move their relationship from that of colleagues to that of friendship.

Dr. Ana Lopez-DeFede, another IFS professor, describes a conversation she had with Dr. Billingsley that would become instrumental in the shaping of her research and scholarship and ultimately much of the visionary work of IFS. Dr. Billingsley posed the question, "What do you want your legacy to be?" This question motivated Ana in many ways. Of significance, it motivated her to more clearly anchor her research interests and further define her professional path.

In the evolving field of healthcare, Ana defined her niche as an applied health services and health policy researcher. Her personal-professional identity fits well with the primary work of IFS. (Funding generated by Lopez-DeFede accounts for approximately 85% of all research funding at IFS.) As Director of the Division of Medicaid Policy Research, she is leading work that examines changes in Medicaid and Medicare policy; disparities in access and utilization of care; changes in health care coverage; the quality of the delivery systems (for example, managed care versus fee-for-service); trends and policies impacting the uninsured; disease management and prevention; payment reform; cost effectiveness of new innovations; health and geographical place; and new models focused on better health outcomes. This interdisciplinary research translates research into policy and practice to improve health outcomes and reduce health disparities both within South Carolina and beyond.

One of Dr. Billingsley's greatest gifts as a mentor is his ability to ask questions and really listen to answers. With pause and reflection, he would offer wise counsel after having listened closely to answers to what were, at times, soul-searching questions. Dr. Billingsley challenged us as faculty, staff, and students, to expand our research, to broaden our views, and to take risks to advance the community. With patience and wisdom (attributes that may have improved with age), he was ever supportive of our efforts.

A Legacy at IFS

Dr. Billingsley is warmly received by the IFS each year as he returns for the annual Robert Smalls Lecture Series. He always provides us an update on his new research and scholarship. He continues to ask us important questions about our work and really listen to our answers. Dr. Billingsley will always remain an integral leader at IFS.

In 2016, the current leadership of the Institute for Families in Society and the African American Studies Program established two annual awards,[69] which are presented annually as part of the Robert Smalls Lecture Series. They were created to pay tribute to Dr. Billingsley's legacy at IFS and his continuing impact in connecting the University and the community. Each reward includes a cash award to support the recipient's ongoing professional work. They include:

1. The Andrew Billingsley Faculty Award, which promotes and honors faculty scholarly and academic research and creative activities that focus on African American families
2. The Andrew Billingsley Community Leadership Award, which promotes and honors the efforts of an individual in the Columbia, South Carolina, community whose work supports and strengthens African American families.

Chapter 22

The Theoretical Contributions of Andrew Billingsley

Robert B. Hill, Ph.D.

A Social Systems Framework

Over the past five decades, Andrew Billingsley has made many important contributions to the fields of sociology and social work. This paper will highlight some of his theoretical contributions to enhance the study of Black families. Walter Allen, in his insightful review article in 1978, stated that a major shortcoming of most research on Black families was the lack of a theoretical framework.[70] He described many Black family studies as being fragmented, static, and ahistorical. Billingsley, however, was convinced that a comprehensive perspective was needed to properly understand all aspects of Black family life. Therefore, in his classic work, *Black Families in White America*, Billingsley adapted the Harvard sociologist Talcott Parsons's social systems paradigm[71] to study Black families. It should be noted that Billingsley was also building on the "holistic" framework that Du Bois argued in 1898 should be used to study Black people adequately.[72]

Consequently, Billingsley depicted Black families as being situated within three concentric subsystems. The inner-most subsystem comprised the "immediate Black family" — that is, all members who resided in that household. The second and larger subsystem comprised the "Black community" — relatives who live outside the immediate household, neighbors, friends, churches, schools, businesses, social clubs, fraternal organizations, and so forth. The third and outer-most subsystem comprised the "wider white society," which includes both institutions (political, economic, educational, health, criminal justice, social welfare, media, culture, values, and institutional or public policies) and social forces (world wars, urbanization, technological changes, industrial shifts, demographic trends, economic cycles, sexual revolution, and immigration).

In order to adequately understand the structure and functioning of Black families, Billingsley's framework would lead investigators to ask the following research questions. First, "What impact do the members of this immediate household have on one another?" Second, "What impact does the Black community have on Black families and vice versa?" Third, "What impact does the wider society have on the Black community and vice versa?" Finally, "What impact does the wider society have on Black families and vice versa?"

It is very important to note that Billingsley added historical and cultural dimensions to his theoretical framework. Following the lead of the 1908 Du Bois study, *The Negro Family*, in his work, *Black Families in White America*, Billingsley felt that it was essential to start with and understand the lives of Blacks in Africa in order to underscore the rich cultural heritage and African legacy that have aided Blacks in America from slavery to freedom.

Black Family Structure

Another major contribution of Billingsley's was to describe the diversity of family structures among Black people. Prior to his work, many researchers thought there were only two types of Black family structures: male-headed families and female-headed families. While most male-headed families were comprised of two parents (the husband and wife), a small minority was comprised of only one parent — the father. On the other hand, the female-headed families were comprised of only the single parent. It should be understood that Billingsley had to use the Census Bureau's original definition of the family, which automatically classified husbands as the "head" of all two-parent households, since that was the only Census data available at the time of his research. However, the Census Bureau has since discontinued this "sexist" definition, and now permits wives to be classified as "heads" of two-parent households.

Instead of two types of family structures, Billingsley identified 12 structures among Black families. These structures were classified into three groups: nuclear, extended, and augmented families. Nuclear families consist of three subtypes: (1) "incipient nuclear," which are composed of husbands and wives with no children; (2) "simple nuclear," which are composed of husbands, wives, and children; and (3) "attenuated nuclear," which are composed of a single parent (either the husband or wife) with children. Similarly, extended families contain three subtypes (similar to nuclear families), with both spouses or only one parent, with or without children, but with the presence of a relative in each type. Finally, augmented families consist of six subtypes (similar to nuclear families), with both spouses or only one parent, with or without children, but with the presence of a non-relative in each type.

Female-Headed Black Families

It is very unfortunate that few studies of Black families have tried to incorporate many of these 12 structures. One of the few exceptions was a study by Isabelle Payton that appeared in the U.S. Department of Agriculture's *Family Economics Review* in the early 1980s.[73] Nevertheless, Billingsley's classifications have major relevance for understanding contemporary Black family structures. For example, most observers readily assume that almost all of the Black female-headed families today consist of single women who are the biological mothers of the children in their households. Yet, nothing can be further from the truth! In fact, almost 40 percent of the current Black female-headed families are headed by single relatives (aunts, grandmothers, or great-grandmothers, etc.) who are caring for related children who are not their own such as nephews or nieces or grandchildren or great-grandchildren. This is due to the large surge in Black ("kinship care") families headed by female relatives as a result of parental incarceration, drug addiction, HIV/AIDS-infection, or abuse and neglect. Thus, many studies of Black single-parent families are very misleading since the researchers treat data on Black families headed by females as if all the heads were the biological parents of the children for whom they were caring. I assert that they should play closer attention to Billingsley's classification of various Black family structures.

Family Functions

Another important contribution of Billingsley's theoretical framework was the identification of family functions. This was not a trivial matter since many researchers (starting with Daniel Moynihan) equated Black family functioning with family structure. They used a simplistic dichotomy: female-headed (or "broken") families are equated with negative functioning or outcomes while male-headed (or "intact") families are equated with positive functioning or outcomes. Billingsley strongly challenged such misguided research. In fact, he asserted that, in many instances, female-headed families often have more positive functioning and outcomes than male-headed families.

Once again, building on Parsons's social-systems work, Billingsley identified two types of family functions: instrumental and expressive. Instrumental functions relate to family activities such as work, child care, providing security and protection that try to meet basic economic and health needs such as food, clothing, and shelter. Expressive functions, on the other hand, relate to family activities such as socialization, affection, companionship, and enhancing self-worth that try to meet the emotional needs of family members. He also observed that while most studies of white families focus on their expressive functions, the large majority of studies of Black families concentrate on their instrumental functions such as the ability of Black breadwinners to meet the economic needs of their families. Consequently, he noted that very few studies of Black families[74] focused on such expressive issues as marital adjustment, dating, happiness, or parent-child emotional relationships. I contend that this fixation on the instrumental functions of Black families — to the exclusion of their expressive functions —continues to exist today. However, Billingsley readily concedes that while all families have both instrumental and expressive functions, some of them are more successful than others in providing those functions and meeting the needs of family members due to greater resources and higher social status.

Social Class

This leads us to another key dimension of Billingsley's theoretical framework: the importance of class stratification. Building on works such as Sinclair Drake and Horace Cayton's *Black Metropolis*, E. Franklin Frazier's *Black Bourgeoisie*, and others, Billingsley's *Black Families in White America* identified three class strata among Black people: the lower class, middle class, and upper class. The lower class, which constituted 50 percent of Black families at the time, consisted of three groups: the nonworking poor (or "underclass"), the working poor, and the working non-poor (or "near-poor"). The middle-class, which constituted 40 percent of Black families, consisted of three groups: skilled blue-collar workers, clerical workers, and professionals. The upper-class, which constituted 10 percent of Black families, consisted of two groups: (1) the "old" upper class — that is, the "old aristocrats," (or "blue-bloods"), who inherited their wealth and status over several generations; and (2) the "new" upper class, the "nouveau riche," (or the newly-rich), who acquired their status and wealth in recent years, mainly through enterprising endeavors. Through the "new" upper class often had more wealth than the "old" upper class, the latter often had higher social status due to their pedigree. The old upper class (or the "Black Brahmins") belonged to lodges, secret societies, and fraternal groups. Unfortunately, the bulk of Black family studies today focus on the lower class (most especially, the "underclass" or non-working poor) — to the exclusion of the middle and upper classes.

Family Strengths

An additional key dimension of Billingsley's theoretical framework was the introduction of the concept of family strengths. Prior to his 1968 work, few scholars conceived that Black families could have any strengths. Up to that time, most researchers assumed that the Black lower class (or underclass) had no positive attributes, but Billingsley asserted that all Black class strata had assets and strengths. Expanding on Billingsley's work in my 1972 study,[75] I identified five cultural strengths among Black families: strong achievement orientation, strong work orientation, flexible family roles, strong kinship bonds, and strong religious orientation. I also provided examples of how these assets functioned among low-income Black families as well as among middle- and upper-income families. Many other scholars, as exemplified in the 1983 work, *Stable Black Families*, also identified strengths of Black families. For example, Joyce Ladner described the assets of young Black women growing up in public housing in her classic work, *Tomorrow's Tomorrow: The Black Woman*. Carol Stack described in detail the positive functioning of Black extended families in her major work, *All Our Kin*. Since that time, many scholars have identified strengths among other people of color such as Native Americans and Hispanics.

Yet, it is necessary to address some myths about research on Black family strengths. Some critics such as Nathan Hare have argued that scholars who focus on the strengths of Black families assume they have no weaknesses or are trying to minimize their negative traits. They also assert that studies of Black family strengths impede opportunities to advocate for social policies to aid Black families in need.[76] Indeed, an important objective of studies on Black family strengths is to provide more balance to the sole fixation with their deficits. Since Black families have both weaknesses and strengths, it is not possible to understand Black families in their totality without describing both negative and positive attributes.

But, a major goal of family-strengths research is to focus more on solutions than problems. In fact, in my updated volume, *The Strengths of African American Families: Twenty Five Years Later*, I assert that it is important for researchers to first identify problems or weaknesses among Black families because it is not possible to solve problems if one does not acknowledge that they exist. However, many researchers of Black families stop after identifying problems and do not provide any solutions to those problems. I contend that researchers take a second step — by offering solutions. The strengths perspective is solution-oriented since it concentrates on positive traits that might help families to become stronger and overcome their weaknesses. In short, such research identifies assets that could be the target of interventions on the part of the Black community or the government through public policies. For example, most studies of single-parent Black families on public assistance focus on why they went on welfare. A strengths approach, however, would address the factors that have helped many single-parents leave the welfare system.

Over the past three decades, more and more scholars are focusing on the assets and positive traits of Black families, especially among the lower class. A major catalyst for this surge in research on positive attributes among the poor was the ground-breaking research in the mental health field focusing on the assets of vulnerable populations. For example, Werner and Smith conducted a study that followed low-income Hawaiian children for over a decade and found that many of them were very resilient and able to succeed against overwhelming odds.[77]   Still, it was the British scholar, Michael Rutter, who coined the term "protective factors" to describe processes that helped disadvantaged people become more resilient and achieve despite stressful situations.[78] Thus, many scholars no longer focus on only the risk factors (or weaknesses) of low-income populations; they also examine the protective factors (or assets) that help those populations to succeed. In short, many studies today examine both the risk and protective factors among disadvantaged populations. This balance was the goal that strengths-oriented research (which was stimulated by Billingsley) was trying to achieve four decades ago.

Black Community

A crucial feature of Billingsley's theoretical framework was to assess the impact of the Black community on Black families. Indeed, many scholars, such as in the 1990 work, *Black Families,* for example, have examined the negative impact on Black families of community poverty, unemployment, crime, inadequate schools, HIV/AIDS, and so on. Conversely, other scholars such as Edith Ross in her 1978 work, *Black Heritage in Social Welfare*, have also described the positive community impact on Black families of extended families, churches, neighborhood groups, social welfare organizations, fraternal groups, and others.

Wider Society

The final critical dimension of Billingsley's theoretical framework was to examine the impact of the wider society on Black families. The wider society influences the functioning of Black families through two mechanisms: societal institutions and societal forces. Societal institutions that may have a positive or negative impact on Black families include political, economic, educational, health, social welfare, criminal justice, media, culture, and values. For example, the criminal justice institution has had a major effect on destabilizing the functioning of Black families for decades by incarcerating fathers, mothers, sons, and daughters. The War against Drugs, especially that pertaining to possession of crack cocaine, and mandatory sentencing has led to exceedingly long prison terms for Black youths and adults. On the other hand, societal forces may have positive or negative consequences for Black families. For example, World War I and especially World War II had major positive effects on Black people since Blacks were able to obtain higher-level jobs as a result of the curtailment of European immigration during both conflicts. Similarly, urbanization and industrialization had many positive consequences for Blacks since it enabled them to obtain higher-paying jobs in many blue-collar industries. On the other hand, deindustrialization, or the exodus of jobs out of inner-cities to the suburbs and abroad, had devastating effects on the functioning of not only low-income Black families but also middle-income families.

Institutional racism is a major attribute of the wider society that continues to destabilize Black families. This form of racism is more pervasive than individual racism since it operates through both societal institutions and societal forces. In their classic work, *Children of the Storm: Black Children and American Child Welfare*, Billingsley and Giovannoni observed that institutional racism in the child welfare system played a major role in the disproportionate removal of Black children from their homes into foster care. Unfortunately, not many studies have directly focused on the impact of institutional racism on Black family instability.

In sum, Billingsley's theoretical framework has made many important contributions toward enhancing this nation's knowledge about the structure and functioning of Black families. More scholars need to incorporate this paradigm in their research on Black families.

References

Allen, Walter, R. 1978. "The Search for Applicable Theories of Black Family Life," Journal of Marriage and the Family, 40 (1): 117-129.

Billingsley, Andrew. 1968. Black Families in White America. Englewood Cliffs, NJ: Prentice-Hall.

Billingsley, Andrew & Jeanne Giovannoni. 1972. Children of the Storm: Black Children and American Child Welfare. New York: Harcourt, Brace & Jovanovich.

Cheatham, Harold & James Stewart, Eds 1990. Black Families. New Brunswick, NJ: Transaction Publishers.

Drake, Sinclair & Horace Cayton. 1945. Black Metropolis. 2 Vols. New York: Harper & Row.

Du Bois, W. E. B. 1898. "The Study of the Negro Problem," ANNALS, AAPSS, I (1): 1-23

1908. The Negro American Family. Atlanta, GA: Atlanta University Press.

Frazier, E. Franklin. 1957. Black Bourgeoisie. New York: The Free Press.

Gray, Lawrence, et. al., 1983. Stable Black Families. Washington, DC: Howard University Institute for Urban Affairs and Research.

Hare, Nathan. 1976. "What Black Intellectuals Misunderstand about the Black Family," Black World, 25 (5): 4-14.

Hill, Robert B. 1972. The Strengths of Black Families. New York: Emerson Hall Publishers.

1999. The Strengths of African American Families: Twenty Five Years Later. Landham, MD: University Press of America.

Ladner, Joyce. 1971. Tomorrow's Tomorrow: The Black Woman. Garden City, NY: Doubleday.

Parsons, Talcott. 1951. The Social System. New York: The Free Press.

Payton, Isabelle S. 1982. "Single-Parent Households," Family Economics Review (Winter): 11-16.

Ross, Edith. 1978. Black Heritage in Social Welfare. Metuchen, NJ: Scarecrow Press.

Rutter, Michael. 1987. "Psychosocial Resilience and Protective Mechanisms," American Journal of Orthopsychiatry, 57 (3): 316-331.

Stack, Carol. 1974. All Our Kin. New York: Harper & Row.

Staples, R. & L. Johnson. 1993. Black Families at the Crossroads. San Francisco, CA: Jossey-Bass.

Werner, E. E. & R. S. Smith. 1982. Vulnerable But Invincible: A Study of Resilient Children. New York: McGraw-Hill.

PART VI

LIFE AFTER RETIREMENT

Andrew Billingsley and former student Howard Dodson, Director of the Howard University Libraries and former Director of Harlem's Schomburg Center for Research in Black Culture, at Andrew's 90th Birthday Symposium in 2016.

Chapter 23

Letters and Reflections on the 90th Birthday Symposium

Ambassador Amy Ruth Davis (Ret.)
Ralph Hurtado
E. Ethelbert Miller
and Evelyn Brooks Higginbotham, Ph.D.

After a fashion, African Americans in this wonderful, but flawed, country are all children of one storm or the other, bringing to mind one of Dr. Andrew Billingsley's books, *Children of the Storm*. However, we have survived as a race and will keep on surviving and thriving because of patriarchs such as Dr. Andrew Billingsley.

I knew Dr. Billingsley before he had a hand in moving Howard University into a new educational and cultural realm. But, I believe his experience just before coming to Howard, at the School of Social Welfare at the University of California at Berkeley, was a formative period for him and for those of us whom he touched while there. Therefore, I would like to shed some light on Dr. Billingsley as one of America's leading scholars of the African American experience; as a dedicated institution builder; and as an unsurpassed mentor, role model, and promoter of education and social work.

I feel very fortunate that Andy Billingsley came into my life when I was a student at Spelman College during his travels throughout the South to recruit students for UC Berkeley's School of Social Welfare. Although he worked hard at recruiting and was relentless, for some reason I was his only catch! I think he felt responsible for me. And what a protector, mentor, and role model he turned out to be! I feel rather sorry that his invitation fell on the deaf ears of so many other students in the South and that they missed such a golden opportunity.

For me, attending Berkeley under Dr. Billingsley's watchful eye was a life-changing experience. Although I never practiced social work *per se*, it was an excellent base from which to launch and succeed in my diplomatic career.

My friend and Berkeley classmate Ralph Hurtado, who did practice social work and who contributed a great deal to California's Latino community, gave Billingsley high marks for teaching him about research and evaluation procedures. Ralph also said:

> Discussions with Andy, when I was a student, were not only fun but helped me understand institutional racism, the importance of a stable income for poor people, and to look at people's strengths. Those basic ideas served me well while working in my own Latino community.

Generally, Americans know Andrew Billingsley as a highly regarded author beginning with his seminal work, *Black Families in White America*. I am very proud to say I was, so to speak, present at the book's creation. He was writing that book when I was one of his research assistants. I feel honored to have contributed to his acclaimed work, which offered insights into African American families in an objective way that highlighted the strengths and the weaknesses of those basic units of our society.

I also served as his and Dr. Jeanne Giovannoni's research assistant as they were writing *Children of the Storm*. Helping them collect data at San Francisco General Hospital, I learned about the quality research and analysis that Dr. Billingsley puts into telling the complex story of our people.

Finally, a word about his irrepressible involvement in institution building.

In 1968, after the assassination of Martin Luther King Jr., African American students vigorously protested the lack of a Black Studies Program at Berkeley. Hispanic students joined, and we all went on strike. Dr. Billingsley was the most prominent voice supporting the students, to the chagrin of the administration. So, as much to quiet him as anything else, the Chancellor of the University asked him to serve as Vice Chancellor, with specific instructions to develop a Black Studies Program. So he did, and Berkeley was all the better for it.

Here again, I am proud of the part that I played. I was out on the picket lines protesting early one morning. At midday, I put my sign down, and rushed to the airport, boarded a plane to Washington, and, with Billingsley's blessings, entered the Foreign Service of the United States.

The first thing I was required to do was to sign an oath that said I would not strike against the U.S. government. "OH! MY, I've been co-opted," I said, and I never looked back! — again fueled by the lessons I had learned from this incredible man.

I truly believe that Andrew Billingsley belongs in the annals of great Americans. I know that we are all the better for knowing him, and that both UC Berkeley and Howard University are much stronger institutions because of the footprints he left behind.

Amy Ruth Davis

Andy and Jeanne Giovannoni were a team when I attended the Master's of Social Work program in the late 1960s at the University of California-Berkeley. From them, I learned about research and evaluation procedures. That knowledge and experience would later serve me well as a grant writer and executive director. I partnered with Julie O'Donnell at California State College-Long Beach. She was an excellent evaluator, and together we raised $23 million in community development funds to serve the downtown neighborhood of Long Beach. We were able to prove our program's effectiveness and ability to create community change. Jeanne also took part in some of the evaluations, and she published several articles on them with Julie. Discussions with Andy when I was a student were not only fun but helped me understand institutional racism, realize the importance of a stable income for poor people, and look at peoples' strengths. Those basic ideas served me well working in my own Latino community. Thank you, Andy, for helping me feel like I made meaningful contributions to social work and the Latino community.

Ralph Hurtado

Between the Vanishing Negro and the Invisible Black Man: Well Wishes and Reflections on the Howard Years

E. Ethelbert Miller, Poet

A few years before Andrew Billingsley arrived on the campus of Howard University, I wrote the following poem:

"HOWARD"
Between the vanishing Negro and the invisible black man,
I look for change.

The unfortunate thing about history is that historians too often write it. Too often, they overlook and misinterpret things. Let us hope this is not the case in the future when someone writes about the contributions Andrew Billingsley made to Howard University. Howard has a tendency, now and then, of looking away from the mirror of reality and seeing only the sleepiness of its own dream. Is it a Capstone or a Mecca? In many ways, the vision of Kelly Miller was similar to that of Andrew Billingsley. In the 1970s, when he walked across the campus, one could feel what Amiri Baraka described as "the motion of history." Things were finally happening on the hill.

I called the Billingsley years the "Golden Era" at an institution that was struggling to define itself as a Black university. Andrew Billingsley attempted to save a culture by trying to change one. He was responsible for bringing Black genius to Washington. He recruited a dream team of artists and scholars to teach at Howard, most notably John Oliver Killens, Haki Madhubuti, Joyce Ladner, and Stephen Henderson. He created a series of institutes to interact with academic units and the community. One accomplishment by this unit was enough to resurrect Du Bois or Woodson.

The sadness of winter is that it too often brings death. When the Institute for the Arts and the Humanities was phased out by the new Howard administration, it was as if we were all distracted again — the way we were at Malcolm's assassination.

Andrew Billingsley was a visionary and a man who understood the beauty and strength of the Black family. His work reminds us not to tire but to endure. Our love for him is what glitters when stars come out, amazed at who we are and the Blackness we must be.

Letters to Professor Andrew Billingsley from a University of Maryland Colleague and Friend

Evelyn Brooks Higginbotham, Ph.D.

Evelyn Brooks Higginbotham, who was a colleague and friend of Professor Billingsley during his tenure at the University of Maryland at College Park, sent greetings to him at the symposium at Howard University honoring him at his 90th birthday celebration. In her second letter, Higginbotham, again in her role as President of the Association for the Study of African American Life and History, wrote to express her greetings and appreciation to him on the occasion of the organization's annual meeting in Richmond. Her comments are reprinted below.

Happy Birthday, Andy! I was an M.A. student at Howard during your years of leadership. I had found an exciting intellectual community of legendary professors and brilliant fellow students, who inspired me to go into the budding field of African American women's history. Later, as a doctoral student in history at the University of Rochester, I recognized the transformative character of your scholarship since *Black Families in White America* played an influential role in revising earlier historical interpretations of the slave family. The noted historians John Blassingame, Eugene Genovese, and Herbert Gutman found persuasive your challenge to the Moynihan Report and used it in their own work on the resilient character of the slaves. They accepted your emphasis on the greater number of dual-headed households and stressed the existence of meaningful family patterns despite the horrors of slavery. In the early 1980s, I got to know you as a colleague and friend at the University of Maryland.

Thank you for all that you have given to the academy and to the Black community. We are in your debt as we celebrate your life of 90 years. You have made and continue to make a real difference in this world.

The Association for the Study of African American Life and History (ASALH) is pleased to celebrate the 90th birthday of our member, Dr. Andrew Billingsley. During Dr. Billingsley's term as Howard University's V.P. for Academic Affairs (1970 - 1974), he recruited such scholars as Robert Hill, Haki Madhubuti, Stephen Henderson, Ronald Walters, Joyce Ladner, John Killens, and Charles Harris. He helped form the Institute for Urban Affairs and Research, the Institute for the Arts and the Humanities, and the Howard University Press, which helped to make Howard an internationally known metropolitan research university.

As a renowned scholar who has received many awards and honors, Dr. Billingsley has published a range of books and scholarly articles, including seminal works on the Black family and on social policy. As we celebrate the 90th birthday of Dr. Andrew Billingsley, we wish him many more years filled with loads of fun, excitement, and beautiful memories. ASALH loves you, Dr. Andrew Billingsley!

Respectfully submitted,
The Officers & Members of The Association for the Study of African American
Life and History (ASALH)
Dr. Evelyn Higginbotham, President

Above: The Billingsley Family — Amy, Angela, Andrew and Bonita — at home in Berkeley, California, while Andrew was a professor in the School of Social Welfare at the University of California, Berkeley, 1966.

Below: The Billingsley Family in Silver Spring, Maryland in 1986, while Andrew was Chairman of Family Studies at University of Maryland, College Park.

A Long and Winding Road

Andrew Billingsley, Ph.D.
(Dedicated to Amy Loretta Tate Billingsley)

This academic career, this "life of the mind," has indeed been long with many turnings, and I have been blessed many times over by the best and by the makers of this book.[79] This chapter and this book are dedicated to Amy Loretta Tate Billingsley, which is proper. She was with me during my doctoral studies in the Heller School at Brandeis University in the early 1960s. There, along with Professor David French, my mentor, and other faculty including Dean Charles Schottland, Professor Arnold Gurin, and fellow students including Ruth and Sydney Bernard they all conspired to make this last stand — my last four years of academic preparation — the best, least stressful, and most engaging of my entire decade of advanced studies. Amy did this while holding down a job as a graduate assistant to a Harvard faculty member doing research on psychedelic drugs (she insists that she did not partake!).

Those four years at Brandeis were also enhanced by a small group of friends outside Brandeis including Vivian and Willard Johnson (whom Amy had first met while doing voluntary service years before in Africa). After making the trek with me to the 1963 March on Washington, led by Bayard Rustin, Dorothy Height, Dr. Martin L. King Jr., and future Congressman John Lewis, she would later accompany me to my first academic post in the School of Social Welfare at the University of California at Berkeley. That's where this long and winding road began, in January 1964, some 46 years ago and counting.

While tending to our daughter Angela and waiting for Bonita to arrive, she helped me prepare my first book for publication. Based on my doctoral dissertation, the book detailed the role of the social worker in the child protective agency and was later published by the National Association of Social Work in 1964. It would take another four years for *Black Families, in White America* to be ready for publication.

The Berkeley Years

In Berkeley, Amy did the lion's share of the raising of the girls, and since we had no boys and a big house, we elected to help my brother and his wife raise some of their boys. Both the older boy, Billy, and his younger brother, Joseph Andrew, came to live with us for a while in Berkeley. Joseph stayed for a year and attended Berkeley High School; he would join us again in Washington, DC to attend Howard University some years later. When their younger brother, Douglass came along, Amy proposed that we take him over completely and raise him along with the girls. Though their mother, Rosalina, was amenable to that, my brother listened carefully to our plea and then told us "no."

While at Berkeley, Amy also took charge of our community relations and extended hospitality to my students (through frequent dinners in our home) and to our white neighbors, especially Tom and Ginger Alexander and their children. She also served as hostess for the periodic Soul Food dinners we shared with the dozen or so Black families scattered through the city. It was during several of these dinners that some historic political campaigns were initiated. They included Otho Green's failed run for California State Legislature; Reverend Roy Nichol's successful run to integrate the Berkeley School Board; and Ron Dellums's successful run to integrate the City Council, and later, his spectacularly successfully run to integrate the California delegation of the U.S. Congress.

While we supported and championed our friends' forays into politics, Amy and I were focused on the struggles taking place on Berkeley's campus. Student groups were actively engaged in the struggle to establish an African American Studies Department (and other Ethnic Studies departments) on campus, which I fully supported. Additionally, the research, eventual publication, and ensuing discussions surrounding my publication, *Black Families in White America*, became my primary focus during this time. Over 50 years later, the impact of this book on my scholarship, and, ultimately my career is undeniable. My tenure at UC Berkeley would culminate with my appointment as the Assistant Chancellor for Academic Affairs, making me the highest-ranking administrator of color at the University.

After Berkeley, Amy continued to help me with my work at Howard and Morgan. However, as the children grew older and went off to boarding school and college, it became my turn to assist her with plans for graduate study and her career, as she had done for me at Brandeis. She would go on to earn an M.B.A. at the University of Baltimore and enter the banking industry soon thereafter. Years later, she made the transition from the private to the public sector and worked as Assistant to the Secretary of the Department of Labor. The administrative support she had provided for me during the early years proved highly beneficial to her role within the Secretary's office.

Though Amy continued to assist me with my book projects, she was no longer my principal (unpaid) research assistant; however, I was then able to hire a research assistant with funds from the Ford Foundation. Though enormously helpful to my research, as it enabled me to fund all aspects of my projects, that help came with a down side: it took me all over the country and overseas, often for long periods. Several years of this extensive research took a toll on the Billingsley family, causing damage beyond repair. As a result, I elected to move to South Carolina alone to work on my Robert Smalls study for a year.

Professor Gary Melton arranged a one-year appointment at the University of South Carolina (USC) that would allow me to finish my project. As the project developed, the year mark came and went. It would take nearly 10 years for my book on Smalls to be completed. Upon completion of that project, I was invited to a book talk at Venerable Venue in Charleston. On one side of the hall sat Robert Small's descendants including his great-great granddaughter, Dr. Helen Boulware Moore; her son, Dr. Michael Boulware Moore; and other family. On the left side of the auditorium, sitting three rows from the front, was a surprise: there sat Angela Billingsley and Bonita Billingsley Harris, with their mother, Amy Loretta Tate Billingsley — in all her glory. Although this was the only one of my books that Amy did not help with, she nevertheless adopted it, and she and Bonita became avid marketers.

Departing USC

When I retired from the University of South Carolina in 2010, I was 84 years old with a number of health challenges. It had been a long, winding road: 14 years at USC, 10 years at College Park, 10 years at Morgan, 5 years at Howard, and 6 at UC Berkeley. I could look back on hundreds of students, dozens of colleagues, and scores of administrators who had joined my families and neighbors in bringing enrichment to my life. Leave-taking was a communal effort. Timothy Jenkins arranged a farewell breakfast with the men of Brookland Baptist Church. Bobby Donaldson from USC came over to help me pack and to designate my personal papers for shipment to the Howard University archives and USC archives. On moving day, Tim came over with his truck, packed my things, and drove me halfway from Columbia, South Carolina, to Chesapeake, Virginia, where Bonita met us with a second truck. After lunch, she drove me the rest of the way to her home in Chesapeake for dinner. Soon thereafter, we made our way to the assisted-living facility, consistent with the recommendation that my doctor and family agreed would be necessary to provide me with the optimal care I needed at the time.

Angela to the Rescue, Again

I had long ago become aware, as I grew older and not fully able to move about on my own, how fortunate I have been to have two adult daughters to come to my aid periodically. Whenever I thanked them, they would often say that they were only returning the favor. After two years of excellent 24-hour care at the assisted-living facility, I longed for more independence and freedom of movement. My doctor agreed that I could leave the institution if I had someone who would be responsible for providing 24-7 care similar to what I had received in the assisted-living facility.

I had come to a fork in the road. I could not move back to Columbia, South Carolina. Bonita's work, family, and the responsibility of small children made her home a less than an ideal residence for me. Angela, who was now living alone in Washington, D.C, came to my rescue, as she had done several times before. I was to live with her, and she would employ a part-time home health care assistant to look after me during the day. So, in December 2012, I moved back to Washington, DC, for the third time in my long career.

This was the ideal arrangement for me: our apartment is located in a high-rise building in the rapidly redeveloping southwest quadrant of the city. The building has a 24-hour concierge, a gym, and a swimming pool right next door. It's an easy walk to the public library, pharmacy, and all manner of other commercial facilities including the famous Arena Stage live theater. Among the other features in our neighborhood is a Presbyterian church that offers live Blues band concerts on Mondays and a Jazz band on Fridays. All of these factors have made acclimating to this new phrase in my life much easier. Most importantly, Angela arranged for me to have a home health care assistant and custodial advisor, O. Tyronne Jackson, who lives in the building. He has provided excellent service and friendship to me for several years. Mr. Jackson is an exceptional, trained agent with the kindest heart and the most attentive manner.

Then Amy soon took me to her new church, Alfred Street Baptist Church, across the river in Alexandria, Virginia. She had left Shiloh Baptist Church in DC, with a few others in a minor schism. The 200-year-old Virginia church was founded in 1803, during Thomas Jefferson's presidency, and lays claim to being the oldest Black Baptist church in the nation, north of Richmond.

Amy works with one of the many community activities the Alfred Street Baptist Church sponsors its annual HBCU College Fair. The event brings together representatives from the various institutions from all over the nation and hundreds of Black Students from the area's numerous high schools. The church invites corporations, fraternities and sororities, and dozens of community, government, and area organizations to serve as co-sponsors of the event. In February 2018, the 16th annual Fair hosted more than 70 HBCUs from 23 states and the District. The institution selected for special recognition and donation was Morgan State University, whose president, Dr. David Wilson, was the special guest speaker for that Sunday morning's services. During his message, he noted that a former president of Morgan was in the audience, and Amy and I stood to generous applause. Then, he asked all Morganites in the audience to stand, and nearly a third of the congregation rose to thunderous applause. This moment of intersection between the church and HBCUs demonstrated the natural connections between the two. That coalition serves as a lifeline between these institutions and reinforces the importance of both entities to the Black community.

A frequent alternative to our Alfred Street Baptist Church's worship service is to attend the Andrew Rankin Memorial Chapel on the campus of Howard University. Again, Amy serves as a member of Rankins' Friends of the Chapel group, along with close friends Patricia Walters, Anita Hackney, Timothy Davis and his wife, Donald Temple, Roberta Polk, and other old timers. The Dean of the Chapel, Reverend Doctor Bernard Richardson — a highly educated, community-minded leader — is a master orator and worthy successor to former Dean Dr. Evans Crawford, who was Dean of the Chapel when I was at Howard during the 1970s.

A special feature of the Sunday morning services is the prayer written and recited by Dean Richardson, a tradition started by the founding Dean of the Chapel, Dr. Howard Thurman. Another prominent feature of the Sunday services at Howard is the participation of student organizations in the conduct and performance of every Sunday service. This spirit of service fostered by the Chapel is not limited to Sunday service, however; Dean Richardson encourages students to abandon their traditional Spring Break plans and join the Office of the Chapel in community service through the University's Alternative Spring Break program. Students are placed in both domestic and international locations to assist communities in service projects, such as rebuilding after Hurricane Katrina and, most recently, Hurricane Sandy; and earthquake clean-up in Haiti and organizing resource distribution during the water crisis in Flint, Michigan.

Finally, the most noted feature of Sunday morning services at Rankin are the sermons, which are always delivered by a rotating, annually recurring cast of the most outstanding preachers in the nation. A sample of these regulars include:

Bishop Vashti Murphy McKenzie
Reverend Dr. Renita Weems
Reverend Dr. Otis Moss II
Reverend Dr. Otis Moss III
Reverend. Dr. Calvin O. Butts
Reverend Dr. Howard John Wesley
Dr. Eric Michael Dyson

Thus, our time visiting Rankin Memorial Chapel is always filled with a divine musical experience and a timely word from the sacred desk.

On My 90th Birthday Symposium

My return to Washington, DC, culminated in a symposium that was held April 20-22, 2016, in honor of my 90th birthday. The idea for the symposium originated from a discussion that took place during a dinner at Amy's house. She asked what I would like for my 90th birthday. I suggested a small dinner party at her house. Since my return to Washington in late 2012, I had been serving as the John and Eula Cleveland Scholar-in-Residence in the Department of Afro American Studies at Howard since 2013. Dr. Greg Carr had asked me to consider the position by phone and again after a campus memorial service for Dr. Ronald Walters in September 2010. He told me the department would put the resources of the Chair behind bringing in anyone I wished for symposia, talks, or other programs I might like to create.

I had been occupying an office on the third floor of Founders Library and working on my memoirs with a small team for a couple of years by the time Amy asked me about my birthday wishes. She then approached Greg with the idea for the birthday symposium. One day, he came up to my office and said, "Get me a list of your former students and colleagues, and we'll bring them here from wherever they are in the country we can celebrate your birthday!" Though I had begun envisioning perhaps a one-day event with morning and afternoon sessions featuring a half-dozen speakers, Amy clearly had envisioned something far more substantial. Given that I was busy with several writing projects, it took me several weeks to get around to making a list of names. Meanwhile, Amy had gone through her extensive files and compiled a list of my former colleagues and students from which we could select a few.

In due course, Amy had assembled a planning committee, which she co-chaired with Dr. Bathsheba Bryant-Tarpeh. Dr. Carr approved the committee, which included, among others, Kamili Anderson and Donald'a Gaddy. (The full committee is listed on the acknowledgments page of this book.) The list of colleagues, students, friends, and relatives numbering several hundred was drawn from all over the nation. People came from all over for the resulting three-day symposium, entitled "Howard University, The Decade of the 1970s." They were from our early years in the 1960s, from my doctoral studies at Brandeis University; from the six years that began my career at U.C. Berkeley; my five years at Howard University; ten years at Morgan State University; and ten years at University of Maryland at College Park; and finally, my years at the University of South Carolina. It was from the remarks and papers given at this symposium that this *festschrift* developed and, as they say, the rest is history.

Endnotes

INTRODUCTION

[1] During this period, Professor Billingsley recruited other scholars whose names are not included in the above discussion, including Robert Cummings, Robert Staples, and Sulayman Nyang.

[2] With special appreciation for the assistance provided by the following: Clifford Muse, JoEllen El Bashir, and Richard Jenkins staff members of the Moorland — Spingarn Research Center.

PROLOGUE

*Bathsheba Bryant-Tarpeh served as the primary editor for the Prologue focusing on Dr. Andrew Billingsley's early life.

[3] Many years later, Billingsley's fourth child, Donald Billingsley, found the first official documentation of his birth upon examining the 1930 U.S. Census.

CHAPTER 1

[4] Andrew Billingsley, in a telephone interview with the author, February 17, 2010. [Except where otherwise documented, this tribute is based on the telephone interview with Billingsley on the aforementioned date.]

[5] Hylan Lewis. Faculty Collection. Hampton University Archives, Hampton, Virginia.

[6] Untitled newspaper article, Press. 6 November 1949. [This partial newspaper article is from the Hampton University Archives, Hampton, Virginia.]

[7] Ibid.

[8] Ibid.

[9] Ibid.

[10] "Hampton Man to Work with Friends Group." *New Journal and Guide.* 25 April 1950.

[11] *Report of the President of Hampton Institute for Ten Years Ending 1958.* Hampton Institute. Hampton, Virginia. April 1959, 7. [From the Hampton University Archives, Hampton, Virginia.]

[12] Ibid.

[13] Claud D. Nelson Jr. "Exchange Students Find 'One World' Atmosphere." *The Hampton Bulletin,* February 1949. [From the Hampton University Archives, Hampton, Virginia.]

[14] *"Report of the President of Hampton Institute."*

[15] Ibid.

[16] Claud D. Nelson.

[17] "Robinson, Billingsley Win Top Council Posts." *Hampton Script*. 14 May 1949. [From the Hampton University Archives, Hampton. Virginia.]

[18] "Billingsley Heads Council: To Speak at Inauguration." *Hampton Script*, 8. October 1949. [From the Hampton University Archives, Hampton. Virginia.] See also John N. Popham, "Hampton Installs First Negro Head." *New York Times* 30 October 1949, 54; Josephus Simpson. "Moron Inaugurated as President of Hampton Institute, Proxy," *Afro-America*. 5 November 1949.

[19] "Student Council Makes Report." *Hampton Script*, 12 November 1949. [From the Hampton University Archives. Hampton, Virginia.]

[20] "Hampton Debaters Beat Morris Brown." *New Journal and Guide,* 15 May 1948. 17.

[21] "Hampton Debaters Hosts to Teams." *New Journal and Guide (1921-2003),* 1 May 1948. D4.

[22] Ibid.

[23] Hampton Debaters Beat Morris Brown.

[24] "Sociological Association Plans Mock Election." *Hampton Script,* 9 October 1948. [From the Hampton University Archives, Hampton. Virginia.]

[25] "Democrats Earn Mock Election Archives, Hampton. Virginia Edge." *Hampton Script*, 30 October 1948. [From the Hampton University Archives, Hampton Virginia]

CHAPTER 5

[26] Ling-chi Wang, "Chronology of Ethnic Studies at U.C. Berkeley," Department of Ethnic Studies at U.C. Berkeley, *Newsletter,* Volume 2, Number 2, Spring 1997.

[27] Vincent Harding, "Toward The Black University," *Ebony*, August 1970, pp. 156-159.

[28] Karen K. Miller, "Race, Power and the Emergence of Black Studies in Higher Education," *American Studies, 31,* 2, fall 1990, pp. 108.

[29] R. David Cobbs Jr. "Black Students in White Schools," *Journal of Negro Education, 445,* 1, winter 1976, pp. 108.

[30] Alex Poinsett, "Howard University: Onetime 'Negro' school shifts emphasis to black curriculum," *Ebony,* December 1971, pp. 116.

[31] James D. Stanfiel, "A Profile of the 1972 Freshman Class at Howard University," *The Journal of Negro Education, 45,* 1, winter 1976, pp. 66.

[32] Orde Coombs, "The Necessity of Excellence: Howard University," *Change, 6, 2,* March 1974, pp. 37.

[33] Alex Poinsett, "Howard University: Onetime 'Negro' school shifts emphasis to black curriculum," *Ebony,* December 1971, pp. 120.

[34] Orde Coombs, "The Necessity of Excellence: Howard University," pp. 37.

[35] Ibid, pp. 39.

36 Ibid, pp. 38.

37 Ford Foundation Annual Report 1972, http://www.forddfoundation.com/archives/item/1972/text/42

CHAPTER 6

38 Charles Hamilton, "Howard Students Continue Sit-in as University Seeks Injunction." *The Harvard Crimson*, March 22, 1968. http://www.thecrimson.com/article/1968/3/22/howard-students-continue-sit-in-as-university/

CHAPTER 8

39 Stephen Henderson, editor 1973. *Understanding the New Black Poetry: Black Speech & Black Music As Poetic References.* New York: William Morrow & Co., pp. 119.

40 Carmichael, Stokely, and Ekwueme Michael Thelwell (2009). *Ready for Revolution.* New York: Scribner, pp. 129-130.

41 Henderson. *Understanding the New Black Poetry*, pp. 199-200.

42 Carmichael, and Thelwell. *Ready for Revolution*, p 119.

43 A Glimpse of History: Scenes from the Howard University 1968 Takeover, see http://www.pbs.org/wgbh/pages/frontline/shows/race/etc/history.html

44 Gregory U. Rigsby, "Afro-American Studies at Howard University: One Year Later," *The Journal of Negro Education*, 39, 3, Summer 1970, pp. 209.

45 Henderson. *Understanding the New Black Poetry*, pp. 212.

46 Ibid, pp. 214.

47 Medina, Tony 2009. "Island Song." *I And I Bob Marley*. New York: Lee and Low Books.

CHAPTER 12

48 Cedric Robinson, "Capitalism, Marxism, and the Black Radical Tradition: an Interview by Chuck Morse," *Perspectives on Anarchist Theory* 3 (1999), http://flag.blackened.net/ias/5robinsoninterview.htm.

49 John Bracey, "Discussant: Graduate Studies in Africana Studies: The Beautiful Struggle Continues" (panel presentation at 40th Annual Conference of the National Council for Black Studies, Charlotte, NC, March 19, 2016).

50 A recent example is Robin D. G. Kelley, "Black Study, Black Struggle," Boston Review, March, 2016, https://bostonreview.net/forum/robin-d-g-kelley-black-study-black-struggle.

51 The metaphor is drawn from Perry Hall, *In the Vineyard: Working in African American Studies* (Knoxville: University of Tennessee Press, 1999).

52 See Karen Ferguson, *Top Down: The Ford Foundation, Black Power, and the Reinvention of Racial Liberalism* (Philadelphia: University of Pennsylvania Press, 2013) and Noliwe Rooks, *White Money/Black Power: The Surprising History of Afri-*

can American Studies and the Crisis of Race in Higher Education (Boston: Beacon Press, 2006).

53 Martha Biondi, *The Black Revolution on Campus* (Berkeley, CA: University of California Press, 2012), 202.

54 See, for instance, Andrew Billingsley, *Black Families and the Struggle for Survival: Teaching our Children to Walk Tall* (New York: Friendship Press, 1974), 36-47; and his *Climbing Jacob's Ladder: The Enduring Legacy of African-American Families* (New York: Simon and Schuster, 1992), 83-95. See also his commentary on Black Studies in Biondi, *The Black Revolution on Campus,* 179.

55 Ladner's edited collection was indeed much larger than a critique of the discipline of sociology; it encompassed the whole of Western knowledge production. See Joyce Ladner, ed. *The Death of White Sociology* (New York: Random House, 1973).

56 On the "success" of Black Studies, see Biondi, *The Black Revolution on Campus,* 249-267. See also Fabio Rojas, *From Black Power to Black Studies: How a Radical Social Movement Became an Academic Discipline* (Baltimore: The Johns Hopkins University Press, 2007).

57 W. E. B. Du Bois quoted in Vincent Harding, *Beyond Chaos: Black History and the Search for the New Land.* (Atlanta, GA: Institute of the Black World, 1970), 4.

58 *Negro Digest* (February 1962).

59 See Abdul Alkalimat, et al., *African American Studies 2013: A National Web-Based Survey* (Urbana: University of Illinois-Urbana Champaign, Department of African American Studies, 2013), http://www.afro.illinois.edu/documents/BlackStudiesSurvey.pdf, 6.

60 The professional organization for Black Studies, see http://www.ncbsonline.org/africana_studies_graduate_programs

61 Greg Carr, "What Black Studies is Not: Moving from Crisis to Liberation in Africana Intellectual Work," *Socialism and Democracy* 25 (March 2011): 178.

CHAPTER 13

62 Elaine H. Kim, 1982. "Chinatown Cowboys and Warrior Women: Searching for a New Self-Image," *Asian American Literature: An Introduction to the Writings and Their Social Context.* Philadelphia: Temple University Press, pp.174–175.

CHAPTER 16

63 Coalition of Urban-Serving Universities. (2007). *Proceedings: Advancing an Urban Agenda in Human Capital, Strengthening Communities, and Public Health.* Retrieved June 8, 2010, from http://www.usucoalition.org/downloads/part2/2007U-SUProceedingsFINAL.pdf.

64 I was Director of IUR for two-and-a-half years, from 1983 to 1985.

CHAPTER 21

65 Andrew Billingsley. *Mighty Like a River: The Black Church and Social Reform.*

New York: Oxford University Press, 1999, p.168.

[66] Ibid, p.189.

[67] Andrew Billingsley. *Yearning to Breathe Free: Robert Smalls of South Carolina and His Families*. South Carolina: University of South Carolina Press, 2007, p. xii.

[68] See Appendix 1.

[69] Appendix 2 provides information on the annual Robert Smalls symposium and the criteria for the Billingsley Awards.

CHAPTER 22

[70] Walter R. Allen, 1978. "The Search for Applicable Theories of Black Family Life," *Journal of Marriage and the Family, 40* (1): 117-129.

[71] Refer to Talcott Parsons's1951 work, *The Social System*, for further explanation of social systems paradigm.

[72] W. E. B. Du Bois, 1898. "The Study of the Negro Problem," *ANNALS, AAPSS, I* (1): 1-23.

[73] Payton, Isabelle S. 1982. "Single-Parent Households," *Family Economics Review* (Winter): 11-16.

[74] An example of this is Robert Staples and Leanor Boulin Johnson. 1993. *Black Families at the Crossroads*. San Francisco, CA: Jossey-Bass.

[75] This study was published by Emerson Hall Publishers as the book, *The Strengths of Black Families*.

[76] Nathan Hare, 1976. "What Black Intellectuals Misunderstand about the Black Family," *Black World*, 25 (5): 4-14.

[77] Emmy E. Werner and Ruth S. Smith, 1982.*Vulnerable But Invincible: A Study of Resilient Children*. New York: McGraw-Hill.

[78] Michael Rutter, 1987. "Psychosocial Resilience and Protective Mechanisms," *American Journal of Orthopsychiatry*, 57 (3): 316-331.

EPILOGUE

[79] A Friend of mine, the sociologist Horace Cayton, titled his autobiography, *Long Old Road*. Moreover, a dear friend, my daughter Bonita's mother-in-law, Mrs. Anne Harris, always greets me with, "I've been blessed by the best, my brother." Both expressions reflect my sense of the career represented in the several chapters or essays in this book. It has been a long and winding road, and I have indeed been blessed and continue to be so — by authors, the faculty, the students, and the various communities represented in this volume.

Index